Class Struggle
and the Jewish Nation

JUDAICA SERIES

William B. Helmreich, series editor

The goal of this series is to make available social science works in the field of Jewish studies that are recognized as having made a lasting contribution to both. Some of these books have been out of print for decades, others for only a short period. What they have in common is the recognition by scholars in the field that they deserve to be made accessible to a wider public as well as to experts in the discipline.

Class Struggle
and the Jewish Nation

Selected Essays in Marxist Zionism

Ber Borochov

Edited with an Introduction by
Mitchell Cohen

Routledge
Taylor & Francis Group

LONDON AND NEW YORK

First published 1983 by Transaction Publishers

Published 2019 by Routledge
2 Park Square, Milton Park, Abingdon, Oxon OX14 4RN
52 Vanderbilt Avenue, New York, NY 10017

First issued in paperback 2019

Routledge is an imprint of the Taylor & Francis Group, an informa business

Introduction © 1983 by Mitchell Cohen.
Copyright © 1984 Taylor & Francis.

Library of Congress Catalog Number: 83-4695

Library of Congress Cataloging in Publication Data

Borochov, Ber, 1881–1917.
   Class struggle and the Jewish nation.

   (Judaica series)
   Translated from Russian and Yiddish.

   1. Labor Zionism—Addresses, essays, lectures. I. Cohen, Mitchell, 1952–   II. Title. III. Series: Judaica series (Transaction Books)
DS150.L4B59   1984   956.94′001   83-4695
ISBN 0-87855-479-3

ISBN 13: 978-1-138-50819-4 (pbk)
ISBN 13: 978-0-87855-479-9 (hbk)

Contents

Acknowledgments

I am grateful to the numerous people who aided me in preparing this volume. Valuable and incisive comments on my introduction were offered by Jonathan Frankel of the Hebrew University, Arthur Hertzberg of Columbia University, Mattityahu Mintz of Tel Aviv University, and Steve Zipperstein of the Oxford Center for Postgraduate Hebrew Studies. Professors Mintz and Frankel did pioneering research in Jewish socialist history, and my essay would not have been possible without their work. Any errors are, of course, my own.

The Borochov family, particularly Ber Borochov's sister the late Nadia Borochov Ovsey, his brother Harry Borochow, and his niece Betty Frank have all afforded me friendship, reminiscences, and encouragement. Being a student of political theory and not a scholar specializing in Eastern European Jewish history, I required the assistance of friends to examine materials in languages I do not read; I particularly wish to thank Yossi Lapid and Jack Jacobs for their generous help. Aviva Cantor has been a source of ongoing encouragement. I also wish to thank J.N. Porter for his assistance in arranging the publication of this volume.

Invaluable assistance was rendered by the Zionist Archives and Library in New York, the library and archives at the YIVO Institute for Jewish Research, and the Bund Archives. New translations in this volume appear by permission of David Borochov in Jerusalem. Gabi Trunk was responsible for transliterations and for making non-English terms consistent throughout the book. It should be noted that several names and terms have been left in their familiar transliterations for the sake of recognition and clarity. Several terms problematic for precise English translation have been left in the original, and a glossary is supplied at the end of this volume.

Parts of the introduction are derived from my earlier biographical portrait of Borochov: "Ber Borochov: Towards a Portrait of a Socialist Zionist," *Response* (Fall 1977).

Before the publication of this volume there existed only one substantive anthology of Borochov's essays in English: Ber Borochov, *Nationalism and the Class Struggle: A Marxian Approach to the Jewish Problem,* edited by Moshe Cohen (New York: Young Poale Zion Alliance of America, 1937). This entire collection, minus its outdated introduction and footnotes, is reproduced here by permission of the successor of the Young Poale Zion Alliance, the Ichud Habonim Labor Zionist Youth Movement. The original translations have not been altered, with a few minor but necessary exceptions. The essay "Our Platform" is condensed (the original would take a volume of almost half this length in itself), and so is "Eretz Israel in Our Program and Tactics," which was excerpted for the 1937 edition from Borochov's 1917 speech in Kiev.

Supplementing the materials that first appeared in 1937 are several essays newly translated for this volume and several short works by Borochov that appeared in English in various publications. "On Questions of Zionist Theory" first appeared in *Sources of Contemporary Jewish Thought 2* (Jerusalem: World Zionist Organization, Departments of Education and Culture in the Diaspora, Organization and Information, and Youth and Hehalutz, 1971), and is reprinted by permission of the World Zionist Organization. "The Aims of Yiddish Philology," ed., trans., and abr. by David Katz, *Jewish Frontier* (June-July 1980). "At the Cradle of Zionist Socialism," trans. Gabi Trunk, *Jewish Frontier* (January 1981). Especially for this volume, Rabbi Mark W. Kiel translated the following from the Yiddish: "Hebraismus Militans," "The Socialism of Poale Zion Here," and "Two Currents of Poale Zionism." The "Declaration to the Hollando-Scandinavian Socialist Committee Submitted by the Jewish Socialist Labor Confederation Poale Zion," which Borochov helped draft, appears as it was published in 1917 by the Poale Zion.

Mitchell Cohen

Introduction:
Ber Borochov and Socialist Zionism

Mitchell Cohen

Not long before the commencement of World War I, a young Russian Jewish exile named Ber Borochov attended a lecture by V.I. Lenin in Liege, Belgium. When the Bolshevik's talk ended, Borochov arose and began presenting the case for Socialist Zionism. Lenin laughed in reply and told his interlocuter that he was trying to be both "here and there." You, said the future leader of the Soviet Union, are trying to sit on two chairs at once. The problem is, you are not even on the two chairs, you are in the empty space between them.[1]

No doubt Borochov, the founder of Marxist Zionism, grasped the full import of Lenin's chide. In Borochov's view Marxists and socialists had, by and large, failed to come to grips with the question of nationalism in general and the Jewish question in particular. If, according to Marx, communism was a specter haunting Europe, for Borochov nationalism was a specter haunting socialism. Indeed, this ghost still stalks today, over sixty years after Borochov's death. Now, as then, there are few socialists (at least in the West) who would call themselves nationalists, certainly not without a grimace. Did not Marx and Engels proclaim in the *Communist Manifesto* that "working men have no country"? Did they not assert that "national differences and antagonisms between peoples are daily more and more vanishing, owing to the development of the bourgeoisie, to freedom of commerce, to the world market, to uniformity in the mode of production and conditions of life corresponding thereto"?

National differences intensified througout the world in the century after Marx's words were penned. Most Marxist theorists—with important exceptions, such as the Austro-Marxists—never fully confronted the issue. Rather than developing a materialist theory of nationalism, they often assumed it to be a temporary phenomenon only (in which case Marx would eventually be proven right), a thoroughly reactionary phenomenon (to be fought under almost all circumstances), or, as in the case of Lenin himself, largely a tactical question (in which national culture per se ultimately had no true value). The very notion of socialist internationalism seemed to negate nationalism: Would it not obfuscate the class struggle?

1

Would it not mislead the proletariat into subservience to a ruling class that would, under the banner of patriotism, send off workers to die for imperialist interests as in World War I?

Such questions became more problematic throughout the twentieth century with the emergence of Third World anticolonial struggles—which were and are almost unanimously supported by the Left. These struggles, however, have generally taken the form of *national* struggles. Orthodox Marxists may argue that the socialist struggle is international in content while national in form. This ignores the fact that the awakening Third World's efforts have been national both in content and form, even when led by socialists. The desire to create a positive, indigenous national content in the lives of peoples drained by European political and cultural domination has been central to such endeavors and analyzed well by writers like Albert Memmi and Frantz Fanon.

Thus the question of nationalism is far from resolved. In supporting anticolonial struggles, an admission of some form of progressive nationalism cannot be escaped. But does internationalism require the assertion that once victory is at hand in a given country, its national culture no longer has value? Is nationalism simply a means in a worldwide struggle against imperialism? And is it not cynical, if not patronizing, to take this argument to its logical conclusion, namely that a national culture is progressive when the nation is oppressed, and reactionary once freedom has been won? If this is not the case, then a different understanding is required of the phenomenon of nationalism, and in the realm of Marxist theory this means a *materialist* analysis of something whose potency was supposed to have vanished long ago. Other questions must also follow. If a form of progressive nationalism is to be allowed—with the obvious corollary that there exists reactionary nationalism as well—what manifestations shall it take? What is its relationship to the state and what meaning shall *self-determination* have for the various nations in a multinational state? When is political independence justified or necessary as opposed to autonomy, within a given state?

Ber Borochov's chief theoretical achievement was an attempted synthesis of nationalism and socialism. He had a very specific national problem in mind—that of the Jews. This volume represents a selection of his essays all of which, in one way or another, revolve around this topic. He did not answer all the questions posed above, and not all his answers will be judged as satisfactory. Yet his represents an important, if largely unknown, effort. One reason Borochov is not well known is the inaccessibility of his writings to the English speaking reader. The sole edition of his writings to have appeared in English (all of which are included in this volume) was published in 1937, reprinted once, yet is not easy to find. Another important reason is that he was a Zionist who tried to synthesize socialism with a form of nationalism that has not been popular on the Left. The Jewish question as a whole, including Zionism, has been almost as troublesome for the Left as the national question. Beginning with Marx's 1843 essays "On the Jewish Question," through Lenin's, Luxemburg's, and Trotsky's espousal of Jewish assimilation, to current hostility in sections of the Left to the very existence of a Jewish national entity—the Jewish question and Zionism have been like a bone in the throat of many socialists (Jewish and non-Jewish alike) who have been unable either to swallow or disgorge it.

Borochov was unwilling to grant Lenin's premise that one could sit either on the chair of socialism or that of nationalism, but not on both. As far as the Jewish question was concerned, either chair alone seemed too wobbly to him. The empty space between them would have to be filled by a movement for Jewish national self-determination and socialism in Palestine. Such an effort would at once affirm the specificity of the Jewish question, solve it, and maintain solidarity with international socialism. Borochov's attempt at a socialist-nationalist synthesis was tied to the immediate problem of Jewish nationalism and oppression. It was primarily grounded in the atmosphere of Russian Marxist and intellectual currents, Jewish politics, and a Jewish community that was facing a crisis of modernity in a backward, multinational, repressive Czarist empire. To fully appreciate Borochov's effort, all these factors must be kept in mind; for he was not just a theorist of Socialist Zionism, but a political renaissance man, the father and leader of a political party, and a pioneering philologist and analyst of Yiddish culture, highly versed in literature and philosophy. To remove his writings from this context is to abuse them. The following pages draw a broad picture of his political odyssey— an odyssey cut short when he was but thirty-six years old, at a time when Bolshevism presented a new reality to his Party in Russia and his comrades in Palestine struggled to build the backbone of a new Jewish nation.

I

Ber Borochov was born on June 21, 1881, in Zolotonoshi, the Ukraine, where his father, a Hebrew teacher, had recently sojourned in an unsuccessful effort to establish a school. Two months after his birth the family returned to their home town Poltava (also in the Ukraine), where young "Borya" was to grow up. The time and place of his birth are significant. In March 1881 Czar Alexander II was assassinated by the populist terrorists of Narodnaya Volya (people's will). In the following month pogroms swept southern Russia. During the next two years Jews—long the victims of repressive Czarist legislation—were attacked, raped, murdered, threatened, and their homes and places of work looted and burned in 200 towns. The Narodnaya Volya, champions of the peasantry (the main source of pogromists), issued a declaration defending the pogroms and accusing Russian Jewry of being "exploiters."

The Jews lived confined to an area in the western Russian empire (including parts of Poland) generally known as the Pale of Settlement. Their status was that of Russian subjects of non-Russian birth, and they were restricted from numerous professions, barred from living outside cities and towns, and not permitted to own rural lands.[2] They lived by the grace of the generally hostile government and local populace. The Czars, with occasional respite, devised numerous schemes throughout the nineteenth century to rid themselves of the Jewish problem, using methods ranging from assimilation incentives to force and coercion. In addition, the Jewish community, traditional until the nineteenth century, was feeling the impact of the Haskalah (enlightenment), whose adherents, the *maskilim,* strove to have contact with the non-Jewish world and its culture. Some Jewish intellectuals became more and more secularized while others remained "enlightened" but very much within a Jewish frame of reference. Still others, hoping for a triumph of liberal values that would throw off the yoke of confinement they suffered as Jews, promoted integrationist ideas.

For this last group, the pogroms of 1881-82 were a rude awakening. It led men like Leo Pinsker—active in the Society to Promote Culture Among the Jews—and Moshe Leib Lillienblum to despair of the Jewish fate in Russia and to become Zionists. The first organized Russian Zionists, the Hovevei Zion (lovers of Zion) appeared, and a trickle of Jews began leaving for Palestine, forming what became known as the First Aliyah (first wave of immigration). Among them was a small, determined group called Bilu, whose members saw themselves as pioneers in the ancient homeland; in their ranks were several volunteers from Poltava. Nineteen years earlier, a German Jewish socialist and former colleague of Marx, Moses Hess, wrote a little-noticed book, *Rome and Jerusalem,* calling for a Jewish socialist state in Palestine. Five years before Borochov's birth a Vilna-born political exile named A.S. Lieberman (see ch. 18 for Borochov's essay on him) had organized the first association of Jewish workers in London, the Agudat Hasozialistim Haivrim (Hebrew socialist union).[3] In the decades after 1881, concurrent with the growth of Russian radicalism and socialism, Jewish socialist circles began appearing in the Pale, leading to the birth of the Jewish Labor Bund and the Labor Zionist movement at the turn of the century.

The town in which Borochov spent his youth was a microcosm of these currents. His close childhood friend Itzhak Ben-Zvi (then Itzhak Shimshelevitz and later the second president of Israel), described it as follows:

> Poltava was a city without factories or industrial plants. Instead, there were numerous mills, as well as many artisans and petty merchants. . . . The population lived mainly by the sales of products brought from surrounding villages. The Jews engaged in petty commerce and artisan trades; occasionally they earned a livelihood as unskilled laborers. Because there were no factories and large plants there was no labor movement.[4]

Poltava would seem, then, an unlikely place for the radicalization of youths. Yet perhaps because the town had no industrial proletariat, the Czarist regime ordained it as an exile place for radicals. At various times this included the future Menshevik leader Martov, different Narodniki, the writer Vladimir Korolenko, and others; the police chief characterized Poltava as a "university for revolutionaries."[5] Ben-Zvi wrote of young Borochov that "with the help of political exiles, he quickly mastered socialism."[6] As for the Jewish community—Jews had begun settling there in the late eighteenth century and by the late 1870s numbered about 4,000, a figure that was to grow to over 11,000 by the late 1890s. It was a well-organized, progressive community and an early center of Zionist activities.

With Zionists and revolutionaries in his home town, the ingredients of Borochov's future ideas were before him. His parents, deeply rooted in Jewish affairs, were *maskilim,* and his father was a leading member of the Poltava Hovevei Zion. As a teacher licensed by the government, Moshe Aharon Borochov was not suspect of harboring illegal literature or radicals—which he and his wife did nonetheless. Young Borya, first of eight children, thus had easy access to an array of "subversive" materials.[7] From the time he was two or three his parents spoke only Russian in the house, because they feared a Yiddish accent would impede him in school. By the time he graduated from the gymnasium in 1900— he was denied honors by an anti-Semitic teacher, thus preventing entry to a university—he mastered the knowledge of literature, sciences, economics, philosophy and several languages including Latin, Greek, and Sanskrit.[8] Borya discussed Palestine with young Ben-Zvi and twice, at ages ten and sixteen (in 1897, the year Herzl founded the World Zionist Organization in Basle), he tried to leave for that far-off land, only to be returned from neighboring towns.

By the time he was seventeen or eighteen he was immersed in the study of philosophy. There was a saying in Poltava: "If you can't get

Kant and Schopenhauer from the Central Library, it is a sign that Borochov and his *hevra* [comrades] are now dealing with German philosophy."[9] When he graduated, the gymnasium's director described him as "quiet, modest, doesn't talk much . . . deals with nonsense."[10] Borya Borochov then moved to Ekaterinoslav (now Dnepropetrovsk), where he would first make his mark in politics. Shmarya Levin, a leading Russian Zionist and, for a period, official rabbi of the city (founded in 1778 by Catherine the Great) described this industrial center on the Dnieper River in the following words: "My first glimpse of this almost virgin city of Ekaterinoslav seemed to open new horizons to me, and I felt renewed in its newness. Here, where the generations had not preempted everything, a man could still write his name into something."[11] The city had an active Social Democratic movement which put out an illegal newspaper, *Iuzhnyi Rabochii* (the southern worker), and had close contacts with some of Russia's leading revolutionaries. By the late 1890s the Jews, numbering 41,000, made up slightly more than a third of the city.

Ekaterinoslav also had a strong Zionist movement centered around one of Russia's leading Zionists—a man who was to have a crucial impact on Borochov—Menahem-Mendel Ussishkin. "Among the closer friends of Herzl," comments Levin, "he was regarded as an opponent of the latter, because he symbolized the old days when Zionism was centered more on Palestine than on the political setting, the days when— so it was said—a goat in Palestine counted for more than the promise of a chancellery."[12] Herzl's Zionism was based on grand diplomacy, the hope of getting a charter for a Jewish state from a great power, while Ussishkin's, like the Bilu's, focused more on the concrete work of settling Jews in Eretz Israel (the ancient land of Israel), although not necessarily to the exclusion of political efforts.

The newly arrived nineteen-years-old from Poltava joined the Russian Social Democratic Party in Ekaterinoslav. He worked as an organizer and propagandist but was soon confronted by the "space between the two chairs." Levin writes:

> He came to the city about the same time as myself, having just completed a course in the gymnasium in Poltava. But he was educated far beyond his years. He had an excellent grounding in general philosophy, had advanced far in the higher mathematics, and had studied with good results Marxian economics. He was, in addition, a man—or should I say boy—of unusual intellectual honesty. He carried on vigorous Zionist activity among the youth under the direction of Ussishkin. But his Marxism gave him no rest.[13]

Borochov was at once caught between socialism and Zionism. His period in the Social Democratic Party was short-lived. One of his associates was a young fellow named Pozdniakov (who had recently been expelled from a Christian theological seminary for atheism). With Pozdniakov he would engage in "heated discourse on Karl Marx and Richard Avenarius," Borochov later reminisced, adding that "both of us—we were all of nineteen—knew Marx's *Capital* by heart, and we'd go agitating among the workers, Jews and gentiles alike, pressing illegal brochures into their hands" (see ch. 17).

Richard Avenarius (1845-1896), together with Ernst Mach (1838-1916), were the leading names associated with the philosophical-psychological school known as empiriocriticism, which had greatly influenced Borochov beginning in Poltava (more on this later). It should be noted that among Borochov's responsibilities for the Social Democrats was teaching A.A. Bogdanov's *Principles of Political Economy* to workers' circles. This volume was one of the most popular educational texts among Social Democrats and its author—later a rival of Lenin for the leadership of the Bolsheviks—became the chief Russian proponent of a Marxist version of empiriocriticism, which he called "empiriomonism," and for which he was the object of derision, first by Plekhanov and then by Lenin. Bogdanov greatly influenced Borochov, who came to refer to himself as a historical materialist and a monist.

It was apparently Borochov's interest in the national question and Zionism, and his insistence on lecturing on Zionism, that led to his expulsion from the Party in May 1901. He later explained:

> I do not remember what turned me into a non-believer. After meeting with both Jewish and gentile workers, I came to see the truth of Socialist Zionism. The committee [of the party] noticed my increasingly deleterious effect on the workers and charged that I was teaching them to think independently. I was quite unceremoniously given the boot by the Russian Social-Democratic Party .
>
> What does a banished Russian Social Democrat turned Zionist "infidel" do? He immediately marches off to a large Jewish home-study student union and converts them into the first Poale Zionists [Labor Zionists] in Russia.[14]

Borochov had already lectured on socialism and Zionism, and it seems that he even debated Levin on the issue. Both Levin and Ussishkin opposed his socialism but found him a valuable asset to Zionism nonetheless. Ussishkin would later reject the opposition of Joseph Klausner (himself eventually a prominent Zionist historian and biographer of Ussishkin) to printing Borochov's articles.[15] By 1905 (along with the future founder of the extreme right-wing of Zionism, Vladimir Jabotinsky) Borochov was one of Ussishkin's chief lieutenants in Russian Zionism.

Borochov had not yet developed the theoretical synthesis for which he would become famous. His claim (cited above) that the Ekaterinoslav Socialist Zionists were the first in Russia was not completely accurate. In 1897 a group calling itself Poale Zion (workers of Zion) emerged in Minsk. But Borochov's group was one of the earliest, and soon other Poale Zion groups were born throughout the Pale. Shortly after the turn of the century Poale Zion groups appeared in Austro-Hungary, the United States, and Britain as well. Nachman Syrkin (1868-1924), born in Mohilev, began formulating a Socialist Zionist position with his articles "The Jewish Question and the Jewish Socialist State" (1898) and "A Call to Jewish Youth" (1901), among other writings. Syrkin helped found a Socialist Zionist organization called Herut (freedom) in Berlin, and was an active, if a minority, voice in the World Zionist Organization.

Syrkin's Socialist Zionism was rather different from Borochov's, as we shall soon see. The former argued that anti-Semitism was the modern guise of a perpetual Jewish-Gentile tension caused by the "unusual historical situation" of the Jews and the forms of social life which gave "root and sustenance" to such hatred. As a landless people, the Jews had a particular problem. Emerging bourgeois society and Jewish cultural and community organizational distinctiveness clashed. Since capitalist society implied *bellum omnium contra omnes,* "an everlasting individual and class struggle," it was inevitable that the Jews would be in a volatile position. Economic competition played a central role in this entire process. Also, unlike religiously based medieval Jew-hatred, Syrkin argued, the issue was now racial. It was worst in declining classes. The peasants and the middle classes—both of which were being destroyed by the big capitalists—made the Jew the butt of competitive tensions.

Socialism and national sovereignty, suggested Syrkin, provided the only solution. A Jewish state would have to be built, and Syrkin wanted it constructed on the basis of cooperative socialist principles from the outset. Palestine would be acquired "in alliance with other oppressed nationalities in the Turkish empire through a common struggle against the Turks." He called for a program of socialist colonization and cooperative settlements—ideas which "classical Borochovism" would reject. Syrkin's philosophy was not Marxist; it was developed independently of and earlier than Borochov's, and lacked the latter's emphasis on class struggle.

Borochov became increasingly close to Ussishkin in Ekaterinoslav. Soon he was working for the General Zionists and drifted far afield from the existing Poale Zion groups, which lacked any central organization.

His first published essay, "On the Nature of the Jewish Intellect" (1902)—which appeared in a General Zionist publication and displayed the marked influences of both Marxism and empiriocriticism—attempted to analyze the geniuses of a nation, in particular of the Jews, as the unique expression of a given culture and history.[16] Originally a lecture delivered at Ussishkin's home, its birth went back to Poltava where Borochov had once debated and greatly impressed V.V. Liashevitch, a philo-Semitic academic authority on Avenarius. Later in Ekaterinoslav, Ussishkin met Liashevitch who, among other things, commented that a young Poltava Jew was one of the few people he had met who actually understood Avenarius. When Borochov appeared one day at Ussishkin's house (it was their first meeting) and requested that the latter arrange to have him lecture either on a Jewish or a general subject, Ussishkin first asked if he was the expert on Avenarius and then, with a certain reluctance, agreed to the youth's request. He invited the best of the city's Jewish intelligentsia and the lecture was a success.[17]

Avenarius and Mach were representatives of one school of German thought in the late nineteenth century particularly interested in epistemological and psychological questions. Theirs represented an attempt to do away with the epistemological subject[18] in an effort to transcend the distinction between matter and idea by claiming that reality could not be properly described as either. Avenarius' "monistic" and biological approach to human knowledge asserted that human thought and experience could be reduced to sensations that were neither physical nor spiritual. Cognition was seen as a response of the central nervous system to the outside world, aimed at equilibrium for the organism. Central to this process was the spending and absorbing of energy in the nervous system. Reducing the subjective and objective to a biological question of sensations, this "monism" tried to do away with philosophical dichotomies between subject/object, physical/mental, and is/ought. It also stressed the mind's tendency to economize and organize knowledge as it is accumulated, a process it viewed as necessary to any science.[19]

Borochov's interest in empiriocriticism thus antedated its rise in popularity in Russian radical circles after 1905—in fact he was by then moving somewhat away from it. Bogdanov's empiriomonism argued that empiriocriticism was a scientific advance that helped rid the world of metaphysics and was as such of great value to Marxism. (Lenin, following Plekhanov, claimed that the entire approach was reducible to Berkeleyan idealism.) Critical of Avenarius on numerous points, Bogdanov tried to corroborate empiriocriticism with a broader social framework.

The epistemological views of Avenarius, Mach, Bogdanov, and Borochov himself are not the central concern here, but rather Borochov the

Socialist Zionist. However, the terminology and frames of reference of the empiriocriticists appear as important elements of Borochov's Zionist formulations of 1905-1906. Organic descriptions, processes leading to equilibria, and the spending and conserving of energy are conceptions embedded within Borochov's analysis of the subjective and objective factors of the Jewish anomaly in the Diaspora. Even in his more orthodox Marxist Zionist writings empiriocritical terminology and ideas play a crucial role, and the reader interested in his epistemological views is referred to Mattityahu Mintz's seminal study of Borochov between 1900 and 1906.[20]

II

In 1902 Borochov returned to Poltava, where he was active in Jewish self-defense work, especially after the Kishinev pogrom of 1903. This violent and vicious anti-Semitic outburst traumatized Russian Jewry, particularly the youth, and Bialik wrote his famous poem "City of Slaughter" about it. That year Borochov's family left for America (to where the eldest daughter, Nadia, had already gone). Poltava province had recently also experienced peasant riots after a bad harvest. Borochov, around whom a group of young Zionists coalesced, was particularly bitter and disappointed by the reaction of Social Democrats to the pogrom. Ironically, in July 1904 he was arrested for a month on charges stemming back to his past membership in the Social Democratic Party. Unable to find evidence against him, the police released him.[21]

At this time, important controversies raged within the Zionist movement and among the Labor Zionists. One major question for the Labor forces was that of political activity in the Disapora: Should they, with their essentially pessimistic view of the Diaspora, be intimately involved in the struggle against the Czarist autocracy? The "Blues," particularly the Minsk Poale Zion, were resoundingly opposed, and Borochov sympathized with that position until the 1905 events. On the other hand, the "Reds" called for intense involvement in the revolutionary struggles. Dispute also arose over the primacy of the demand for Jewish autonomy in the Diaspora. As if to make matters more complicated, the Zionist movement as a whole, and the Socialists within it, were torn apart by a British offer to the World Zionist Organization to establish a Jewish home in East Africa (the Uganda Plan). Many General and Socialist Zionists (like Syrkin) became Territorialists, arguing that the immediate traumas of the Jews had to be paramount. To focus on Palestine was romantic in their view; the Jewish problem could be solved by territorial autonomy in *any* land.

A different political perspective came from the Vozrozhdeniye (renaissance) group which originated in 1903. Non-Marxist, close to the Russian Social Revolutionaries and the eclectic Jewish thinker Chaim Zhitlovsky, the Vozrozhdeniye accepted the principle that territorial autonomy would be needed to solve the Jewish question but claimed that this was a distant prospect and the struggle for autonomy in the Diaspora had to be a major concern in the meantime. The Vozrozhdeniye, whose influence went way beyond its numbers because of its journal, stressed that securing national rights for Jews in the Diaspora was a necessary step in solving the Jewish question. Borochov was among those who were impressed by this group which, in 1906, merged into a new party, the Sejmists (or SERP—the Jewish Socialist Workers Party). Based in the Ukraine, the Sejmists pressed for Jewish national autonomy on what was called a national *personal* basis, rather than on a territorial basis. They imagined each of the various nationalities in the Russian empire possessing its own Sejm (parliament) within a confederated framework. In direct contrast to the Vozrozhdeniye and the Sejmists was the Zionist Socialist Labor Party (the Z.S.), which minimized the question of autonomy and became, in effect, Socialist Zionists without Zion, i.e. socialist territorialists. Emotionalism, they claimed, led to the Zionist stress on Palestine. The Jews needed a land—any land—immediately. Among their leaders was Nachman Syrkin.

Borochov, in the meantime, was a Zion Zionist working with Ussishkin.[22] The latter feared that Jewish youths would be swept away by either territorialism or revolutionism. In 1904 he published a pamphlet entitled "Our Program." It is possible that Borochov had a hand in writing it. Ussishkin was vehement in his opposition to territorialism— Eretz Israel alone would carry the Jewish future in his view. "Our Program" outlined his ideas on guaranteeing Zionist success in that land. "In the political revival of any people," he stated, "three elements play a part: the people, the territory, and outward conditions." To build a "politically free" national center, a high national consciousness was required along with disciplined organization. It was necessary to "be ready to sacrifice the interests of the *present* for the sake of the future."[23] Just as important:

> Long before a state is established the territory must actually belong, in an economic and political sense, to that people which desires to form a center in it. Its whole life must be dependent on this people, which must be possessor *de facto,* even though not as yet *de jure.* The people must be bound to the land by eternal ties of heartfelt love and devotion. The earth must be moistened with its blood and sweat.[24]

To be victorious Zionism had to act simultaneously in three directions: diplomacy, cultural work, and concrete work in the Land of Israel. Previously, said Ussishkin, the Zionist movement failed to coordinate all such efforts. He went on to stress that:

> In order to create a Jewish autonomous community, or rather a Jewish state in Palestine, it is above all necessary that the whole soil of Palestine, or at least the major portion of it, should be in the possession of Jews. Without property rights to the soil, Palestine will *never* be Jewish, no matter how many Jews there may be in the cities and even the villages of Palestine. The Jews would then occupy the same abnormal position which they do today in the Exile. They would have no ground on which to stand.[25]

To hasten the "normalization" process, Ussishkin suggested establishing cooperative colonies based on Jewish labor and, harking back to the Bilu, called for a self-sacrificing "Jewish Universal Society of Workmen," composed of strong, young, unmarried men, who would volunteer for three years in Palestine of "military duty to the Jewish people, not with musket and sword but with plow and sickle."

Borochov was struck by these ideas, and two of his essays from 1905, "On Questions of Zionist Theory" (originally drafted sometime earlier) and "To the Question of Zion or Territory" reflect this. His tone in both essays is far from Marxist in many respects. These essays represent his ideas right before the formulation of "Borochovism."

In "On Questions of Zionist Theory" (see ch. 1 of this volume), Borochov stresses the need for immediate Zionist action: "We must not wait" are its passionate opening words. He proceeds to argue on the basis of the Weber-Fechner Law, a nineteenth century psychological formulation based on the work of E.H. Weber and G.T. Fechner.[26] This law claimed that the intensity of a sensation increases as the logarithm of the stimulus, or, as Borochov explains:

> If we translate this law from the language of mathematics to the language of life, it means that sensation increases at a much slower rate than the changes that take place in the environment, that as time goes by the individual pays less and less attention to these changes. Therefore, the more a person's situation improves, the greater will be his demand for further improvement, and the longer he will have to wait to feel a real improvement in his environment that he regards as satisfactory.

Thus the oppressed are likely to be content with and "the least sensitive" to their own situation. However, "the surest way of making a slave dissatisfied and demanding is to alleviate the harshness of his lot." So far as the Jews were concerned, matters had objectively improved—

Borochov foresaw no future mass expulsions or inquisitions (how wrong he was)—but subjectively the Jews would need more. In short, he presented a theory of rising expectations.

Those expectations would not be fulfilled by relying simply on "progress." Borochov criticizes, in quite un-Marxist terms, those who put their faith in progress as the ultimate salvation of the Jews. Such optimism was, in his view, totally unwarranted, for "in the *Galut* [exile] there is no salvation for the Jewish people." He even asks whether history's evolution can be called progress. Underlying this is a questioning of the price of progress for the Jews and whether advocacy of "progress"—when it means embracing universalism and negating particular Jewish needs—does not catch the Jews in a painful bind. "Progress," he writes in a striking passage, "is a two-edged sword. If the good angel in a man advances, the Satan within him advances also." As an example he cites the situation of the Jews in Morocco. Progress there meant a justified revolt of the indigenous population against European colonialism that had dominated the country. In such an event the Jews, being neither a true part of the indigenous (Moslem Arab) population nor part of the French colonial culture and apparatus, would be caught in the middle.

All social groups, argues Borochov, use others for their own purposes; they will assimilate other groups if it benefits them, but will never share material possessions with outsiders. All creatures, and analogously all nations, need food to replace used energy. Nations, like the body, assimilate other nations when their possessions are needed. But there is a major difference between two nations living in adjoining lands and a nation which lives—like the Jews—as a stranger in the midst of another. Borochov speaks of a "primordial and elemental fear of the stranger" extending to all sectors of society.

The Jews must not only cope with their foreignness—their economic structure in the Diaspora is an "abnormal" one. Having been invited originally into societies to play a restricted economic function, the Jews were segregated and overrepresented in middleman roles and as artisans. With the development of capitalism and, concurrently, of an indigenous middle class and bourgeoisie, the Jews gradually became superfluous. Eventually this led to displacement, migrations, and expulsions. The Jews were economically dependent on the peoples around them and lacked a material base, especially since there was no Jewish agricultural class (which Borochov called here the foundation of all societies).

> We are foreigners, and nowhere in the world do we possess the social power that could make us masters of our fate. We are cut off from nature and have no agriculture. All this has left us hovering in the air. Our history

in the *Galut* has never been shaped by our own powers; our fate has always depended on external ties.

In this essay Borochov stresses the sociopsychological rather than the economic factors in anti-Semitism, despite the above claims. His presentation of national groups parallels the empiriocritical view of the functioning of the central nervous system in terms of sensations, reactions to outside stimuli, assimilatory processes, and attempts to reach equilibria. It is clear that he believes neither external nor internal equilibria are possible for Diaspora Jewry, which he sees as an alien minority within a foreign body. Social change, says Borochov, will alter the social system, not human feelings. Furthermore, the revolution will occur in the distant future "if at all." The solution to the Jewish question is therefore Zionism and the negation of the Diaspora.

In the same period Borochov published his onslaught against territorialism, which he called "a failure which has been elevated to an ideal." He accused Territorialists of only seeing the negative basis of Zionism, i.e. Jewish misery, and not its positive values—nation, culture, homeland. He accused the worst of the Territorialists of "hatred of Zion." More important, he presented a broader argument that was in many ways similar to "Our Program." Borochov saw a pathological element in the Jewish situation. Denying that he advocated an organic theory of society (while using organic images again and again), he pursued one of his favorite analogies, that of a doctor and his patient. A physician would not try to cure tuberculosis with methods that encourage bacteria to multiply and strengthen. Similarly the social analyst could not recommend a cure for the Jewish problem by using what enhanced anti-Semitism. New forces had to be brought into play. A new scene of action other than the Diaspora was needed, and the problem could not be expected to simply work itself out; indeed therapy was needed. Zionism must be a "therapeutic movement" that would analyze the problem, the obstacles preventing its resolution, and *consciously* begin work on the basis of a prepared program. The effort must be organized and planned. Borochov contrasted this with "evolutionary movements" which worked out their problems within the natural flow of history—Marx and Engels, he said (somewhat inaccurately), did not discuss in the *Communist Manifesto* how to reach their goal.

Borochov called for an elite mobilization of organized, conscious, Bilu-like pioneers to lead the way in Zionism. Eventually Zionism would move from such an avant-garde enterprise to a "national undertaking," at which time "the inner historic necessity of Zionism" would focus on the internal forces of the people rather than the conscious efforts of the original voluntaristic elite. Zionism would then be an evolutionary rather than a therapeutic movement.[27] Borochov's position changed radically in the following months and no doubt the Russian revolutionary events had much to do with this. The Marxist Zionism of Borochovism, worked out primarily in late 1905 and early 1906, went far beyond his earlier psychological assertions (although very important components remained), and presented a more materialist approach that cast aside the idea of a new Bilu for a focus on class struggle. The theory of Borochov's "Our Platform" was more of an "evolutionary" approach. Nonetheless, it is important to note that many of his future ideas existed in embryo in his earlier essays, particularly the notion of abnormality of Jewish economic structure. And of course Borochov vehemently opposed a Jewish nationalism that looked to any land outside of Palestine.

III

Territorialism preoccupied the World Zionist Organization until its Seventh Congress in Basle in the summer of 1905. Borochov attended as a delegate from Poltava. During the congress and before—at a conclave of Zion Zionists organized by Ussishkin at Freiburg and at a preconference meeting of Russian Zionists—Borochov, acting in tandem with the Russian Zionist leader, found himself at odds with many of the Poale Zionists and Socialist Zionists. He had bitter exchanges with Syrkin and the Territorialists as well as other Poale Zionists who had been influenced by the Vozrozhdeniye. The Territorialists were defeated at the congress, the Uganda Plan was buried, and its adherents split from the organization.

Mattityahu Mintz shows that Borochov's anti–Uganda Plan activities, even before the congress, were largely aimed at Poale Zion groups and against *Gegenwartsarbeit* (taking part in Russian politics). His orientation was fixated on Palestine. After the congress, the Vozrozhdeniye-oriented Poale Zionists made efforts to unify the Poale Zion groups throughout Russia. This alarmed both Borochov and Ussishkin, and the former returned to Russia several months later enthralled with a new revolutionary spirit and preoccupied with the establishment of an all-Russian, anti-territorialist Poale Zion party. Throughout his efforts in this direction he remained in close contact with Ussishkin, who gave him assistance.[28] Yet his overall perspective was changing, and his distinct theoretical formulation was soon to emerge. "He had gone abroad as a 'general Zionist,'" writes Itzhak Ben-Zvi, "when he returned, he joined the Labor Zionist movement and set himself the task of working for the consolidation of the new party, for its unity and cohesion."[29]

Immediately after the Zionist Congress he went to a meeting of Poale Zion activists in Zurich together with Liuba Meltzer, whom he had recently married. "Borochov attended as a visitor," reports Rachel Yanait (later Ben-Zvi's wife), "he was still hesitant as to whether his place was among the 'Blues' or the 'Reds' in the Poale Zion and for the most part kept quiet."[30] The next few months were spent in Switzerland and Berlin where, among other things, Borochov pursued one of his favorite pastimes—exploring libraries.[31] It was also in Berlin that Borochov wrote one of his seminal essays, "The National Question and the Class Struggle."

By the fall of 1905, months of revolutionary disruption had shaken the Czarist regime. In late October a wave of pogroms again rocked the Jews. Caught up in the fervor of the times, Borochov demanded "money and arms" from the head of the German Zionist organization and made his way back to Russia, where Ussishkin sent him on a speaking and organizing tour throughout the Pale.

By December Borochov developed a center of his own Poale Zion followers in Poltava. That same month he matched wits with the Vozrozhdeniye at a conference in Berdichev. Borochov and the Poltavists argued that immediate work in Palestine was as important as the struggle in the Diaspora (which they now supported). Their foes presented the reverse argument and claimed that priority had to be placed on Jewish autonomy in the Diaspora, which was a necessary step to the far-off goal of territorial concentration and national autonomy.[32] The two positions could not be reconciled. Borochov turned to creating his own party and the Vozrozhdeniye became part of the Sejmists shortly thereafter.

"In the night of Purim 5666 [1906]," wrote Itzhak Ben-Zvi, "delegates from Poale Zion groups from all the regions of vast Russia, from Lithuania, from the Ukraine, from Poland, and from the Crimea, assembled at Poltava in the Ukraine. . . . At this conference all the existing little groups were fused into one party. It was a decisive step at a decisive moment. . . . It led to ideological consolidation and the creation of an organization and political body of Socialist Zionists. Borochov was its ideological center."[33] Most of the meeting took place in a bakery on the outskirts of the city, where the Jewish Social Democratic Workers Party–Poale Zion was founded. The participants were eventually forced out of town by police raids.

The stars of the conference were Borochov and Ben-Zvi (then using his underground name Ovadiah). The latter was the only participant who had actually been to Palestine. Borochov proclaimed himself a "prognostic Palestinian": based on his analysis of Jewish realities, he believed that Diaspora Jewry was in an impossible position and that a mass migration of Jews was an historic necessity. This migration would occur through a "stychic" (elementary, spontaneous) process resulting from the inner dynamics of Jewish history. His key ideas were formulated in "Our Platform," which he wrote for the newly united Poale Zion.[34]

IV

Three essays included in the present volume, "The National Question and the Class Struggle" (1905), the selections from "Our Platform" (1906), and the later "Economic Development of the Jewish People" (1916)—reveal the full dimensions of Borochov's Marxist Zionist synthesis. "The National Question" begins by attempting to define the relation between class and nation in materialist terms. Marx stated in his famous preface to *A Contribution to the Critique of Political Economy* (1859), that in "the social production of their lives" men enter into "relations of production" which are independent of their will. The relations of production constitute the property relations at the economic base of the society. Revolution, said Marx. results from conflict between the developing forces of production and the existing relations of production. For example, as new, capitalist productive forces grew within the womb of feudal society, that society's relations of production, i.e. the feudal property system of lord and serf, became (to use Marx's terminology) a fetter on those emerging productive forces. Thus a revolutionary bourgeoisie was eventually bound to confront the feudal ruling class.

Borochov believes this analysis is essential to a materialist understanding of modern society, but insufficient to understand nationalism (which Marx, of course, was not trying to explain in his preface). Production, says Borochov, is dependent on different conditions in different times and places. Thus not only are their relations of production to be considered, but also varying *conditions of production*. These conditions "are geographical, anthropological and historical. Historical conditions include both those generated within a given social entity and those imposed by neighboring groups." The natural, geographical conditions first predominated in the historical process of separating groups. As civilization progressed, historical and social conditions became primary. "We may," says Borochov, "and do speak of a *relative distinctiveness* of social groups only because there is a relative distinctiveness in the *conditions* of production under which each group must develop its life." Thus Borochov asserts that there are two basic types of human groups as a result of material, historical development: "societies," defined by conditions of production (peoples, nations, etc.,) and "classes," defined according to relations of production.

Whereas class struggle originates in the conflict between relations and developing forces of production, national struggles occur when the development of a nation's forces of production demands better conditions of production. As such, "*the national problem . . . arises when the development of the forces of production of a nationality conflicts with the state of the conditions of production.*" Unlike "On Questions of Zionist Theory," Borochov here argues that the national struggle is to be understood primarily in material, economic terms. However, his materialist analysis is a concretization of the assertions he already made in his earlier essays. The claim in "The National Question" that national conflicts are the result of a nationality's quest for better conditions of production is a materialist version of his empiriocritical argument in "On Questions of Zionist Theory" that all creatures, like nations, need food to replace energy and assimilate other nations when their possessions are needed.

"The National Question" goes on to develop several definitions. Borochov states that a "people," i.e. a social group developed under similar conditions of production, can be called a "nation" when its members develop self-consciousness. Thus the "*feeling of kinship, created as a result of the visioned common historical past and rooted in the common conditions of production is called nationalism.*" And territory is the critical condition of production for all other such conditions. For nationalism to emerge, the conditions of production must be nationalized, as it were, unified over a given piece of land. Historically, this happens with the rise of the bourgeoisie.

Under normal conditions of production, class antagonism intensifies, whereas under abnormal conditions—and this is crucial for his analysis of the Jewish question—class and national consciousness tend to obfuscate each other to the disadvantage of the oppressed. For the proletariat, all this has special bearing because the worker is affected by the national question through his place of work, his territory. Class struggle can only take place where the worker actually toils:

> The system of production of oppressed nationalities is always subject to abnormal conditions. The conditions of production are abnormal when . . . a nation is deprived of its territory and its organs of national preservation . . . or when it is hindered in the full enjoyment of these. Such abnormal conditions tend to harmonize the interests of all members of a nation.

This hinders class struggle. Yet there is a *progressive* nationalism, that of an oppressed proletariat, that struggles to create for itself normal conditions of production, thus assuring a "strategic base" for class struggle.

"Our Platform," the lengthiest statement of Borochovism, takes many of these ideas and applies them more fully to the Jewish question as well as in criticism of the Poale Zion's rivals—the Z.S., Bund, Vozrozhdeniye, etc. The selections of "Our Platform" appearing here concentrate on Borochov's Zionist formulation. In *Galut* the Jews are a classical abnormal, expatriated nation, says Borochov. Lacking material conditions of their own, the Jews are "helpless in the national competitive struggle." Borochov denies that any struggle is equally in the interest of all classes in a nation, and sees the roots of anti-Semitism in the competition between Jewish and non-Jewish petty bourgeoisie and proletarians. He develops his argument by analyzing Jewish class structure and tendencies. Jewish capital, he says, is largely invested in production of consumer goods rather than in the more basic means of production. Because of anti-Semitism Jewish labor is largely employed by the Jewish middle bourgeoisie. As that bourgeoisie is pushed out by national competition, it is forced to migrate and the Jewish proletariat will follow: "The Jewish question migrates with the Jews."

In "Economic Development of the Jewish People" Borochov shows through use of the 1897 Russian census statistics that the percentage of Jews in any given level of production "varies directly with its remoteness from nature," in contrast with other "normal" nations. At least 50 percent of Jewish workers were in trades producing directly for the consumer. The root of the problem was landlessness. He also argues that the Jews faced a special problem as capitalism developed further. According to Marx's *Capital*, constant capital (i.e. the actual means of production, machinery, etc.) grows at the expense of variable capital (wages). Using a somewhat loose definition of Marx's terms, Borochov claims that as machines displace workers, the Jews will face an even greater problem, for in the production of the means of production, few Jews were to be found. Jewish labor was increasingly being displaced.

Borochov's argument is that anti-Semitism, national competition (in which the Jews, lacking a territorial base, are at a disadvantage), and the continuing development of capitalism force a continual pattern of Jewish migration, and make the abnormal Jewish conditions of production more and more insecure. Jewish labor, not employed by non-Jews, follows the migration of Jewish capital, and because of competition the Jewish petty bourgeoisie becomes more and more proletarianized. Yet if "the Jewish problem migrates with the Jews," then a radical solution that does not simply lead to another inhospitable roadside inn is needed. The solution was proletarian Zionism; the "conscious Jewish proletariat" had the task of directing the migration. In the final analysis the abolition of capitalism *and* national liberation were the salvation for the Jewish working class.

The Poale Zion, under Borochov's leadership and consequent to his new analysis, now actively involved itself in the revolutionary struggle in Russia.[35] However, since the Jewish proletariat developed in abnormal conditions of production, Diaspora struggles—including that for national autonomy which Borochov now supported—could only be palliatives. They failed to provide, in his view, a *radical* solution to a *radical* problem. He stressed that the Jewish proletariat lacked a strategic base. Employed mostly by the small Jewish capitalist, the striking Jewish worker had little impact on the equilibrium of the entire system of exploitation. "A chained Prometheus," he declared, "who in helpless rage tears the feathers of the vulture that preys on him—that is the symbol of the Jewish proletariat." As such, the Poale Zion maximum program was socialism, to be achieved by class struggle. The minimum program was Zionism: solely by attaining political and territorial autonomy in Palestine would the Jews occupy all levels in production, have a normal class structure, and a strategic base to join in the international struggle for socialism. In Palestine the Jewish class struggle would take place.

Not only does Borochov argue against territorialism and for Zionism, he tries to argue that the Jews would migrate to Palestine out of historical necessity. Real conditions, not just emotions, would lead them there because Jewish territorial autonomy "is being realized by means of processes inherent in Jewish immigration." Borochov argues that as migratory labor follows migratory capital, and since Jewish capital is being excluded from areas where there are possibilities for widespread land colonization and large industrial investments, Jewish migration will ultimately tend toward a land where its labor and petty capital can be directed toward basic industry and agriculture: "The country into which Jews will immigrate will not be highly industrial nor predominantly agricultural but rather semiagricultural. Jews alone will migrate there, separated from the general stream of immigration. The country will have no attraction for immigrants from other nations." And, "*The land of spontaneously concentrated Jewish immigration will be Palestine.*" This was Borochov's theory of a spontaneous, or "stychic," process leading the Jews to Palestine, a theory that has become closely associated with his name, but which is one of his least convincing arguments and was eventually rejected by him.

Palestine was ideal because it would be, in Borochov's view, the only land available to the Jews. It lacked advanced political and cultural development, and would be a land in which big capital would find no possibility while Jewish petty and middle capital would. Thus Borochov was an antiterritorialist Palestinist by "prognosis" rather than by "principle," i.e. he claimed that the Jewish historical connection to the land of Israel was not the key factor. The argument is rounded off by a strategy of capitalist development for Palestine, leading to a normalized Jewish class structure, class struggle, and finally socialism.

Borochov had effectively reversed his earlier advocacy of an elite vanguard and now depicted Zionism as an evolutionary movement. "Stychic" in Greek means "elementary" and the Russian *Stikhinost* refers to elemental spontaneity. The movement in Borochov's thought parallels a basic tension that permeated the nineteenth-century Russian intelligentsia. Leopold H. Haimson notes that the intelligentsia, alienated in Russia by their attraction to Western ideas, yet tied to Russia and confronted by the unreality of such ideas in their homeland, found themselves in internal contradiction. They looked to the West intellectually but could not be reconciled with their Russian feelings at the same time. Haimson says:

> It is in this process of dissociation in the psychic life of the members of the intelligentsia, just as much as in their alienation as a "conscious" minority from the "unconscious" masses, it is in the contrast between the elevated sentiments that they could incorporate in their world view and the more undisciplined feelings that they tried to repress or ignore that one must look in part for the origins of the duality of *soznatelnost* and *stikhinost,* consciousness and elemental spontaneity, the two basic conceptual categories under which so many of the intelligentsia were subsequently to subsume the conflicts in their own existence and the evolution of the world around them.[36]

This conflict later manifested itself in numerous variations: faith in the ability of an elite to make the world anew versus fusion with "elementary" forces represented (or rather idealized) in the peasantry, Marxists versus Narodniki, Bolsheviks versus Mensheviks. One can see the therapeutic as opposed to the "stychic" Borochov within this broad light as well.

For the Jewish world, it was not Borochov's particular formulation of the "stychic" process that mattered, but rather his presentation of a coherent ideological synthesis for those who were attracted to socialism *and* Zionism. By his advocacy of both socialist Palestinism, participation in Russian revolutionary events, and support of national autonomy in the Diaspora, he offered a clear alternative to the Bund's anti-Zionism, the Vozrozhdeniye's postponement of a territorial solution to the Jewish question, and finally to the Z.S.'s non-Palestinian territorialism.

V

The Jewish Labor Bund, founded in Vilna in 1897, rapidly had become an important force in the Jewish world and in the Russian Social Democratic movement, and was the largest Jewish socialist organization. As socialists, the Bundists were at first hostile to nationalism. Yet within the first decade of its existence, internal pressure as well as external (i.e. the growth of Zionism) forced the Bund to reevaluate the national question, leading to the advocacy of nonterritorial national cultural autonomy for the Jews, focused primarily on Yiddish culture. Nonterritorial autonomy meant that Jews on a personal basis throughout the empire were to be considered part of a Jewish nation and territorial concentration was unnecessary. Zionism, in the Bundists' view, was a utopia based on the fantastic notion that a Jewish state could be re-created. The real world, life, and the future of the Jews were to them in Eastern Europe, not in Palestine.

The Bund's move toward a national position was not a painless process. Vladimir Medem (1897-1923) played a leading role in attaining a reevaluation. In his essays—published as a booklet in 1906 and entitled *Di sotsyal-demokratye un di natsyonale frage*—he tried to synthesize a Marxist approach with an analysis of the national question. His key concept at that time was *neutralism,* to which not all Bundists subscribed. Medem attacked both assimilationists and nationalists and sought an alternative path for Social Democrats. He opposed Lenin's view that a nation had to be defined on the basis of language and territory, and argued that ultimately socialism alone would solve the Jewish question.[37] The continuation or destruction of the national culture of any particular group should be left to the workings-out of history: "We . . . will not expend any energies," he argued, "either to hinder this process, or to support it. We do not interfere; we are neutral."[38] The oppression of a nationality must, however, be fought on all accounts. A nation was defined as "the totality of all individuals who belong to a certain historic-cultural group, independent of the fact that they live in different territories."[39] Thus Medem's program suggested that nationalities, defined on a cultural-personal rather than territorial basis, should have their own decentralized, autonomous institutions to conduct cultural affairs—and *only* cultural affairs. *Political* autonomy was not included. Medem called for a policy of *neutralism* on the pros and cons of the future of the various nations. In the aftermath of the 1905 revolution, the Bund, and eventually Medem himself, developed a more positive approach to national survival.

The fact that Jews once possessed substantial autonomy in a multinational Eastern Europe set the backdrop for these discussions as well.

Before the nineteenth century they controlled their own internal affairs through administrative councils. The question of autonomy for nationalities also became a major concern for Marxists in the multinational Austro-Hungarian empire. Since Social Democrats in Russia looked west for guidance on many theoretical matters, the impact of Austro-Marxists Karl Renner and Otto Bauer should not be overlooked. These two thinkers formulated an understanding of nationalism that paralleled that of Bundists in many respects.

Renner's *Der Kampf der öesterreichischen Nationen um den Stadt* (1902) envisioned a state organized as a federation of nations rather than as a union of citizens. A nation was defined in personal rather than territorial terms.[40] Bauer's *Die Nationalitätenfrage und die Sozialdemokratie* (1907) conceived of a nation in terms of "a common history as the effective cause, common culture and common descent as the means by which it produces its effects, a common language as the mediator of common culture, both its product and its producer."[41] Bauer did recognize that lack of a common territory played a disruptive role in the life of a nation, but did not make territory essential to defining a nation. His "comprehensive" definition said that "the nation is the totality of men bound together through a common destiny into a community of character."[42] As a solution to the national problem Bauer, like Renner, suggested a federal state and national autonomy. Of assimilated Jewish parents, Bauer admitted that the Jews were a nation, but believed they were losing their national characteristics. Tied by their class structure to capitalism, the Jews were doomed, as was capitalism.

Socialists were not alone in discussing *autonomy* at this time. Simon Dubnov (1860-1941), one of the greatest of Jewish historians, presented his own liberal, nonsocialist conception of a nation. He proposed three periods in the historical evolution of nations: tribal, territorial-political, and cultural-historical (or spiritual). He argued that "a test of the full development of the national type comes in the case of a people that has lost its political independence, a factor generally regarded as a necessary condition for national existence."[43] Such a nation is bound by its cultural, historical, and spiritual aspects rather than by land or economic interests, which are important primarily on a lower level of national existence. The Jews represented such a nation to Dubnov, for they were bound together by Judaism as a "body of culture," not simply as a religion. The main criterion of a nation's existence was its consciousness: "I think of myself as a nationality—therefore I am."[44] To protect itself, he argued, the Jewish nation must oppose both the thesis of isolationism and the antithesis of assimilation. Instead, a new synthesis of autonomy must be asserted: "The chief axiom of Jewish autonomy may thus be formulated as follows: Jews in each and every country who take an active part in civic and political life enjoy all rights given to the citizens, not merely as individuals but also as members of their national groups."[45] Such autonomy would focus on three institutions: the community as a whole, language, and education.

While Dubnov was close in many ways to the spiritual Zionism of his friend Ahad Haam and did not oppose the development of the Palestinian Jewish community, he considered political Zionism as a political messianism that would be unable to solve the Jewish question. He was bitterly opposed to any negation of the Diaspora; as a liberal who formed his own *Folkspartei* during the storms of 1905-1906, he also opposed the Bund bitterly. He attacked the Bund's claim to being the "sole representative" of Jewish workers, and shortly after the pogroms of 1905 stated:

> They talk of "the right to self-determination" and even "national cultural autonomy," among the principles of universal freedom, but they do not care for the concrete development of national Jewish culture, for the organization of autonomous communities, or for national education, as a shield against assimilation which they consider a natural phenomenon.[46]

This last comment was aimed at Medem, who himself attacked Dubnov on a variety of points, including the idea that there was a *world* Jewish people. Lacking a unified Jewish environment, Medem wrote in 1911, one could not speak of a worldwide cultural community of Jews—in each country the Jews were more identified with the local culture. Perhaps, he suggested, a time would come when one would speak of several Jewish nations.[47] This did not represent an isolated position in the Bund. During discussions in 1917 to create a Russian Jewish Congress, the Bund opposed making the problems of non-Eastern European Jewry an issue.

For Dubnov, the Bund's approach was a thorough misconception. He argued that its emphasis on class rather than national politics was a catastrophic error for an oppressed nation like the Jews:

> To all the arguments that the class struggle is natural and necessary, I answer: Yes, it is natural and necessary in so far as it stems from the true relationship between the forces of capital and labor among our people; but it has not yet reached a stage of such decisive importance as to justify its claim to be the supreme principle and sole guide in our social and national life. The class struggle is one of the factors, but not the only factor, and not even the most important one, in our life, and its influence on our national politics must be set in proper perspective and not artificially exaggerated and inflated. Even if we grant that the class problem will become the chief factor for us in the distant future, even then national

politics will not have to yield its supremacy to class politics if this entails a danger to the unity and integrity of the nation.[48]

Seen in light of these theories, Borochov represents a middle ground that interweaves various aspects of them while parting company on the final issue—the ultimate future of the Diaspora. Like Medem and the Bund, Borochov sought an analysis of nationalism and the Jewish question that would both remain within the Marxist framework and face Jewry's immediate crises. Borochov alternated between high praise of the Bund's organizing and self-defense efforts and condemnation of its national program. Like Dubnov, he derided the Bund's claim to be the Jewish proletariat's sole representative. Borochov could accept neither Bauer's nor Medem's final conclusion vis-à-vis the Jews, i.e. their disappearance with socialism's advent in the former case and neutralism toward such a possibility in the latter. A Dubnovian theory of the spiritual individualism of a nation was insufficient as an analysis of the concrete realities of national existence for Borochov, as much as he recognized the role of spiritual factors and supported Diaspora autonomy as a halfway measure in the struggle for Jewish survival. Like the young Marx, Borochov believed that the Jews survived because of history, not in spite of it. And for the Marxist-Zionist, positive national struggle did not necessarily preclude class struggle, although he very much recognized potential contradictions (which were ultimately the result of the abnormality of Diaspora existence). The Borochov of Borochovism—unlike his earlier formulations and those of many General Zionists—insisted on class struggle in the Diaspora, struggle for Jewish autonomy in the Diaspora, struggle with progressive forces against autocracy, *and* concurrently, the struggle for Zion.

Most important was the radical opposition between Borochov's prognosis for the Diaspora and that of his ideological foes. For Borochov, unlike Dubnov, Medem, the Bund, the majority of Russian Social Democrats, and the Vozrozhdeniye (but like the Territorialists), the Jewish condition required radical surgery. Disapora autonomy, a necessary palliative, was simply not enough and failed to take into account the anomalous reality of *Galut*. In fact, autonomy offered nothing radical at all. The Jews had once possessed an autonomous structure in eastern Europe. To argue that autonomy was *the* solution was to argue for a modernized version of what once was, albeit in new conditions and shed of religious domination. The Bund's demand for autonomy in a socialist Russia was a call for a cultural, nonpolitical reconstruction of Jewish internal self-rule. But it offered no truly radical critique of the Jewish situation, and certainly did not offer an economic or political form of self-determination. Similarly, the Vozrozhdeniye, in supporting territorial autonomy "in the long run," negated the urgency of the Jewish question while Dubnov, in opposing class politics, was a liberal who didn't fully grasp the motor of history. A Socialist Zionist synthesis was the only real alternative.

VI

On the same evening in June 1906 that Czar Nicholas II disbanded the Duma, Borochov was arrested in Poltava. The police found arms in the home of Ben-Zvi's father and the Poale Zion leader was taken by the police after the arrest of Ben-Zvi's entire family (with the exception of Ben-Zvi himself who managed to escape). Borochov spent several months in prison where he wrote (mostly on ethics) and conducted a "people's university." As a result of his lectures there, several Ukrainian nationalist groups later referred to themselves as "Borochovist." Fearing that he might end up in Siberia, Borochov's friends raised funds for bail and then arranged for him to disappear. After a period of living under a pseudonym, he left Russia for an exile that lasted a decade.

The following few years were a time of European travel, party work, and research. He began writing in Yiddish in 1907 (his earlier works were written in Russian) and became a pioneering scholar of Yiddish philology. "The Aims of Yiddish Philology" (included in this volume) and "Library of the Yiddish Philologist" appeared in 1913, the same year in which he spent months researching an unfinished manuscript, *History of the Yiddish Language and Literature,* at the British Museum. Borochov vociferously attacked those who, in their zealous advocacy of Hebrew revival, totally negated Yiddish culture. Among those heated polemics was "Hebraismus Militans," which is also included in this volume. After helping found the World Confederation of Poale Zion at the Hague in 1907, he led the fight in the Socialist International for Poale Zion representation and then for an independent Jewish section of the International. One of his chief adversaries was the Bund, and it was not until the close of World War I that Poale Zion was accorded full rights in the International.

The different national sections of the Poale Zion were not uniform in their approach to Socialist Zionist goals. Borochov, based in Vienna in the period before the Great War, was the leader of the left wing. Internal battle-lines were usually drawn between Borochov (leading the Russians), the Austrians (led by Shlomo Kaplansky), Palestinians (led by Ben-Zvi), and the Americans (who by then had Nachman Syrkin in their ranks). Among other things, Borochov opposed cooperation with the World Zionist Organization, which was dominated by bourgeois elements, and led the Russian Poale Zion out of the W.Z.O. Important strategic disputes in the Poale Zion emerged in the fall of 1909 when a series of conferences, first of the Russian Poale Zion, then of the World Poale Zion, and finally of the World Zionist Organization, took place. The Austrian Poale Zionists were advocates of cooperative settlement schemes in Palestine, along lines advocated by the German Jewish sociologist Franz Oppenheimer and favorably explored by the W.Z.O. Oppenheimer's goal was to turn Jewish city-dwellers into farmers in cooperative agricultural settlements based on profit-sharing and self-reliance. The Jews would, as such, become "normalized" by the building of a laboring class tied to the soil. Such was the path by which Zionism would retrieve the land of Israel. As Oppenheimer put it:

> We shall spread a net of farming colonies over the country which we wish to win. When one wishes to spread a net, one first drives in stakes at the points between which it is desired to place the net. Then one extends between these stakes powerful ropes, and between the ropes string cords are knotted, thus forming a coarse meshwork which may be made as fine as one pleases by working in smaller cords.[49]

It can be readily seen how far this conception was from Borochov's notion that Palestine ought to be developed along a capitalist model (as a prelude to the class struggle). Yet even Borochov's friend and comrade Ben-Zvi now supported this idea. The Palestinian Poale Zionists, having actually lived in the land, concluded that the Russian Poale Zion's perspective was untenable. Even before 1909, Rachel Yanait records, the Palestinians' view was that they "were moving far from the dogmas followed by Poale Zion abroad. Our movement here [in Palestine] was shaped by the new life, by the actual needs of the workers who were winning the Land back by the work of their hands. The movement abroad must adjust itself to this new reality."[50] Kaplansky argued for the creation of a Jewish peasantry organized cooperatively, for he asserted that only those working a land could own it. In contrast, Borochov argued that the industrial sector was more important than the agricultural, and cooperative settlements would only succeed with outside (bourgeois) backing and therefore bourgeois control. In a country moving toward capitalism, such cooperatives would become isolated socialist islands. The strategy should therefore be one of a more normal class development, class struggle, and socialist revolution.[51]

Borochov lost on this and several other matters. The debate seems to have been one in which Borochovism was defeated by those affirming many aspects of Borochov's earlier approach—a Ussishkin-Bilu-Oppenheimer pioneering synthesis. In retrospect it also paralleled in some ways the ongoing dispute between Marxist and anarchist models of reshaping society—the former through mass struggle, the latter through alternative community building. Indeed, during the period of the Second Aliyah (1904-1914), a second labor party (apart from Poale Zion) was formed in Palestine called Hapoel Hatzair (the young worker), whose orientation was much closer to the ideas of Proudhon and Gustav Landauer than to European social democracy.

When placed within the context of Palestine and the Zionist efforts there during 1900-1920, the picture becomes more complex. Borochov assumed a model of normal capitalist development in that land, leading to a proletarian class struggle against the bourgeoisie. However, while the new Jewish nation in Palestine was being "normalized" to the extent that Jews were more and more occupying roles in all sectors of the economy (like most other nations, but unlike Diaspora Jewry), this evolution did not take place in conditions that could be characterized as normal. The Zionists found themselves in battle with the Turks, the British, and the Arabs. Facing vehement opposition to their very presence, Borochov's class-struggle model was hardly tenable. Ironically, this was because of the realities of the national struggle between the Jews and the Palestinian Arabs. Given these adversities, the foundation of a Jewish laboring class became cooperative Jewish settlements which was then followed by an urban sector and trade union movement. On the other hand, while this labor movement led the way to statehood, Israeli society later drifted further and further from socialism and, as Borochov predicted, the kibbutzim more and more became islands of utopian socialism.

VII

Borochov made plans numerous times to go to Palestine, but circumstances always seemed to bar his way. With the outbreak of World War I he was forced to leave Austro-Hungary, after being briefly arrested (he was, after all, a Russian citizen, and Russia was at war with Austro-Hungary). Via Italy he went to the United States in late 1914. By now the epitome of the wandering Jew, he must have been haunted by his own words—"the Jewish problem migrates with the Jews." He spent two and a half unhappy years working for the American Poale Zion, editing and writing for several Yiddish publications, including *Di Varhayt* and the Poale Zion's *Yidisher Kemfer*. He was constantly at odds with the Poale Zion leadership, led a "social democratic opposition" to them, and resigned more than once from party positions. In 1915 he launched a vociferous attack accusing them of class collaboration and calling for their withdrawal from the W.Z.O. He refused to pay his dues to the W.Z.O. and was even suspended from the party for a period.

Borochov's Social Democratic current in the Poale Zion fought the dominant Socialist faction. He accused the latter of being 85 percent Zionist and 15 percent socialist whilst his own faction, to the contrary, was "100 percent socialist and 100 percent Zionist." Two polemics from this debate appear in English for the first time in this volume: "The Socialism of Poale Zion Here," and "Two Currents in Poale Zionism," both from 1915. It is also worth noting that rather than arguing for a radical negation of the Diaspora, he argues here *as a Zionist* that "*Galut* and Zion" must each be regarded as ends unto themselves. As World War I led to a worsening of European Jewry's condition, Borochov called for a total mobilization of world Jewry to aid them. He played an important role in agitating for the creation of democratic World- and American-Jewish Congresses to confront the realities of the war, to prepare Jewish demands for the peace afterwards, and to reorganize Jewish life. The Poale Zion "was to act as a spearhead of the entire Congress movement at the socialist and at the general level of Jewish politics."[52] In this battle Borochov fought the Bundist dominated Jewish Socialist Federation, the major established Jewish organizations (like the American Jewish Committee), and the philanthropies which dominated Jewish life.

Borochov's Marxist Zionism demanded that he support progressive politics in America, which he did, including approval of Morris Hillquit's 1916 candidacy for Congress against the Democrat Tammany Hall, who ran as a Zionist. In an article entitled "Socialism and Tammany Hall," Borochov denounced Hillquit's foe for debasing the Jewish national idea.[53] He also had little patience for many of those who spoke in the name of Marxism. On March 20, 1915 he wrote in *Di Varhayt:*

> I can imagine Marx arising from his grave. Upon seeing his present disciples, he motions them away and utters, "I—God forbid—I am no Marxist."
>
> Marx was undoubtedly the greatest thinker of the 19th century. . . . But because Marx is dead and because new problems have arisen, we must think independently and arrive at our own solutions.

As a Jew, a socialist, and a former guest of the Czar's prisons, Borochov could only be pleased when, in February 1917, the world came crashing down around the "little father" of the Russian people. Despite his enthusiasm for the revolution, he warned that "the two most important problems of our time—the social oppression of the working class and the national oppression of weak nationalities shall, despite the present revolution, remain unsettled."[54]

It was time now to return to the land of his birth. On his way, Borochov stopped in Stockholm to await permission to enter Russia and to help prepare a Poale Zion statement for the Holland-Scandinavian Socialist Committee, a group of socialists from neutral countries who had banded together to develop a socialist peace conference and postwar program. The Poale Zion had continuously struggled to gain support from international socialism which was now badly divided by the war. Borochov met with the committee's leaders and the Poale Zion demands were included in the committee's "Peace Manifesto."[55] The Poale Zion statement (see the Appendix to this volume) greeted peace efforts, attacked the "imperialistic governments" responsible for the carnage, and urged the international proletariat to lead the "bleeding human race" to deliverance. It praised the idea of a League of Nations, insisted that the Jewish problem be placed on the international peace agenda, and demanded equality for Diaspora Jewry and national autonomy for Palestine Jewry.

Poale Zion became legal in Russia as a result of the revolution, and Borochov arrived in Kiev in September for its Third Congress (the First was the Poltava meeting in 1906, the Second in Cracow in 1907). His Russian supporters were shocked, for when "Comrade Borochov" spoke he sounded, in many respects, like a pre-Borochovism Borochov. The party, already racked with divisions on Jewish, Russian, and general questions—there were Bolsheviks, Mensheviks, and Internationalists—now found many of its members crying to "save Borochovism from Borochov."

Borochov's speech, subsequently known as "Eretz Israel in Our Program and Tactics," renounced his earlier conception of the stychic process, and supported the idea of constructivism in Palestine, including Oppenheimer's experiments. He spoke concurrently of the need for class struggle and the "dictatorship of the toiling masses." It is evident that he had not yet thoroughly rethought his changing ideas; it is certain that in 1917 he no longer spoke as a prognostic Zionist as he had in 1906. Ben-Zvi recalls that at one of his last meetings with Borochov in the United States, Borochov sided with him and with David Ben-Gurion— both of whom were then in the United States, having been expelled from Palestine by the Turks—in asserting the need to claim Jewish "historical rights" in Palestine.[56]

In Kiev, Borochov said that while past debates with the Bund and General Zionists had imposed a "kosher" terminology on his formulations, more emotional words could now be employed: "Now we can and must proclaim 'Eretz Israel'—a Jewish home!'" Mattityahu Mintz has shown that Borochov's new approach led to such a storm that later the party only presented a censored version of the events for publication.[57]

In the ensuing three months Borochov was apparently at odds with the Russian Poale Zion over numerous issues. In the Ukraine, efforts were underway by nationalists to guarantee independence or at least autonomy for the region. Borochov was willing to go much further than the Poale Zion leadership in support of Ukrainian claims. As a delegate to the Nationalities Congress, he called for a Socialist Federated Republic for Russia, and proposed a Russia much more decentralized than the Poale Zion advocated. His own party's publications gave him little coverage, and many of his public actions on the Ukrainian issue were taken while other Poale Zionists officially represented the party.[58]

What direction Borochov would have taken after the Bolshevik Revolution can only be the subject of speculation. That autumn he fell ill and on December 17, 1917 he died in Kiev, apparently of pneumonia. The Russian Poale Zion eventually split as a result of the revolution and was, in due time, suppressed like all other parties in the USSR. One Left faction actually survived into 1928, and a "Borochov Brigade" fought with the Red Army during the civil war. Two years after Borochov's death the Palestine Poale Zion merged with several other groups to form a new party, Achdut Avodah (unity of labor), which played a crucial role in creating the Haganah (defense), the chief Zionist underground military force during the British Mandate years, and the Histadrut, which soon became a powerful trade union federation. In 1930 Achdut Avodah merged with Hapoel Hatzair (the young worker) to form MAPAI (acronym for Israel's Workers' Party), which soon became the leading force in the Zionist movement. At its head was David Ben-Gurion, who began his political career in the first decade of the twentieth century in the Poale Zion in Plonsk, Poland, and who, in May 1948, 31 years after Borochov's death, read the declaration proclaiming the birth of the Jewish state.

How is Ber Borochov to be evaluated today? What is his legacy? This has been perpetually debated since his death. Borochov tried at once to be a Marxist and a nationalist. He sought to fill what Lenin called an inevitable empty space between two chairs because that space was, for him, potentially an abyss. Yet in this endeavor he became a pioneering social scientist of the Jews, constructing an argument based on history and the analysis of class and social structures. His doctrine helped galvanize a political party whose successors led Zionism to victory, although that party parted company with much of Borochovism. When compared with his competitors in Russian Jewish left and liberal circles, his pessimism about the future of the Diaspora and particularly Eastern

European Jewry, seems to have been borne out. While the catastrophe that befell European Jewry during World War II was not the dissolution of Jewry that Borochov foresaw, and while the stychic process did not take place, underlying Borochov's argument was a deep-seated belief that, given the evolution of Russia and modern capitalism, the Jewish situation was untenable.

Borochov's legacy is thus that of a theorist and political figure who insisted on asserting the particular needs of his people without negating the internationalist spirit. His internationalism refused to be self-denying. In this century, when Jews have been advised to disappear for the sake of progress, or have been simply exterminated by fascism, Borochov's vision still has much to say to those who hope for a different world.

Notes

1. Liuba Borochov, *Prakim meyoman hayai* (Givat Haviva: Givat Haviva Press, 1971), pp. 24-25.
2. Sidney S. Harcave, "Jewish Political Parties and Groups and the Russian State Dumas from 1905 to 1907" (Ph.D. diss., University of Chicago, 1943), p. 7.
3. For more on Lieberman see Jonathan Frankel, *Prophecy and Politics: Socialism, Nationalism and the Russian Jews, 1862-1917* (Cambridge: Cambridge University Press, 1981); Moshe Mishkinsky, "The Jewish Labor Movement and European Socialism" in H.H. Ben-Sasson and S. Ettinger, eds., *Jewish Society through the Ages* (New York: Schocken Books, 1971); William Fishman, *Jewish Radicals* (New York: Pantheon, 1974).
4. Itzhak Ben-Zvi, "Labor Zionism in Russia," in J. Frumkin, G. Aronson, and A. Goldenweiser, eds., *Russian Jewry (1860-1917)* (New York: Thomas Yoseloff, 1966), p. 209.
5. Jonathan Frankel, "Socialism and Jewish Nationalism in Russia, 1892-1907" (Ph.D. diss., Cambridge University, 1961), p. 357.
6. Ben-Zvi, "Labor Zionism," p. 210.
7. Author's interview with Borochov's sister, Nadia Borochov Ovsey.
8. Ibid.
9. Itzhak Ben-Zvi, "Neurei B. Borochov," in Ber Borochov, *Ktavim nivharim* (Tel Aviv: Am Oved, 1954), p. 9.
10. L. Borochov, *Prakim*, p. 22.
11. Shmarya Levin, *The Arena* (New York: Harcourt, Brace, & Co., 1932), pp. 190-91.
12. Ibid., p. 183.
13. Ibid., p. 262.
14. B. Borochov, *Di Varhayt*, May 13, 1916. See ch. 17 of this volume.
15. Frankel, "Socialism and Jewish Nationalism," pp. 371-72.
16. The essay itself is in Ber Borochov, *Ktavim* I (Tel Aviv: Hakibbutz Hameuchad and Sifriat Poalim, 1955). Valuable discussions of it are in Mattityahu Mintz, *Ber Borochov: Hamaagal harishon 1900-1906* (Tel Aviv: Tel Aviv University

and Hakibbutz Hameuchad Press, 1976), and in Frankel's chapter on Borochov in *Prophecy and Politics.*
17. Mattityahu Mintz, *Ber Borochov,* pp. 35-36.
18. Leszek Kolakowski, *Positivist Philosophy* (Middlesex: Pelican Books, 1972), p. 125.
19. This discussion is summarized from and based on the relevant chapters in Kolakowski, *Positivist Philosophy;* Kolakowski, *Main Currents of Marxism,* vol. II (Oxford: Oxford University Press, 1978); F. Copleston, *A History of Philosophy,* vol. 7, part II (Garden City: Image Books, 1965).
20. For the complex influences of Avenarius, Mach, and Bogdanov on Borochov see the lengthy discussion in Mintz, *Ber Borochov;* and Mintz, "Borochov veBogdanov," *Baderech* I (1967).
21. Mintz's *Ber Borochov* should be consulted for a more detailed biography. This award-winning volume covers the period up to 1906 and examines Borochov's intellectual development in much depth.
22. See Mintz, *Ber Borochov,* on the relation between Borochov and Ussishkin. See also Borochov's correspondence with Ussishkin, edited by Mintz, "Igrot Borochov le'Ussishkin," *Tzionut* II (Tel Aviv: Tel Aviv University and Hakibbutz Hameuchad Press, 1978).
23. Menahem-Mendel Ussishkin, *Our Program* (New York: Federation of American Zionists, 1905), p. 1.
24. Ussishkin, *Our Program,* pp. 1-2.
25. Ibid., p. 11.
26. The work of Weber (1795-1878) in experimental psychology was supplemented by Fechner (1801-1887), a Leipzig physicist and psychologist. For a short discussion of their theories see Copleston, *A History of Philosophy,* pp. 148-49.
27. See the essay itself in Ber Borochov, *Ktavim* I, pp. 18-153.
28. See Mintz, *Ber Borochov,* for a detailed account of this matter.
29. Ben-Zvi, "Labor Zionism in Russia," pp. 213-14.
30. Rachel Yanait Ben-Zvi, *Coming Home* (New York: Herzl Press, 1964), p. 199.
31. Rachel Yanait Ben-Zvi also later recalled a discussion with Borochov in Berlin on feminism, a subject which apparently had captured his interest. She recounts, "Borochov felt that there were no limits to what women could yet accomplish in intellectual and artistic fields. I used to go with him to the library every day, and one day among other things, he talked of the problems of women. He was doing research on the subject and had gathered three hundred notes on the position of Jewish women from Biblical times to the present." It seems he later lost these notes, much to his dismay. See Rachel Yanait Ben-Zvi, *Coming Home,* p. 199.
32. See Mattityahu Mintz, ed., "Shalosh te'udot me'yomai pulmus 'vozrozhdeniye,' erev ve'idat poltava shel mifleget hapoalim hayehudit hasotzial-demokratit 'poale Zion,'" in *Tzionut* V (Tel Aviv: Tel Aviv University and Hakibbutz Hameuchad Press, 1978).
33. Itzhak Ben-Zvi, "First Steps: The Beginning of Borochov's Zionist Work," *Itonut Avodah,* November-December, 1942, p. 7.
34. It is generally assumed that Borochov wrote most of "Our Platform." Zalman Shazar's memoirs report that Borochov was responsible for the theoretical analysis, Itzhak Ben-Zvi for material focused on Palestine, and a third Poale

34   Class Struggle and the Jewish Nation

Zionist named Vitebski for part of the polemics. Rachel Yanait Ben-Zvi also writes that her future husband was responsible for the Palestine section. See Zalman Shazar, *Morning Stars* (Philadelphia: Jewish Publication Society of America, 1967), pp. 157-59; Rachel Yanait Ben-Zvi, *Coming Home*, p. 209.

35. See Harcave, "Jewish Political Parties," for an analysis of the Jewish parties in 1905.
36. Leopold H. Haimson, *The Russian Marxists and the Origins of Bolshevism* (Boston: Beacon Press, 1966), p. 7.
37. See Oscar I. Janowsky, *The Jews and Minority Rights (1898-1919)* (New York: AMS Press, 1966), pp. 83-85. For additional information (in English) on Medem see Vladimir Medem, *The Memoirs of Vladimir Medem* (New York: Ktav Publishing House, 1979); Jonathan Frankel, *Prophecy and Politics.*
38. Janowsky, *The Jews and Minority Rights,* p. 83.
39. Ibid., p. 84.
40. Ibid., pp. 30-31.
41. Otto Bauer, "The Concept of the 'Nation'," in T. Bottomore and P. Goode, eds., *Austro-Marxism* (Oxford: Clarendon Press, 1978), p. 103.
42. Ibid., p. 107.
43. Simon Dubnov, *Nationalism and History* (New York: Atheneum, 1970), p. 80.
44. Ibid., p. 98.
45. Ibid., p. 137.
46. Ibid., pp. 208-209.
47. Koppel Pinson, "Arkady Kremer, Vladimir Medem, and the Ideology of the Jewish 'Bund'," in A. G. Duker and M. Ben-Horin, eds., *Emancipation and Counter-Emancipation* (New York: Ktav and the Conference on Jewish Social Studies, 1974), pp. 311-13.
48. Dubnov, *Nationalism and History,* pp. 218-19.
49. Franz Oppenheimer, *Co-operative Agricultural Colonization in Palestine* (New York: Federation of American Zionists, 1910), p. 5.
50. Rachel Yanait Ben-Zvi, *Coming Home,* p. 96.
51. See Frankel's discussion of this in chapter 8 of *Prophecy and Politics;* Ber Borochov, "Haavodah be'eretz israel," in Ber Borochov, *Ktavim* II (Tel Aviv: Sifriat Poalim and Hakibbutz Hameuchad, 1958); Ber Borochov, "Leshe'elat hapoalim be'eretz israel," in Ber Borochov, *Ktavim* III (Tel Aviv: Sifriat Poalim and Hakibbutz Hameuchad, 1966).
52. Jonathan Frankel, "The Jewish Socialists and the American Jewish Congress Movement," E. Mendelsohn ed., *Essays on the American Jewish Labor Movement* (New York: YIVO Annual of Jewish Social Science, no. 16), p. 209.
53. Norma Fain Pratt, *Morris Hillquit* (Westport: Greenwood Press, 1979), p. 152.
54. Joseph Rappaport, "Jewish Immigrants and World War I: A Study of American Yiddish Press Reactions" (Ph.D. Diss., Columbia University, 1951), p. 280.
55. Janowsky, *The Jews and Minority Rights,* pp. 250-51.
56. Ben-Zvi, "First Steps," p. 10.
57. See Mattityahu Mintz's introduction to *Have'ida hashlishit shel 'Poale Zion' berusya, 1917 (te'udot)* (Ramat Aviv: Tel Aviv University Press, 1976).
58. Mattityahu Mintz, "Ber Borochov vehaukrainim beshnat 1917," *Shvut* 4 (1976): 53-61.

1

On Questions of Zionist Theory

(1905)

We must not wait.

The Jewish people has suffered so much that greater affliction is inconceivable. Regarded objectively, our situation today, compared with the suffering experienced by our forefathers, can almost be envied, and there is every reason to believe that as time goes by our troubles will diminish. This gives support to the optimists among us, who take a hopeful view of the future in their opposition to Zionist action that aims to bring about a radical change in our situation and to put an end to the *Galut* episode with all its achievements. These optimists, since they value these achievements, try to prove to us that there is no need to be alarmed by the slowness of progress, on which they pin rosy hopes.

Objectively speaking, our position is already assured in a number of respects. The Inquisition—it is safe to assume—will not be renewed. Nor will mass expulsions ever occur again. But can the same be said when the question is viewed subjectively? On the basis of numerous experiments, psychologists have laid down the so-called Weber-Fechner Law, according to which the intensity of a sensation increases as the logarithm of the stimulus. If we translate this law from the language of mathematics to the language of life, it means that sensation increases at a much slower rate than the changes that take place in the environment, that as time goes by the individual pays less and less attention to these changes. Therefore, the more one's situation improves, the greater will be his demand for further improvement, and the longer will he have to wait to feel a real improvement in his environment that he regards as satisfactory. This explains the well-known fact that the most oppressed people are the least sensitive to their plight; they are content with their lot and only rarely complain. The surest way of making a slave dissatisfied and demanding is to alleviate the harshness of his lot. Some claim that our position has improved. I agree. But this very improvement has made us more sensitive: a reed of straw oppresses us more today than did the most savage torture rack in the past. The hostility of the environment, the restriction of civil rights, the pogroms, which in the past were facts of life we learned to live with, now strike us as horrible disasters. Our optimists fail to grasp this; for them progress has the brightness of the sun. But in reality, through the hazy glass of the Weber-Fechner Law, its light is becoming ever dimmer.

We have acquired more culture; we have lost our earlier faith in the world to come, in redemption by the Messiah, in our divine election— by virtue of which we allowed ourselves to look down on other nations, ignore their humiliating attitude, and regard it as conduct of creatures greatly inferior to us; hence they were unable, even by their most barbarous deeds, to upset our composure. One does not despair or lose his self-confidence just because he has been bitten by a dog. Today it is no longer a dog but one like ourselves who bites us, and his insults injure our honor. Formerly, religion and the ghetto constituted a wall that protected us against the enemy; but that protective wall has been undermined, and like all peoples of culture we have become sensitive to every affront to our rights, while externally our situation is much more difficult than theirs. Our optimists advise us to wait, to join forces with the progressive elements among the other nations, to help them in their struggle for the universal human ideal; they promise us and them victory over the reaction that oppresses us all.

But we Jews must not wait—and we Zionists cannot wait. Some among us fear that in the course of time, as a result of our stay in the *Galut* and the destructive effects of progress, the Jews will disintegrate and lose their national selfhood and national distinctiveness. Others say that the persecutions will not cease and the forces threatening us will assault us again after a short interval—half a century at the most—when they will attack with even greater ferocity. Finally, there are those who, disregarding these apprehensions and dangers, think that this is the most opportune time for the Jews in their struggle for self-expression and national distinctiveness to pass from the purely passive resistance they have practiced for eighteen centuries to concrete, territorial creation. In any event, all of us regard our position in the *Galut* as unstable and our prospects gloomy, not only from a subjective viewpoint but even from an objective-historical one.

Be that as it may, it is our deep conviction that in the *Galut* there is no salvation for the Jewish people. We do not rely on progress; we know that its overpious proponents inflate its achievements out of all proportion. Progress is an important factor in the rapid development of technology, science, perhaps even of the arts, but certainly in the development of neurosis, hysteria, and prostitution. Of the moral progress of nations, of the end of that national egoism that is destroying their best—it is too soon to speak about these. Progress is a two-edged sword.

If the good angel in a man advances, the Satan within him advances too.

It is hard to say which is the more amazing in our optimists: the naiveté of their enthusiasm or the dullness of their perception. They continue to sing hymns of praise to progress at a time when "cultured" England is cruelly grabbing from the Boers their last possessions—to the thunder of cannon and the applause of all classes of the English people; when "cultured" America is guilty of wanton despoliation of the Negroes; when Germany is threatening the entire world with its arrogant militarism; when the strong nations are prepared to trample one another for a piece of land in Turkey or China; while the weak nations groan in the world of the strong, yet pass up no opportunity to steal from one another or to demonstrate their might to peoples even weaker than they are. Most important, however, is that no one has yet succeeded in proving that he is right in trusting in the saving power of progress and in its real value. The rhetoricians and the believers are naive. It has not yet been proved that the historical process, the development of nations and society, is *progress.* Is it not improper to propose to the Jewish people to wait and put its trust in progress, when no one has yet succeeded in convincing us that such a thing actually exists?

But let us assume that it is true that all of mankind—including the inhabitants of Tierra del Fuego, the Fiji Islanders, the Japanese and the Kurds, and the anti-Semites of all varieties—will all be pacified and accept the peaceful reign of progress. But even you will not deny that such happiness cannot be attained without war and battles, you know that this war, which began some time ago, has cost and will cost mankind much blood and tears. What, then, is the price that we Jews will have to pay for it?

Let us take a small community, such as the Jews of Morocco. There are 300,000 Jews there, descendants of the exiles of Spain and Portugal in the fifteenth and sixteenth centuries, of the stock which gave to Judaism generations of distinguished personalities—scholars, poets, philosophers, and rabbis. A group of such superior descent deserves particular attention. But if the achievements of your progress must be attained by rivers of blood, by the degradation and torture of those Jews, is not the price of this boundlessly cruel idol of yours too high? For whom is the progress of Morocco desired? For those very Moroccans who drank the blood of Jews with such lust in the pogroms of 1903 and who violently abused women and children? The scraps of information available from the press show that the Moroccans have proved beyond any doubt that no upheaval will take place among them without bringing catastrophe to the Jews.

Certainly, progress cannot pass Morocco by; European states have already laid their predatory hands on that primitive country. Is it conceivable that the achievements of civilization will not arouse the hostility of the Moroccan masses, who hate everything foreign or European? Will such a revolution not be the end of the Jews in that country? Will nationalist hatred not be directed against the defenseless Jews because it cannot be directed against the well-protected predators of Europe? And will the Moroccan authorities be able to prevent this bloodshed, even if they should want to come to the aid of the Jews? Will they even want to? Will they not be pleased to divert the national passions away from themselves to the line of least resistance? Remember that even during the civil war over the throne, the Jews served as an excellent lightning rod the moment popular resentment threatened to burst over the heads of the pretenders to the throne.

The same fate awaits the Jews of Persia and the other Eastern countries. These Jews will pay with their lives for the first steps of militant progress. Meanwhile, the Jews of the Moslem countries are sitting on a volcano, and those wise enough to foresee the future, who have joined the Zionist movement, are well aware of the horror of the situation. This is another reason why the Zionists cannot—have no right—to wait. Certainly, let all the nations enjoy the fruits of progress, but we do not wish to be their scapegoat. Even if we leave the *Galut* mankind will pay in blood and tears for every upheaval that occurs in its history, except that Jewish blood is not taken into account—it only serves as amusement for the raging mob. There are thousands of Moslem and hundreds of thousands of Jews; let progress be content with the thousands of Moslems.

It will be said that these fears are unreal. Such fears cannot arouse or give direction to a solid national movement, first because passing phenomena are liable to give rise to spontaneous eruptions rather than to conscious activity, and second, because a solid movement cannot expect quick success when immediate rescue from danger is called for. I agree with that entirely. I will go even further and say that the Jews in the past have been saved from graver dangers; they may have lost a tooth or an eye, but they have nevertheless been capable of a new and higher development. We are experienced in the tribulations of bondage. And it is not my intention, nor that of any thinking Zionist, to tie the need for the realization of our goal exclusively to the possibility of outbreaks of anti-Semitism. I trust I have shown how little good we are promised from this much-heralded progress. Now let us examine how our fate is affected by certain laws that operate in society.

One fundamental and practically unique impulse in the life of society is egoism. If, with respect to the individual, there are grounds for arguing that man is not the miserly egoist depicted in certain ethical theories, the egoism of the group cannot be denied. For the benefit of the group, its members eschew personal gain and individual pleasure, conferring on the group's interest a supreme moral imprimatur. The individual sacrifices himself for the good of the group, and in so doing nourishes the group's crude lack of consideration. On the other hand, nothing is done in the life of the society that is not to the advantage of the dominant classes who are in full control and have the power to forbid or permit.

Aside from this, human society, by virtue of the iron laws of historical development, is divided into tribes, nationalities and nations, and that has consequently prepared the ground for dividing man's attitude toward others in a striking manner: with respect to "ours," the laws ensure equality of duties—I may not coerce, deceive, or cause unpleasantness to "mine"—while with respect to *others* there are no limitations, everything goes: the crudest infringement of rights, the most deceitful betrayal. I do not mean to say that this unfair demarcation will exist forever, but no one can prove it is destined to change in the foreseeable future. For the time being it is a fact of life; although its force is gradually weakening, it still must be taken into account.

It is man's nature to try to fit others to himself. This pure desire, which has nothing to do with the seeking of advantage, the desire to spread ideas, to impart feelings or ideals, is found in every person who relates to his existence with any degree of religious feeling or awe, and who appreciates their value not for himself alone. A man scatters his spiritual treasures willingly, and in this respect often reveals a degree of generosity that borders on heroism. Those whose ideas are being persecuted, are prepared for any suffering and sacrifice that will provide them with victory. And those whose views already hold sway over the consciousness of the masses—even though they are incapable of attaining such spiritual heights—are zealous in making converts, and their generosity is tremendous.

But my advice is to avoid becoming enthusiastic about such generosity; for spiritual possessions are not expropriable, and thus not only do not perish from this prodigality but even increase and improve in the process of preaching. By letting you share in my faith I may be giving you much, but I am still not depriving myself of anything. This is not the case with material or earthly possessions, measurable or not. Here man is generally not at all a squanderer, and social groups are even less so. It follows that every group is ready and willing to assimilate outsiders so long as it does not thereby surrender anything of its own, but faced with sharing material possessions with outsiders, no social group has as yet proved itself capable of such generosity.

Let us examine the meaning of this ambition, so often encountered in history, on the part of some nations to assimilate others, and the national conflicts that result. Every living creature that wishes to live requires food to replace the energy lost in every motion. For this purpose, the body acquires—i.e. assimilates to itself—energy from without. And just as the living creature, striving to expand its sphere of independent life draws and assimilates from without whatever he can swallow, without distinguishing between nonorganic parts and compounds on the one hand, and animals like itself on the other—so it is with society.

Society, all of whose functions are designed to expand its patterns of life, imbibes energy both from the nonsocial area and from other national groups, and is limited only by its ability to conquer and incorporate them within its own flesh and blood. These foreign people have no importance in themselves for the society that assimilates them. All it requires of them is their possessions and functions. There have been groups, including some quite developed ones—not to mention tribes of ancient times—who would kill babies born with a defect that made it unlikely that they would ever be able to bring any benefit to the society. This was the practice in Sparta, for example. The direct assimilation of other peoples by swallowing up their possessions—their land and the culture that flourished there—is still the ambition of all peoples, even in our day. And it is not so long ago that nations also strove to assimilate the functions of weak groups by making slaves out of them, forcing them to serve without any hope of taking part in the division of the assets accumulated by the enslavers. For a contemporary example, it is enough to cite the minor fact that the enlightened Americans bar the gates of their land to immigrants who are ill or unable to work. There is no need to mention the base exploitation of the Indians by England.

Here we must take account of the distinction between two cases so different from one another that the widespread failure to distinguish between them is enough to account for the current confusion concerning this matter. There can be no comparison between the position of two nations that live in adjacent territories, and two nations one of which lives amidst the other, in the latter's territory. In the first instance, the stronger of the two will strive to assimilate directly the possessions of the members of the other, and where possible, their functions as well. In the past this was done quite simply by wiping out the members of the second nation completely, or else by enslaving them, taking their property as a matter of course. In our time, international relations having become more complex, this method cannot be adopted. The effort is therefore made to assimilate the foreign country, and the cultural assets it has developed indirectly, by assimilating the population dwelling in it. Precisely the same objectives now being sought by German or Magyar assimilation of border areas would have been achieved in an earlier day by much more simple, direct, and efficient methods.

This clearly proves that no nation is interested in assimilating another without good reason. The assimilation of foreigners is actually in itself a most unpleasant business, and hence also undesirable. New people mean new candidates for benefits from the accumulated public assets, new hands hungrily stretched out for a share of the common loaf of bread. In order for a nation to desire the assimilation of another social group, it must first see in it something so valuable and attractive as to make it worthwhile despite all the inconvenience of including new partners in the distribution of the assets.

Today the functions performed by the foreigner can no longer constitute such an attractive commodity. Increasing recognition of the freedom and rights of the individual proves that the nature of social relations in our time is making the exploitation of someone else's toil by compulsion quite superfluous and even harmful. Society now requires only free workers, and these are available everywhere and in whatever quantity required, i.e. there is no longer need of the functions of the foreigner. Hence, if even today we witness the deliberate assimilation of a social group, it can only be for the sake of its wealth. For a nation to permit a foreign people to share in its unexpropriable spiritual assets, to graft onto its language, ideals, world-view, laws, and customs without thereby giving up anything tangible of its own, and yet to be able to do as it pleases with the expropriable material possessions of the foreign people— this is an extremely worthwhile exchange, which is still not renounced by nations in our day.

It should be noted that even though social bodies also act on the pleasure-seeking impulse, they do not reveal very farsighted reasoning in this matter. The gratifying hope at the time of assimilation is generally something like this: one day, when we succeed in getting the owners of the desired wealth to adapt themselves to such a degree that they no longer resist the policy of conquest, we shall be able to seize this wealth by force and stop bothering with this expensive business of assimilation. The trouble is that as the process of assimilation, which was at first only a means, turns into an end in itself—since opposition intensifies the ambition—the assimilators no longer think of the ultimate benefit. Assimilation becomes a chimera that lives by its own power, the supreme mission of the ruling groups, and gives rise to such tension and waste of energy that all the foreign wealth is not worth the effort. Therefore discernible men among cultured nations, who have not confused ends and means, have already pointed out that a policy of assimilation is unlikely to yield any benefit. It is safe to assume that as awareness of this fact spreads and the failures of this policy become more apparent, the idea of assimilation will eventually die out, and nations will renounce the ambition to control other peoples' property.

If the assimilation of peoples who live on their own land and have accumulated certain cultural assets has already become unprofitable and is soon likely to become undesirable, the assimilation of a people that lives on the land of strangers, that possesses no material or cultural assets of its own, can certainly not be of use to anyone. We know, for instance, that American society rejects the Negroes, who in turn would give all they have for the chance of assimilating among the Whites, and dream of ways of changing the color of their skin. We know that this was the attitude of the Spartans to the Helots and of the Indians to the pariahs. If, for example, we see the English and French dwelling in peace in Canada, it is only because they are equal in numbers and are both equally rooted in the land.

As for us, the Jews, other people have willingly let us share their cultural possessions, so long as this sharing did not mean confiscation, so long as this sharing did not raise us from our degraded position. Our opposition to assimilation and the enthusiasm of the priests to make converts brought cruel persecution upon us. Our stiff-necked attitude aroused the stubbornness of our enemies, who longed to assimilate us within them. To convert Jews to Christianity was often regarded by priests as a sacred duty, to the point where they momentarily forgot what was best for themselves. Thus, in order to attract Jews to embrace Christianity they would grant apostates special privileges. Good Christians, in order to draw Jews unto the fold, even agreed to set aside part of their material assets for apostates. But this was only for appearance's sake. Who is so naive as to believe seriously that the privilege promised to individual converts would be granted to the Jews as a whole if they should come in large numbers to seek refuge in the shade of Christianity? Most likely they would be expected to content themselves with having acquired eternal life in the world to come; in this world they would no doubt remain the same dirty Jews, with the addition of a new epithet, *apostates.*

Is not our assertion borne out by the attitude toward the Marranos in Spain and their persecution by the Inquisition? When Jews were converted individually it was customary to grant them favors for their act, and full confidence was placed in them. Many became pillars of the Catholic Church, and by their false charges against Judaism they brought more affliction to the Jews than anyone else. But when the Jews of Spain began to convert to Christianity in their tens of thousands, the attitude of the Catholic clergy toward the Marranos underwent a profound change. The converts were subjected to the closest scrutiny because of the suspicion that they were still loyal to their former religion. Naturally this only served to fan the spark of faith in the religion of their forefathers that still glowed in their hearts, and the Marranos began secretly and even openly to observe Jewish customs.

This by no means displeased the fanatical priests, for one does not persecute only that which is undesirable. On the contrary, the Inquisitors were pleased with the Marranos' reaction, for persecution by the Inquisitors brought the authorities tremendous wealth by expropriating the suspects' property. For who were the main victims of the persecutors but the rich and the well born, from whose wealth they could benefit. In short, those at first so keen on assimilating us now had second thoughts and hastened to seize those earthly assets they had granted us so liberally as a supplement to our heavenly salvation, which had not cost them anything.

It will be said that my explanation is somewhat exaggerated, that the clergy in those days used to strangle all heretics and expropriate their property. But what explains this wholesale suspicion of the Jewish converts if not their prior mistrust of the Jews generally, simply because they were strangers? What explains the zeal of the Inquisition's interrogations if not the desire to recover the property the Church had lost when, in a moment of religious enthusiasm, it presented it to the Jews? If it is recalled that most of the heretics in Spain were Jews and Moors who had been converted to Christianity—all foreigners—then perhaps this explanation will be accepted after all. They have always treated us like strangers. We have never been seen as members of another people but as strangers, so small in number that our very weakness and vulnerability served as a stimulus to various kinds of persecution and acts of violence, and so numerous that we became a thorn in the flesh of the people of the land, always the object of its animus and awaiting its next blow. The vulgar person is by nature hostile to anything foreign. He never distinguishes between fear and distrust on the one hand and hatred and contempt on the other. All these feelings fuse within him into one tight bundle.

What is foreign is not regular, so it arouses suspicion—and for the vulgar this means hatred. What is foreign is strange and therefore ridiculous, which to the vulgar means deserving to be treated with contempt and cruelty. What is foreign is mysterious and hence potentially dangerous, which to the vulgar means an enemy and a bearer of destruction. So the threat implicit in the existence of the foreigner must be repelled. And it is not surprising that although the weak individual foreigner encounters only an attitude of curiosity mixed with suspicion and sometimes even sympathy for his plight—as proved by the ancient custom of showing hospitality to the stranger—the moment foreigners become a dangerous force—and they need not be very numerous to be regarded so—they gradually become the object of great suspicion and of the most burning hatred. The dominant group frightfully exaggerates their numbers and power.

Thus, for example, the simple Russian peasant believes in all earnestness that "the *zhidi* are tremendously greater in number than we are," and that all the treasures of the world are hidden among the *zhidi,* and he listens attentively to all sorts of fabrications about the cunning, the machinations, and the power of the Jews. The fear of Jewish plots in the abstract does not interfere with recognizing very well that the Jew of flesh and blood is weak and defenseless, which makes it possible to maltreat him at will. This primordial and elemental fear of the stranger is supplemented by the hatred of foreigners who conspire to take part of the fat of the land. This is why the Jews are tolerated only where their activity is needed. This is also the reason why the Jews have never been permitted to assimilate naturally the way two people fuse, who are of equal vitality, who live in one territory, cannot oppress one another, and who do not regard the weakness of the other as an excuse to enslave him. If all the Jews were to convert to Christianity their plight would become even worse. This would intensify the resentment against foreigners who want to penetrate what is "ours."

We see, then, that there is no comparison between the attitude prevailing between two peoples who live in contiguous territories and the attitude of an indigenous people to a foreign group, conspicuous but weak, who lives among it. In the former case, the one strives to assimilate his neighbor if he sees no other way of gaining control of his possessions, while the other opposes the assimilatory designs of the first. In the latter case, the hatred that is engendered in the indigenous people when a foreign mass penetrates it invariably repels the foreigner and prevents him from assimilating even if he should desire to do so. So long as the foreigner joins only to benefit from the host's unexpropriable assets, no one objects, and sometimes he is even being encouraged; as far as religion is concerned, it may even be forced on him. But once there develops a threat of equalizing the foreigner's rights with those of the dominant group, pressure against this dangerous tendency begins. Here too the shortsightedness of social egotism is revealed. Because of its zealous preoccupation with ensuring that not a single crumb of "mine" should fall into the hands of the foreigner—who possesses no rights and who may rightly be persecuted—the ruling class completely ignores the fact that if it were to draw the foreigner in, he would become a most beneficial element. Hostility toward strangers and all related manifestations of violence are obviously harmful to the perpetrators, for they corrupt the indigenous people and educate them to lawlessness.

Furthermore, the foreigners manage, in one way or another, to link themselves to the interests of the natives since, being cut off from the land, they could not survive for a moment without such ties. Hence, all the disturbances directed against the foreigners have an ill effect on the natives too, although to a lesser degree. This is why discerning persons in the society, who always oppose policies of forced fusion of groups living in adjacent territories and who preach the principle of nonintervention, regard it as their duty to aid in the assimilation of foreign groups living amidst their own society, and raise their voice against the hostile expulsion of foreigners, which is practiced by most of the society. However much they may try to conceal it from themselves and from others, their attitude toward the foreigners in their land is always one of expediency: the guiding principle is the advantage to the dominant people and, by the same token, a disregard for the natural needs of the foreign people. Members of the progressive classes of society well understand that foreigners can perform valuable functions, but the foreigners' personality is not their affair, and they treat them as animals. In order to exploit our talents they want to assimilate us and dissolve us among their masses.

In the past, even these measures were unnecessary: progressive rulers, who recognized the benefit of Jewish activity, would grant the Jews special privileges in return for the performance of these functions and would make no effort to bring about their assimilation. This was the case, for example, with the privileges granted to the Jews by Casimir the Great. He opened wide the gates of commerce and finance and ensured them freedom of religion and safety of life and property, but at the same time isolated them completely from any external influence and removed them from Poland's political life. This treatment was appropriate to the economic positions of the Jews and the peoples about them. In that period the Jews functioned as middlemen and artisans. The surrounding society had no use for Jewish labor developed outside the guilds; its consumers were the Jews themselves. But commerce was then an important factor in the economic development of Europe. Farsighted kings and princes often even facilitated matters for the Jews in the performance of their functions; but the shortsighted masses, the tyrannical clergy, and the ignorant nobility, although they benefited from the services of the Jewish merchants and moneylenders, were still unable to overcome their hatred for the Jews and harrassed them as much as they could.

The position of the Jews was then much more alarming than it is today, but at least they stood on firm economic ground: they were useful; they promoted the factors from which present-day capitalism and the bourgeoisie developed. They were by no means the poor, unfortunate multitude they are today. And even if they were eventually despoiled, they had the opportunity of arising and shaking off their degradation, because there was no one else to perform their unique economic functions. When it happened that the Jews were banished from a country that had not yet managed, by virtue of Jewish activities, to reach a stage of development that would enable it to do without them—i.e., where a vigorous and capable, commercial bourgeoisie had not yet arisen—the expulsion of the Jews caused the country's decline, as occurred in Spain.

As for the banished Jews, the way was still open to countries that were already in need of middlemen but had not yet produced such a class from among their own people. The trend of Jewish expulsions in the Middle Ages was from Western to Eastern Europe. Here the course of capitalism overtook that of the *Galut*. Where the Jews had previously been of use they eventually became altogether superfluous. But the authorities did not wait until that stage was reached; they hastened to expel the Jews while the time was ripe, when the local bourgeoisie that was competing with the Jews was just beginning to stand on its own feet.

The expulsions as such were no innovation in the *Galut* process, which was an historical necessity. If the Jews had not been expelled then, they would have been ousted from their economic position eventually, since, being prevented from owning land, they had no chance of competing with the natives and would sooner or later have emigrated from those countries. Only the expulsion from Spain was an exception to this rule, accomplishing at a relatively early stage what was bound to occur eventually—but this deviation was caused by special circumstances which need not be explored here. Such crude expulsions of masses of Jews are out of the question today. Consequently, the anti-Semitic society and government in countries where the Jews have become superfluous do not wait until they have become totally redundant, but hasten to drive them out of the country. Such a policy in Rumania led to a large-scale Jewish exodus.

Our economic position has always been distressingly dependent on that of the peoples among whom we live. The reason for this is that the economic life of society is always based on its relation to nature; only through a struggle with nature can man obtain the materials and means necessary for his survival. The basis of every society is the agricultural class. This truth is valid independently of the theory of the Physiocrats.

Any social group that has no such basis is compelled to form strong ties with other groups who are based on the land, and from whom it can obtain agricultural products. The entire life and fate of the Jews in the *Galut,* long ago cut-off from the land and with no agricultural class, depend entirely on finding a society which, because it needs the services of the Jews, will give them in return agricultural products, cattle, or manufactured goods.

But the peoples who have never needed us and those who have ceased to need us will try—as we now see—to drive us away by means of restrictive laws or, if humane feelings rule out legal discrimination, will destroy us by a persistent boycott; at best, competition will put an end to the Jews. For even where the Jews are numerous, only a few can become big capitalists while the rest, the middle and lower middle classes, cannot withstand the competition of the local bourgeoisie, whose strength lies in its land and its blood-ties with the rest of the population. At present there is hardly a need for us anywhere. We have become superfluous. There can be only one fate in store for us—complete economic degeneration—and consequently physical and cultural degeneration.

In our generation the signs of the degeneration process are already discernible in terrifying forms. Prostitution has made its appearance among us. Poverty has reached unparalleled proportions. The slightest economic tremor ejects us by the thousands from our petty bourgeois position into the arms of the *lumpenproletariat,* into the desperate poverty of the *sansculottes.* Furthermore, most of the Jews are concentrated in countries where capitalism did not develop organically and steadily, but suddenly swept the whole economy into its whirling vortex: Russia, Galicia, and Rumania were sucked into the process of industrial capitalism by the tempest of inevitability. This stunned everyone, but especially the Jews, who possessed no land and were economically weak.

The extent to which we are hanging in a vacuum can easily be seen from the following example. Ask an old Jewish merchant whether he has not noticed that the number of his Christian customers has declined; his answer will be that he used to deal mainly with Christians and now deals only with Jews. Has he not noticed that lately the Jews are resorting to credit, and that on this basis they are making a living from one another and not from the Christians? You will see that the structure of Jewish commerce is built on the sand of perpetual reciprocal credit.

The Christians already have merchants of their own to whom they turn more readily than to the Jews. The Jews used to buy agricultural products, bread, cattle, iron, and the like from the local populace, and would pay for them in cash, using the money they had earned from them through trade and interest. With what will they pay the Gentile now, if he does not buy from them at all? It can only be from past savings, which of course are gradually decreasing. The possibility of making up the difference with income from the surrounding populace is diminishing, with the result that Jews who have not managed to acquire considerable property will suffer utter impoverishment.

We are foreigners, and nowhere in the world do we possess the social power that could make us masters of our fate. We are cut off from nature and have no agriculture. All this has left us hovering in the air. Our history in the *Galut* has never been shaped by our own powers; our fate has always depended on external ties. Can progress in the *Galut* redeem us from this dependence and insecurity? So long as Jew hatred exists, hatred of us as strangers, progress will only make our position more sensitive, more passive; the difficulty of our position, subjectively, will become intolerable. Jew hatred could conceivably come to an end as a result of a thorough social revolution, or through gradual atrophy. Many of our optimists think that the roots of Jew hatred lie in the economic forces of the times and that if there is a basic reform of the existing social order, Jew hatred will disappear.

If I could permit myself to digress here and examine all the fundamental principles of systematic Zionist thought—something I cannot do in the limits set for this essay—it could be proved, first, that Jew hatred does not stem from economic factors but from the sociopsychological sphere; that its roots lie in certain forces that necessarily operate in every society. Second, the Jews are not exploited, nor is it the alleged exploitation practiced by the Jews that has aroused this hatred. Competition is not the explanation of anti-Semitism, which often manifests itself most violently precisely among those social classes not even in the position of competing with us—such as peasants, laborers, or clerks. Even national competition can explain nothing in this case, since the Jews have no basis for competing. Third, basic changes in the social system can strike directly at legal institutions but not at human feelings, among which Jew hatred is numbered. And feelings, when deprived by the revolution of the legal institutions which formerly embodied them, will establish new institutions for their needs. Fourth, the social revolution, on which our optimists pin their hopes, will be a long time in coming, if at all. Finally, Jew hatred as an independent feeling or evil spirit—that is, a feeling long-freed from any solid reason or excuse—which manifests itself as hatred for the Jew simply because he is a Jew, can be eliminated only in the course of protracted, peaceful social development atrophying for lack of nourishment as, with society's progress, its causes gradually disappear.

If we wait for redemption we shall wait a very long time, so long that in the meantime we might have created not one but several Jewish states. In the meantime we shall become completely superfluous, and the reserves on which we have been subsisting until now will have been consumed. On the other hand, it is no secret that in the countries still open to us, such as the United States and England, we have already become too conspicuous, and there are places there where our presence arouses a burning Jew hatred. Our poverty-stricken masses are already so crowded in the ghetto that they are compelled to rebuff without mercy all the new immigrants who arrive. Restrictions are already being placed on our entry to those countries, and soon they will be barred to us completely. The desire to emigrate has grown under the pressure of the stifling atmosphere in the Pale of Settlement, but new outlets for the flow of emigration have not yet opened up. For who is willing to take in the homeless and impoverished members of a foreign nation, who are not even able to do productive labor?

The Zionists wish to exploit the force of this emigration to achieve their objectives, but until Zionism begins to be realized in concrete terms, the Jews have nowhere to turn. Some try to comfort us by saying that the Pale of Settlement may soon be abolished. The difficulty is—where can we go from there? There are enough merchants in Greater Russia without us, and there are hosts of unemployed workers. Moreover, the attitude of the population there toward the Jews is more hostile than in the Pale of Settlement. This is known to anyone who is familiar with the peasants' attitude toward the Jews in the Pale; it is also known that they generally constitute the bulk of the pogrom mobs. If these peasants hate us in our Pale of Settlement, why should they hate us less in their own area of settlement? Even assuming that in Greater Russia we are left alone initially and are treated humanely, will the proportion of the Jewish population change from what it is today?

Is there such a great difference between the conspicuousness of 5 million Jews among a population of 50 million in the Pale of Settlement and that of 5 million Jews among a population of 100 million in all of Russia? It should be remembered that the Jews will continue to live only in the cities. This will attract attention to them both among the city-dwellers and the villagers, exactly as now occurs in the Pale of Settlement. Was there no Jew hatred in Greater Russia before the Jews were enclosed in the Pale? Were there not cruel persecutions in Nizhniy Novgorod? Will not professional inciters of Jew hatred make their appearance and create around the Jews a poisonous atmosphere, ostracism, and a systematic exclusion from all fields of endeavor? In what way does Greater Russia hold out greater blessings for the Jews than Galicia or the United States? Briefly, perhaps the abolition of the Pale would temporarily relieve the position of some Jewish groups, but it would extend the Jewish question to a much greater area without getting to the root of the matter. The root is in the lack of land, the conspicuousness of the mass of foreigners that catches the eye of the local populace, the fate of becoming superfluous, and of sinking into an abyss of rootlessness and grinding poverty.

For the bulk of Jewry, which is crowded together in Russia and Galicia, the present situation is critical; if deliverance does not come now it will perish, for no legal concessions can stop the inevitable process of historical necessity. Just as in the Middle Ages there were no legal restrictions or persecutions except those resulting from the internal and irresistible necessity of the *Galut,* which brought capitalism victorious on the heels of the Jews, so today it would be shortsighted to assume that the "temporary laws" of the Pale of Settlement and the like are simply the doing of governments that dislike the Jews.

Here as in the Middle Ages, considerations of what was advantageous to the state emerged, and merely anticipated and forced what would have come about sooner or later of itself, more gradually and without the assistance of legal restrictions, by virtue of historical necessity. From this standpoint, by recognizing the inner law operating in the *Galut—* which I have only sketched here in broad outline—we shall also understand that the *Galut* is drawing to an end. And by virtue of that same irresistible necessity we shall also understand that the law that determines our fate obliges us to take action that will speed the end of the *Galut.* We must hasten its death, and not prolong the death throes by a struggle to ease the condition of the Jews in the Diaspora, by letting ourselves be drawn after the mirage of emancipation, of legal amelioration, and of progress.

2
The National Question
and the Class Struggle

(1905)

The Twofold Division of Human Society

In the preface to his book, *A Contribution to the Critique of Political Economy,* Marx states: "In the social production which men carry on, they enter into definite relations that are indispensable and independent of their will; these relations of production correspond to a definite stage of development of their material powers of production." In order to live, men must produce. In order to produce, they must combine their efforts in a certain way. Man does not as an individual struggle with nature for existence. History knows man only as a unit in a social group. Since men do live socially, it follows that between them certain *relations* are developed. These relations arise because of production. Indeed, Marx terms them *relations of production.*

"The sum total of these relations of production constitutes the economic structure of society—the real foundation, on which rise legal and political superstructures and to which correspond definite forms of social consciousness." Thus, the relations of production in China or in France, for example, are the basis for the entire "social order" of Chinese or French society. But when we refer to societies by different names, we imply that there are *several* societies. These societies are in some manner *differentiated* one from the other. If this were not so, we could not speak of an English bourgeoisie and a German bourgeoisie, of an American proletariat and a Russian proletariat. Then we would speak only of mankind as a whole, or at least of civilized humanity, and no more. But the English and the Germans, the Americans and the Russians, are all part of mankind, and if you will, of civilized humanity, and yet they are differentiated from one another. We therefore see that humanity is divided into several societies.

The above is common knowledge, and it would never occur to anyone to deny it. The question is, however, how can we explain the causes which make for this division of humanity. Many explanations have already been offered. One has but to inquire of those who speak in the name of "national ideologies," a "pure Russian spirit," a "true German spirit," of "Judaism," and so on. The problem for us, however, is to explain this in terms of materialism, which teaches us to seek the basic causes of every social phenomenon in economic conditions.

We know why men are divided into classes. We know that all members of a given society are not in the same position in the relations of production. Each group in society takes a different part in the system of production (feudal or capitalist). Each group bears a specific relation to the means of production. Some are the entrepreneurs, others the workers, a third group are peasants, and so on. The groups which are so differentiated from one another represent the different *classes*. Every society is therefore divided into classes. But what is responsible for the differences between the various societies which give rise to the national question and its concomitant struggles? On what grounds do these differences arise, and what are the conclusions to be drawn from the previously stated Marxist theory?

Conditions of Production

We stated above: in order to live, men must produce. In the process of production various *relations of production* arise. But the production itself is dependent on certain *conditions,* which are *different* in different places. Citing Marx above, we said that the nature of the relations of production is independent of man's intellect and volition. The character of the *relations* of production depends on the state of the forces of production that are in the control of man. But the state of the forces of production and their development are dependent primarily on the natural conditions which man must face in his struggle for existence. The condition of the forces of production is therefore dependent on the geographic environment, and the latter is, of course, different in different places.

What is true of the forces of production is also true of the development of production. This development is always influenced by certain naturally and historically different conditions, which result in *different* economic structures among different peoples. The conditions of production vary considerably; they are geographical, anthropological, and historical. The historical conditions include both those generated within a given social entity and those imposed by the neighboring social groups. These conditions are recognized by Engels in his second letter in the *Socialist Academician.* He states therein that among the many factors that make for different economies are also the geographical environment, the race, and even the human type, which has developed differently in different places. In the third volume of *Capital* Marx also states that one and the same economic base can develop in different ways because of different conditions, such as natural environment, race, and external historical influences. Therefore we see that according to the teachers of historical materialism one and the same process of development of productive forces can assume various forms according to the differences in the conditions of production.

Of the above-mentioned conditions of production, the natural, nonsocial factors predominated first. As society develops, however, the social and historical environment gain in importance over the nonsocial, natural conditions—just as man in general assumes mastery over nature. In this conception of the "conditions of production" we have a sound basis for the development of a purely materialist theory of the *national question.* For in it is contained the theory and the basis of national struggles.

For scientific accuracy we must add the following explanation: the foregoing citation from Marx speaks about historical influences acting *from without.* By "from without," we mean that the thing which is being influenced is a *distinct entity* from the other. It therefore has an internal and external life. But is there anything in the world that is an absolute totality in itself? No. And yet we do speak of certain totalities. It is common knowledge that to the present day humanity must still be considered an aggregate of certain entities which are *to an extent* distinct one from the other. Thus, for example, everyone knows that the French masses are distinct from the German masses, and so on. Scientists very often do speak of various things which are in some measure connected one with the other, and yet are considered distinct entities. Why is this so?

As we have emphasized, there are many things which are to a certain extent totalities in themselves. True, they are not absolute, but only to an extent so, i.e., relatively distinct entities. Humanity must to the present day be considered an aggregate of *relatively* distinct entities. It is therefore apparent that when speaking of such relatively distinct entities, we can also speak of *internal* and *external* relations. By speaking of "influences acting from without" Marx recognizes the relative totality of modern societies. What brings about this relative totality of the social life of a certain group, so that we may consider it a closed entity? Why do we consider England as something different from France, although both have an identical capitalist system of production? We may speak, and do speak of a *relative distinctness* of social groups only because there is a relative distinctness in the *conditions* of production under which each group must develop its life. Sometimes such a group is called a socio-economic organism.

We, therefore, come to the following formulation and explanation of the two kinds of human grouping: (1) The groups into which humanity is divided according to the differences in the conditions of the relatively distinct productions are called *societies,* socioeconomic organisms (tribes, families, peoples, nations); (2) the groups into which the society is divided according to their role in the system of production itself, i.e., according to their respective relations to the means of production, are called *classes* (castes, ranks, etc.).

The National Struggle

Having ascertained the causes for the division of humanity into societies, we can proceed to a discussion of the national struggle and the grounds from which it arises. We know that class struggle arises because the *conditions* of the various classes in the production system are different. The position of one class may be better or worse, more advantageous or less so, than the position of a second class. The striving of the various groups within a given society to gain a more advantageous position or to retain an already achieved position, results in class struggle.

Class struggle assumes the character of a social problem wherever *the development of the forces of production disturbs the constitution of the relations of production,* i.e., when the constitution of the relations of production is archaic, obsolete, and no longer suitable to the further development of production. The same is true of *national struggle.* The situation in one set of material conditions of production may be more advantageous than the situation in another, and a striving of the same character as that previously described develops in connection with the class struggle. The result of this striving is a struggle between social entities.

Nor is it even necessary that the conditions should differ regarding relative advantage. For no matter how advantageous the position of a given society may be in the sphere of its usual conditions of production, it may nevertheless strive to expand its production, to increase the sum total of its energies. It therefore becomes necessary in the process of enlarging the scope of its conditions of production to annex those of other social entities. And here we perceive the same phenomenon: one body seeks to annex the field of the other, or to defend itself against that other; in other words, we are witnessing a national struggle.

We have thus demonstrated two cases which give rise to the struggle between social entities. We may quite simply state that a national struggle takes place whenever the development of the forces of production demands that the conditions of production belonging to a social group be better, more advantageous, or in general be expanded. In other words, a national struggle comes about when the existing conditions of production are no longer compatible with the further development of production. *The national problem therefore arises when the development of the forces of production of a nationality conflicts with the state of the conditions of production.*

Every social phenomenon is primarily related to the material elements of society. A struggle is waged not for spiritual things, but for certain economic advantages in social life. Class struggle is waged not for spiritual values, but for the means of production. So too is national struggle. Class struggle is waged for the material possessions of the classes, i.e., for the means of production. The means of production may be material or intangible. Material wealth is for the most part something that can be expropriated, such as machines. Intangible assets are those which cannot be expropriated, for example, technical proficiency, skill, and so on. Despite the fact that the struggle between classes very often assumes the form of a conflict between cultural-spiritual ideologies, such a struggle is not waged for the possession of intangible assets, but for the control of the material means of production.

National struggle is also waged for the material possessions of social organisms. The assets of a social body lie in its control of the *conditions of production.* These, too, may be material or spiritual, i.e., such as can or cannot be expropriated. The material conditions consist of the territory and all the products of the material culture which have been developed by man, particularly the tangible conditions of production. The spiritual conditions consist of languages, customs, mores, *Weltanschauungen*— namely the historical conditions of production. The national struggle is waged not for the preservation of cultural values but for the control of material possessions, even though it is very often conducted under the banner of spiritual slogans. Nationalism is always related to the material possessions of the nation, despite the various masks it may assume outwardly. But first it is necessary to determine what nationalism is. The terms *nationalism* and *national question* are directly linked with the term *nation,* and it therefore becomes imperative to ascertain precisely what we mean by this latter term.

Peoples and Nations

The terms *people* and *nation* each denotes a different stage or degree of development in the life of a given society. To better understand the distinction between the two, we bring as an illustration the single word *class,* and the interpretation of which it is capable. It is well known that the meaning of the word *class* as employed by Marx is ambiguous and somewhat complicated. On the one hand, Marx considers as a class every social group that differs from other groups in the same society in its participation in production or in its relation to the means of production. It is in this sense that Marx and Engels claimed that the history of humanity is a history of class struggles. But then again we find passages in Marx indicating that he employed *class* in another, much narrower sense, where it appears he understands a class to be not merely any economic group occupying a special place in the system of production, but such a group as has already achieved a measure of self-consciousness and has appeared on the political arena with clearly expressed interests and demands.

These two meanings of the word *class* are to be found in Marx's *The Poverty of Philosophy.* In one instance we find, "The working class will substitute, in the course of its development, for the old order of civil society an association which will exclude classes and their antagonism. . . ." In another case he says, "So long as the proletariat is not sufficiently developed to constitute itself as a class, so long as, in consequence, the struggle between the proletariat and the bourgeoisie has not acquired a political character. . . ." And in still another instance, "Many researches have been made to trace the different historical phases through which the bourgeoisie has passed from the early commune to its constitution as a class." In these last two examples we have the second meaning of *class.* Marx distinguishes here between the two different conditions of the group: one, when the group is a class only in relation to the other groups; and second, when it enters the political arena and becomes a class in its own consciousness.

An entire society may also find itself in one of these two conditions: when it appears as a relatively distinct entity only in relations to other social organisms, or when it appears as a social organism with a consciousness of its own. When we wish to denote the respective states of groups which developed under different conditions of production, we have two terms. Thus, a social group which developed under the same conditions of production is commonly called *a people.* And the same social group which is united also through the consciousness of the kinship between its members is commonly called *a nation.* A people becomes a nation only on a higher plane of its development.

Nationalism

The psyche of every personality adapts itself, in a greater or lesser extent, to the conditions under which its group lives. In this way a group psychology develops, and definite earmarks of a group character emerge. The keen observer will always discover in these traits a relationship to the material conditions of a given system of production or to a definite stage in the development of the system. This relationship may, however, often be obscure. Furthermore, although the members of each group— a class or a society—may have certain generally common characteristics, it does not yet follow that this similarity denotes the community and solidarity of their interests. And even where there is such community of interests, there may not always be any consciousness thereof.

There are some groups among whose members there can be no mutuality of interests, because they are in constant conflict with one another as a result of inner-group contradictions. And even groups that indeed have common, harmonious interests do not easily become conscious of them, for this consciousness can develop only in the course of a more or less extended period of time. But in groups that are organized so harmoniously that their individual members adapt themselves uniformly to their environment, sooner or later there also develops a consciousness of this harmony. Thus we see that because the group lives under uniform and harmonious conditions or relations of production there sometimes develops, in addition to the group character, a group consciousness. All the emotions which result from this group consciousness give rise to what is commonly called the feeling of kinship or affinity.

Life under similar *relations* of production, which are harmonious for the individuals of a group, evokes *class solidarity*. Life under the same *conditions* of production, which are harmonious for the members of a society, evokes the *national consciousness* of that society and the feeling of *national kinship*. This kinship is felt by individual members as something associated with their common past. Naturally this does not always mean they really have a long common past. Sometimes the antiquity of the common past is purely fictitious. *This feeling of kinship, created as a result of the visioned common historical past and rooted in the common conditions of production, is called* nationalism.

Nationalism and Territory

I stated previously that in the last analysis nationalism is always related to the material resources of the nation. What are these material resources of a nation? The resources of a society, I have pointed out, are the conditions of its system of production. These may be material or spiritual. *The most vital of the material conditions of production is the territory.* The territory is the foundation on which rise all other conditions of production, and it serves as a base for the introduction of all external influences. In addition, every nation has also fashioned certain instruments for the preservation of its resources—its political unity and institutions, its language, national education, and nationalism itself.

It is necessary to remember that a nation is divided into classes (in both senses of the word). These classes are in different positions in the system of production of the nation—their places in the *relations* of production are not the same. Therefore, the conditions of production can under no circumstances be of equal value to all. Each class has a different interest in the national wealth and therefore possesses a different type of nationalism. If we should define nationalism as a striving to preserve the national interests, which are always in some way or other related to the *base* of the conditions of production—the *territory*—and to its instruments of preservation, then because of the diversity of national interests, we also have *various types of nationalism*. National interests may be directed internally or externally; they may be conservative or progressive, aggressive or defensive. All this accounts for certain variations in the types of nationalism.

The Origin of Nationalism

There can be no nationalism where the conditions of production have not yet been nationalized, i.e., where the relatively distinct society has not yet become segregated from without and united from within. Both conditions mentioned above—the segregation from the outside world and the internal unity—must be met. The feudal system satisfied only the first condition—it only served to segregate one society from another, but it did not unite the members of each society with a strong internal bond. The feudal era did not possess harmonious wholeness in the conditions of production. Consequently it had no conception of the existence of nations but only of peoples, and therefore, had no conception of nationalism and the national question.

The nationalism of ancient times was purely political in character. It often flared up spontaneously when the external relations between peoples became sharply strained. This sort of nationalism came to life and subsided together with the great wars, which were not waged because of national interests and were not, therefore, national in character. When commerce began to develop out of the feudal system, a great revolution was set in motion. Nationalities, nationalism, and consequently the national question gradually came into being. The first simple national policy—that cannot yet be termed national—shifted from without to within the society. Instead of being purely occasional and accidental as heretofore, it assumed permanent and regular features. And only by this shift to *within* the society did it become national. The development of capital slowly shook the foundation of the existing order, and with its aid the consolidation of the land began and great monarchies developed.

We may well ask what interest prompted the movement which nationalized the conditions of social production. I shall answer this question in the next chapter. Before concluding this chapter, however, I wish to point out that the first protagonist of national ideas, the bourgeoisie (the mercantile and industrial bourgeoisie), which was so young and progressive in its day, waged an energetic struggle against the old order and created a new world. Needless to say, it could not at the same time also defend the traditional concepts. *From its very beginning nationalism has been independent of traditions.* Those who berate nationalism as something obsolete and reactionary, as traditional, are remarkably shallow and ignorant. Nationalism is a product of bourgeois society—it was born simultaneously with it, its reign is as old as that of the bourgeois society, and it must be reckoned with as much as any other phenomenon of bourgeois society. Speaking from the proletarian standpoint, we must therefore say that the proletariat is directly concerned with nationalism, with national wealth, and with territory. Since the proletariat takes part in production, it must also be interested in the conditions of production, and there must develop a specific proletarian type of nationalism—as is, indeed, the case.

One of the prerequisites of the capitalist system of production is freedom. Commerce and industry develop only through free competition, i.e., when there is freedom to transport capital and goods and to trade with them. The worker must also be free to sell his labor power; he must be able to move about freely, for only then can surplus value— the lifeblood of capitalism—be created. The freedom to travel is the first and most essential of all liberties; without it all others have no value. Travel and transportation, naturally, depend on territory. The prerequisite of freedom of transportation is a free territory. And this makes clear what led the bourgeoisie to engage in the struggle to free the land. The struggle was first waged to free a specific territory with definite boundaries, which marked off the whole territory in which a given language was spoken. It also became necessary to emancipate the population living within this territory and to abolish the feudal barriers that covered the land like a network and obstructed the freedom of transportation. Thus the bourgeoisie created a relatively segregated social organism, freed it from serfdom, and harmonized the conditions of its production. That is why it was nationalistic. In addition it emancipated the whole population of the country—with the aid of the masses. It united with all classes against one class—the lords of that period. This strengthened and encouraged all the more its militant and progressive nationalism.

Thus the European *peoples* became *nations*. Among each people a national consciousness developed, and the members of the nation became imbued with the feeling of kinship arising from their common historical past or—to use the materialist terminology—from the common conditions of their system of production. The various peoples, who now desired to develop their national wealth, realized that such wealth did exist but that it was necessary to wrest it from the toils of the reigning feudalism. Thus each nation began to love its territory—the homeland, the fatherland, that is, the common base of its conditions of production. Each nation began to love its instruments of preservation and to cultivate the national language, and aspired to a truly national commonwealth.

After the French Revolution, however, the division within the society itself was clearly manifest; it became evident that the nation consists of different classes. And after the national wealth had been emancipated and the controlling powers proceeded to the division thereof, the *class struggle* broke out in all its fury. The harmony and solidarity of which they formerly spoke were dispelled like smoke. The fundamental postulate—"the people"—proved to be a fiction. The "homeland," "our" land, "our" language, "our" culture—all these conditions of the system of production remained a part of the *national* wealth, but they no longer appeared as the common possession of all members of the nation. Even the basic feeling of kinship arising on the ground of the common historical past lost its original aura. It lost its passion, and remained a mere experience; *it became a tradition.*

The above is true regarding free nations, which oppress no one and are not oppressed themselves, i.e., nations which live under normal conditions of production. With them the feeling and consciousness of kinship has become a tradition, an historical reminiscence. Life itself has helped to further this condition. The material conditions of life, which gave rise to class antagonism, have pushed aside this tradition and prevented it from exerting any social influence. Each class has assumed its social position, and each values a particular aspect of the national wealth—that aspect with which it is mostly concerned. Free nations, which do not oppress others and are not oppressed themselves, lack the environment in which all national interests may merge. In other words, there is no instance in the conditions of production in which the common interests of all members of the nation are affected. Such nations have no dynamic nationalism, but one that expresses itself in weak sympathies only, in "love for one's own," so to say. This "love" may simply mean that, *all other* conditions being equal, an individual will help his own more readily than a stranger.

Among certain classes of free nations, there may exist sometimes a latent sort of nationalism. But this is no more than a potential (a repressed) nationalism, which may manifest itself strongly at the first opportunity. It must always be remembered that this occasion will arise only when the national resources are affected, and only the material resources at that. These must be affected in such a manner that the interests of some class are also involved, because the center of gravity of free nations lies not in their national existence—for their conditions of production are normal—but in their class structure, in the relations developed within the confines of the system of production itself. As long as the national interests of some class are not endangered, the propaganda of nationalism serves only to dampen class consciousness; and on that consideration it is harmful. It goes without saying that when the conditions of the system of production of a certain nation are in an anomalous state, its nationalism assumes an altogether different aspect.

Nationalism and Class Consciousness

It must be noted that all anomalies in the conditions of production affect adversely the relations of production—the class structure. It is commonly known that under normal conditions of production class antagonism becomes more acute, whereas under abnormal conditions of production it abates somewhat. Normal conditions of production denationalize the people and dull its national consciousness, whereas abnormal conditions of production (i.e. when some part of the national possession is lacking or its organs of preservation are curtailed) harmonize the interests of various classes of the nation and heighten its national consciousness. Therefore, there is a kind of antagonism between *class consciousness* and *national consciousness* of a given group, and the two are wont to obfuscate one another. It sometimes happens that the interests of the individuals of various classes in a nation, under abnormal conditions of production, are in reality harmonious in some respect, and yet certain irrational ideologists ignore these national interests, which are also of great significance to their own class. They attempt to blunt the national consciousness, which in this case should not be obscured because it would be harmful to the interests of their own class too. The same effect is created by carrying on nationalistic propaganda within a nation which is living under *normal* conditions of production, or where the propagandists will have the people believe that the common interests are broader and more harmonious than is really the case. In the latter case nationalism blunts class consciousness and is therefore detrimental to the whole nation, since it hides the real relations between the various groups within the nation. This results in self-deceit, illusions, and social myopia.

It is always harmful to obscure the class or national consciousness of a given group, irrespective of whether this is a result of class or national demagogy. Whether it is class or national interests which are being obscured, or whether it is the real conditions of production or the relations of production which are being falsely interpreted, is immaterial, since either attempt is reactionary. The ruling classes of free and of oppressed nations take advantage of this fundamental contradiction between national and class consciousness, and are often inclined to carry on hypocritical nationalistic propaganda in order to obscure the class consciousness of those whom they oppress. But we should not be misled by this condition into believing that these ruling classes are in reality nationally inclined. The ruling classes are not national but *nationalistic.*

All propaganda and every movement that is rooted in the character of the conditions of production of a given society is either national or nationalistic. Whenever it attempts to blunt the class and civic consciousness of the members of that society, and whenever it ignores the class structure and the antagonism between the interests of the classes, it is nationalistic. If, however, it does not obscure the class structure of the society, it is *national.* The phrase *national spirit,* all sorts of "cultural-historical essences," and all other exaggerated traditions are the best warning signals against a confusion of the two. Nationalistic speeches are always liberally dotted with them. Empty phraseology, crammed with these and similar conceptions, is not national but nationalistic.

Taking into consideration the existence of a common national character that is the same for all members of the nation—a person who thinks *nationalistically* is inclined to forget on that account all the social differences between the individuals making up the nation. On the other hand, a person who thinks *nationally*—even when he recognizes the existence of a common character created in the environment of common conditions of production—realizes first, that it is rather difficult to define this national character and the national-cultural type, for they are too intangible, and second, that within every nationality the separate characteristics of each class appear much more acutely and can be more readily discerned.

Finally, a person who thinks nationalistically believes that all members of society should be nationalists; he conceives of nationalism and patriotism as a holy imperative. But a person who thinks nationally does not consider it traitorous when he discovers that certain classes of the society are wholly free of nationalism, while others understand nationalism in different ways, according to their respective class interests.

The Nationalism of the Great Landowners

The great landowners are the class which lives from land rent. Naturally, their income consists in part of interest derived from their capital, but the principal source is land rent. As a result they are mainly concerned about immobile things, about their estates. They cherish the territory only in as much as it represents a piece of land from which they can exact their rents. Their nationalism is inherently a land nationalism. It is affected only when some other neighboring people attempt to annex the soil itself; for should such conquest be achieved, the landowners would lose their source of income. They are not concerned with the fact that the territory also serves other classes of their nation as a national market, and it would hardly trouble them should a foreign people, foreign capitalists, attempt to wrest from its own bourgeoisie the domestic market offered by the territory. However, other incidental interests oblige them to give some attention to those matters.

For the landowning class occupies a transitory position in the history of social development. This class is rapidly becoming capitalist and is therefore beginning to find itself in a new relationship to the national wealth and to the instruments of national preservation; the landowning class is but a remnant of the feudal system, whose death knell social progress has long since sounded. Landowners have lost their economic power and are losing more and more of the political power which they still retain in some countries. It is inevitable that these changes should affect their nationalism, the nature of which is utterly chauvinistic. In some backward countries where the landowning class has to a certain extent preserved its identity, it still exerts a greater influence on the state than do other classes.

One must bear in mind that the present-day state is a class state. The respective interests of the various groups in a state are different. Naturally, not all groups in the society are in a position of power. The state regime is intimately associated with one class. As far as possible, however, the state strives to gain the confidence of the whole population, irrespective of class. In order to exert its influence the state pretends to steer a middle course between all classes. It can maintain such a position only when it can raise one issue above all antagonism within the social organism. This issue is nationalism.

Wherever they still retain the political power in their hands, the big landowners do precisely that. We frequently behold the following phenomenon: the same adherents of feudalism, who formerly had no conception whatsoever of "national ideals" or "the national mission," are now the first to shout these slogans. In reality, though, they acquired this idea from their former enemy—the bourgeoisie. This phenomenon can be explained only by the fact that the landowners are forced to pretend to a position *above* all classes. In order not to awaken any dissatisfaction in the subordinated populace, they ferret out everything that has any semblance of national value and go to all extremes to preserve it, thus pulling the wool over the eyes of the populace. That is also why the great landowners are so sensitive about national honor, and are so exaggeratedly finicky in a nationalist sense. They are, so to speak, the permanent gunpowder-barrel of nationalism, and are always ready to explode on the slightest provocation.

The nationalism of the landowning class has another characteristic: this class has preserved the whole store of traditions amassed during the feudal period. And although nationalism itself had nothing in common with traditionalism when it made its first appearance—the landowners nevertheless enmesh it in the toils of old traditions.[1] In the countries where the bourgeoisie is in control and the landowners are powerless, the traditional nationalism of the latter class manifests itself clearly, as does the reactionary and barren nature of its tactics. Sensing its imminent doom, it strews its grievous path with no less grievous scandals. This is the type of nationalism we find in France. The number of scandals is an inverse index to the number of days which this class still has to live.

The Nationalism of the Great Bourgeoisie

As was stated previously, the great bourgeoisie is independent of traditions. We can safely say that if it is nationalistic, its nationalism is in no way related to traditions. It is but mildly concerned with the internal national market and with the national language which prevails therein. The great bourgeoisie long ago transcended the narrow bounds of the national market and the national language, and now stalks head-up across the great expansive world market. In the disposition of its wares, the great bourgeoisie is not confined to the environment of the national language, for it has no direct relations with the consumer. The consumer speaks not with the manufacturer but with the dealer. The manufacturer himself need know no other language save his mother tongue, for he can employ correspondents and agents to conduct his business with foreign firms. And the financier, the money capitalist, whose clutches are on the whole course of modern economy, has even less contact with the domestic market than has the great industrialist.

The great bourgeoisie, therefore, is not concerned with domestic national politics. It strives for the world supremacy of its national capital. It seeks to crowd all "foreign" capital out of the world market, so that its own profits may be the greater. For this purpose, a strong navy and a well-trained army are essential. Such noble matters as "the national cultural spirit" and so on seldom interest it. It is much more interested in bayonets, shrapnel, and battleships. It has but little concern for such things as language and national education, and is much more concerned with the budget of the army and navy. But in order to have its way about the latter, it must gain political power; and the real basis for political power is, of course, the territory. *Thus, the territory and its boundaries are of value to the great bourgeoisie as a base from which to capture the world market.*[2]

The Nationalism of the Middle Class

Unlike the landowning class, the middle class regards the territory as something more valuable than a piece of land. *The territory serves this class in the capacity of a consumer market.* The boundaries of this market coincide with the bounds wherein the national language prevails. The immediate buyer must speak the same language as the immediate seller. It follows that the middle class is interested in having more and more people speak its language. The nationalism of this bourgeois group draws its whole sustenance from the interests of the national market. Therefore, this element is the mainstay though not the sole supporter of the political suppression of foreign languages. For to this class the essence of nationalism lies in language and all that flows from it, such as traditional culture, education, and so on.

It sometimes happens that the great landowners of a certain ruling nation desire to annex the land on which an oppressed people lives. They therefore strive to assimilate these inhabitants. They assume the guise of culture crusaders, crush the language of the nation they desire to assimilate, and strangle its education. The middle class is always the readiest partner of the landowners in this noble task, for the former presumes to be the devoted "knights" of the "culture crusade." To be convinced thereof one has but to remember the assimilatory *politik* in Prussian Silesia. The middle-class ideologists employ the same phraseology as the landowners. They also resemble the latter in occupying the middle position between the two main classes of society, and in pretending to stand above the class struggle. In reality they fear every social upheaval, for it might signify their death warrant. They sanctify orderliness, and mortally fear revolution. They cling fast to whatever property is still in their possession, and tremble lest that too be wrested from them. They are therefore the bulwark of law and order, and are ready to defend with fire and sword the existing order of things. They are vexatious, as might be expected from an element which is on the downgrade to pauperization and which cannot fight for its future or face it squarely. Everything that is in whatever degree unusual or strange, appears to them as rebellious, traitorous, and subversive. Their poor, dull wit will not permit them to rise above their drab possessiveness.

All this has provided excellent soil for various nationalistic prejudices and superstitions. The poor head of the petty bourgeoisie is filled only with "we" and "they," "native" and "alien." Incidentally, the members of this class are always at one another's throat because of mutual competition, and there is no common meeting ground whereon their class interests may converge. They are incapable of developing a *class* consciousness, and therefore their *national* self-consciousness emerges with greater vigor. This group also creates its own ideals. But this is not the place to dwell upon them.

It is of importance to us that the middle class, being unequivocally interested in the protection of its domestic market, indirectly supports the chauvinistic domestic and foreign policy of the landowners. This wretched type of nationalism plays no independent role, and when it loses its strong ally—the landowning class—it will completely die out. The more rapidly this propertied class becomes declassed, and its members distributed among the proletariat and the great bourgeoisie, the quicker will this type of nationalism become extinct.

Some elements of the middle class and petty bourgeoisie who are concerned with the national culture—teachers, historians, writers, artists— are inclined toward a peaceful, honorable, respectable, "cultural" nationalism. They place great hope in the recognition of the right of every nation to its own self-determination. They have no desire to destroy every other nationality and do not wish to swallow anyone. In domestic politics they are liberal, frequently even radical, and they maintain the same position in international politics. And yet, they do love the native more than the alien; somehow, the traditions of their own culture are dearer to their hearts. They are not nationalistically "snobbish," but they feel that they must protect their national prestige. The more intellectually developed and progressive elements do not even deny the class structure of society. Nevertheless, they are not concerned therewith because they loath conflict and disorder. They have only managed to preserve in a petrified state the earlier sentiment of prerevolutionary, bourgeois nationalism with its old national-democratic traditions.[3]

Until now we have considered the nationalism of the ruling classes. As we have seen, it is multifaceted. Naturally, it is difficult to distinguish between the national ideals of the landlords, of the great bourgeoisie, and those of the middle and petty bourgeoisie. It is even difficult to determine the economic line of demarcation between these classes. There are innumerable transitional forms which make one type of nationalism approximate another, and to the unexperienced eye they all seem to fuse into one whole. However, the materialist conception of history teaches us always to distinguish between the basic characteristics and their variations, and always to resolve into its original elements what may superficially appear to be one compounded whole.

The Nationalism of the Proletariat

It is wrong to accept the widespread fallacy that claims the proletariat has no relation with the national wealth and therefore also has no national feelings and interests. No class in a society is outside the conditions of production of that society. It follows that the state of these conditions of production is of vital concern also to the proletariat. Let us forget the flippant and dangerous conceptions about this question usually entertained by progressive elements. If the general base and reservoir of the conditions of production—the territory—is valuable to the landowning class for its land resources and as a base for its political power; if this territory serves the bourgeoisie as a base for capturing the world market, and serves the middle class as the consumer market; and if the organs of preservation of the national wealth have for each of the above-mentioned classes their respective worth—then *the territory also has its value for the proletariat, i.e. as a place on which to work.* The organs of preservation are also of special value to the proletariat.

Were the worker a thousand times over a "god in human form," as certain demagogic agitators try to convince us, he would still have to eat and therefore work. Unemployment is not a very pleasant thing for him. Even Marx recognized the existence of a degree of competition among workers for the place of work when he said: "The great industry masses together in a single place a crowd of people unknown to each other. Competition divides their interests. . . . This combination has always a double end, that of eliminating competition among themselves while enabling them to make a general competition against the capitalist." Among certain uncultured workers, this competition often results in physical conflict between urban workers and laborers from other communities even of the same country. More cultured workers have a higher, finer concept of competition; they will not engage in physical conflict with workers from the provinces. But when there is a great influx of immigrants from other countries who beat down the wage scale, then the interests of even the most cultured workers are affected and they can no longer remain indifferent.

Some individuals whose abilities to think have been stultified by partisan phraseology and vulgar agitation will protest that we are desecrating the holiest of tenets when we demonstrate the verity of our above contentions through facts. What more convincing proof is needed than the fact that Volmar's *Munchener Zeitung,* for example, is always quick to raise an alarm when Bavarian private or governmental contractors hire Italian instead of German workers. And Volmar is at the head of a great party. He is a revisionist, but nevertheless, at the party conference in Jena, he is a very esteemed comrade. Or consider for instance the Australian government's policy regarding immigrants. It is manifestly clear that the immigration restrictions there are not in the interests of capital, but of the workers. Nor is it necessary to go into the attitude and behavior of the American proletariat toward the Chinese coolie; the horrible facts of pogroms perpetrated on Chinese workers are sufficiently well known to the reader. And is not the fact that this accursed problem is by no means alien to the proletariat further manifested by the growing interest of party leaders in the national question? The most vital way in which the national question affects the worker is through the territory as place of employment.

Other workers' interests related thereto are the cultural interests of language, education, and literature. All these are valuable as media for the development of class consciousness, which is nurtured not so much by the culture as by the processes of the class struggle itself. But the class struggle can take place only where the worker toils, i.e. where he has already occupied a certain work place. The weaker his status at this position, the less ground he has for a systematic struggle. As long as the worker does not occupy a definite position, he can wage no struggle. It is, therefore, in his self-interest to protect his position.

From whatever angle we may approach the national question to determine the scope of its existence for the proletariat, even if we should primarily approach it by way of its cultural needs, we must always arrive finally at its material basis, i.e. at the question of the place of employment and the strategic base of struggle which the territory represents for the proletariat.

The problem of employment has not only a class aspect, but also a national one. Thus, the English worker must protect his place of employment not only against the profit considerations of the capitalist, but also against the immigrant worker. It follows that as long as the national work place is not secure, the national problem overshadows the labor problem. And as long as the workers of a given nation have not yet made their place of employment secure, the problem of work is of far greater importance to them than the issues of the class struggle.

Consequently we have the following results: first, the masses who are just becoming proletarized and are looking for work, are generally incapable of readily becoming class conscious, and are therefore only nationalistically inclined; second, the class consciousness of even the cultural proletariat is greatly obscured by its national consciousness whenever the proletariat is forced to defend its national place of employment. Thus the constant immigration of new workers into England and the United States is a threat to the security of the places of employment of the English and American workers, and as a result the national consciousness of the latter is heightened, deterring the development of their class consciousness. This is one of the main reasons why the labor movements in those countries have not yet developed beyond their present trade-unionist framework.

The orthodox Marxist dogmatists have not as yet been able to explain this extraordinary backwardness of the English and American proletariat. Nor can they beg the question. This fact does not bear on the *relations of production,* and therefore they cannot explain it. In order to explain this fact, we must analyze the *conditions* of the English and American production respectively. The national question must be considered more deeply and honestly; it is necessary once and for all to break with unfounded prejudices. We must understand that class consciousness cannot develop normally unless the national problem, in whatever form it may exist, has been solved.

Those students who ignore the role of the conditions of production and devote themselves exclusively to a study of the relations of production are not in a position to understand the national question. Therefore, the following contradictions in the capitalist economy must forever remain for them an insoluble mystery. They cannot explain why, on the one hand, the capitalist system appears as international, destroys all boundaries between tribes and peoples, and uproots all traditions, while on the other hand, it is itself instrumental in the intensification of the international struggle and heightens national self-consciousness. How is it possible that at the same time when the various societies are drawn closer together economically and their respective and relative distinctions are modified, the national problem is intensified and various national movements develop? Unless the materialist can answer this problem, he must entangle himself in a mesh of contradictions.

Kautsky made several attempts to explain this problem, but in so doing he deserted his materialist concepts. Nevertheless we must admit that in a recent series of articles on the national question, he gradually approaches the theory which we have developed here. And according to this theory, the solution of the above-mentioned riddle is quite clear. If we take into consideration that humanity is divided into groups of production, we will understand that the inherent striving of capital to expand must result in friction between these relatively distinct groups. One aspect of the above-mentioned contradiction is the cause, the other is the effect. This is one of the many contradictions with which modern society is burdened.

I have previously stated that the national question, and also the conversion of the various peoples into nations, is a result of the capitalist mode of production. It might therefore be presumed that the *national struggle* must disappear together with the *class struggle*. But this conclusion would be too far-fetched. Every serious student must consider as even more far-fetched and hazardous the contention that *national differences* will be eradicated simultaneously with the eradication of *class differences*. It is inconsequential to dwell on this question, and furthermore no definite factual answer can be given at the present moment. As far as I am concerned, the national question is a concrete reality today, and I cannot prophesy what will be the condition a hundred years hence—whether the nations will remain intact or will fuse with one another.

Summary

During the feudal period the various social groups—each of which was engaged in the struggle for existence under a different and relatively distinct complex of conditions of production—emerged as separate *peoples.* The physiognomy and character of each people have their relatively distinct qualities. But the feudal period also gave birth to capitalism. Consequently there soon appeared the following twofold material, socioeconomic contradictions in the current system of production: on one hand, because of the higher degree of their development, the forces of production were no longer compatible with the ossified feudal relations of production; and on the other, the forces of production which were affected by the development of capitalism were no longer compatible with the petrified system of the conditions of production. For the feudal system had disintegrated the people and their territories by the innumerable barriers erected by its feudal barons, thus hindering the development of capitalism.

As a rule, every disparity between the *forces of production* and the *relations of production* results in a social problem which can be solved only by the emancipation of the oppressed *class.* This type of contradiction, which appeared at the beginning of capitalism, was felt most severely by the bourgeoisie, who therefore took the initiative to wipe it out. They succeeded in achieving this purpose through the French Revolution.

Every disparity of the second sort, i.e., between the forces of production while they are in the process of development, and the conditions of production which hinder this development, results in a national problem that can be solved only by the emancipation of the oppressed nation. This type of contradiction, which manifested itself at the very beginning of capitalism, was felt by all classes of the society of that day. Therefore, all oppressed classes at the time of the French Revolution were imbued with the feeling of a common nationality which was being oppressed by the upper strata. It was generally believed that there was a common national harmony of interests, and only the ruling classes of that period were excluded from this ostensible harmony. Nationalism then assumed the form as we understand it today.

The development of the capitalist economy created the basis for the feeling of kinship which we call nationalism. This development transformed what had been peoples into modern nations. Nationalism, therefore, first became manifest not in the external politics of the ruling classes but in the internal struggle of the oppressed classes. Nationalism—in the present sense of the word—was carried over to the sphere of external politics only later, when the national question made its full appearance.

Soon after the newly developed capitalism had superseded feudalism, it became evident that the expansion of its forces of production was impeded not only by the state of the conditions of production *within* the relatively separated societies, but also by the relative distinctness of the various conditions of production. Striving naturally to expand the sphere of its conditions of production, every society comes into conflict with neighboring societies which offer it resistance. Thus, the development of the capitalist system places the national question in the limelight. The root of the national question lies in the conflict between relatively distinct socioeconomic organisms, and is manifest in international competition.

International competition is not a result of some despotic, egotistic trait of the ruling classes. It is a result of the unconditional need of the capitalist economies to expand while they are developing. This competition develops certain sentiments and emotions in predisposed individuals, who are concerned thereby. And although these sentiments and emotions are deeply enrooted in economic life, those people believe that they are in no way related to the material life. They fail to see the deep economic basis of these feelings, and therefore lose every possibility of understanding their own motives, which to them appear holy and far removed from materialism. From these sentiments arise multifarious fantastic nationalistic ideologies, which are prone to obscure the national consciousness and emphasize the antagonism between the latter and class consciousness. The capitalist system engendered the national question not merely for the bourgeoisie but also for all other classes of society, since each class is in one way or another affected by this international competition. The territory is of value to them all as the base of the conditions of production.

Among *free* nations who oppress no one and are not oppressed themselves, nationalism is but so much conserved energy. However, at the first opportunity this energy becomes kinetic. The *ruling classes* are the first to lose their balance. They are always imbued with the desire to capture the world market or to expand the domestic market. Once this equilibrium is destroyed, hitherto latent nationalistic feelings suddenly flare forth in an all-consuming conflagration. The nationalism which arises from the desire to expand the market is aggressive and of a consciously bellicose nature. The weapons employed are the conquest of foreign territory and the forced assimilation of national minorities.

The striving of the proletariat to expand its labor market and work sphere cannot, however, express itself in the form of a policy of conquest. The proletariat and the proletarizing masses have no direct influence on international politics. The only means of expanding the work sphere is the peaceful emigration to foreign lands. The emigrating masses, who are wandering all over the world in search of work, introduce no new national policy. The migrating worker, who has been expelled from his sphere of conditions of production, feels no deep ties for his former home. And were it not for external circumstances such as the traditions of his early education or his blood relationship with those who have remained at home, the emigrating worker would not even manifest those weak sentiments for his fatherland to which he sometimes gives expression.

The situation is quite different with regard to the proletariat of the countries to which the workers emigrate. They evidently endeavor to retain for themselves the work places, and this is accompanied by an intensified national self-consciousness. In the case of the proletariat of a free nation, this latter phenomenon assumes the character of a militant defensive against the "pernicious foreigner." This is evidenced to an even greater degree by the attitude and sentiment of the proletarizing masses, because they are interested even more than the proletariat in retaining the integrity of their national work place. We see, therefore, that as far as the proletariat is concerned, the question of emigration and immigration is fundamentally connected with the national question. Thus the localistic character of proletarian nationalism is made clear. We see too that in the case of free nations which are not oppressed nationalism has multifarious forms, because it depends on who is exhibiting it—the ruling class or the oppressed classes.

The nationalism of oppressed nationalities assumes a more peculiar form. The system of production of oppressed nationalities is always subject to abnormal conditions. The conditions of production are abnormal when, as we stated above, a nation is deprived of its territory and its organs of national preservation (such as political independence and the freedom of language and cultural development), or when it is hindered from full enjoyment of these. Such abnormal conditions tend to harmonize the interests of all members of a nation. This external pressure not only lessens and dissipates the influence of the conditions of production but also hinders the development of the relations of production and the class struggle, because the normal development of the mode of production is hampered. Class antagonism is abnormally mollified while national solidarity exerts a more potent influence.

Not only the special interests of every class are affected by this external pressure, but also every individual in the nationality feels it and understands that the source of this pressure is national. It derives from a foreign nation and is directed against his own nationality as such. Under such circumstances, the mother tongue, for example, assumes greater significance than that of a mere means to preserve the local market. When freedom of language is curtailed, the oppressed person becomes all the more attached to it. In other words, the national question of an oppressed people is detached from its association with the material conditions of production. The cultural aspects assume an independent significance, and all the members of the nation become interested in national self-determination.

In the course of the struggle for national emancipation, however, the class struggle and class psychology manifest themselves. One can usually identify the middle and petty bourgeoisie, and above all the clerical elements and landowners, as those groups of an oppressed nation that are vitally concerned with traditions. The dabblers in national education, in national literature (teachers, writers, etc.), usually garb their traditionalism in national hues. The chief protagonists of national emancipation, however, are always the progressive elements of the masses and the intelligentsia. Where these latter elements are sufficiently developed and have already freed themselves from the bonds of traditionalism, their nationalism assumes a purer character. Fundamentally the emancipation process is not nationalistic but national; and among such progressive elements of oppressed nations there develops a genuine nationalism, which does not aspire to the preservation of traditions, will not exaggerate them, has no illusions about the ostensible oneness of the nation, comprehends clearly the class structure of society, and which does not seek to confuse anyone's real class interests. It is the aim of this type of nationalism to achieve the real emancipation of the nation through the normalization of its conditions and relations of production.

Genuine nationalism in no way obscures class consciousness. It manifests itself only among the progressive elements of oppressed nations. The genuine nationalism of the progressive class—of the organized revolutionary proletariat of an oppressed nation—expresses itself in the strong, clearly-defined demands embodied in its minimum program. It is the purpose of these demands to assure the nation normal conditions of production, and to assure the proletariat of a normal base for its labor and class struggle.

Once this goal has been achieved, the purpose of genuine nationalism has been realized. Instead of the former solidarity of national interests engendered by certain emancipation processes—a forced and abnormal solidarity—a healthy class structure and a sound class struggle appear in a new and clear form.

Notes

1. Because the great landowners are in the limelight of political life, there are some observers who conclude that nationalism and traditionalism are synonomous. Such a superficial conclusion does no honor to those who believe in nationalism. Only in the case of the great landowners do nationalism and traditionalism have an identical meaning. Their nationalism is *aggressive* in foreign policy and is the chief supporter of militarism; it is *conservative* in domestic policy and is the chief supporter of the status quo. These nationalists lable as *antinational* and *traitorous* every movement of the oppressed. They wish to obscure any difference between the "internal" and "external" enemy, presenting the first as an ally of the second.
2. Among the intelligentsia there are almost no ideologists who concern themselves with the formulation of a *Weltanschauung* for the great bourgeoisie. Only the daily press caters to the great bourgeoisie, for the press is not too particular in its choice of chauvinistic propaganda.
3. We have already pointed out that this type of nationalism is called *spiritual nationalism*, which should not be confused with the pseudospiritual nationalism of the great landlords. The landlords and their allies merely shout phrases and are not concerned with the content or meaning of their spiritual fictions. Such is not the case with the middle class. This class attempts to understand its spiritual nationalism, though its approach is essentially dogmatic.

3
Our Platform
(1906)

The national problem arises when the development of a nation's forces of production conflicts with the state of conditions of production. The most prevalent national conflict is the result of the development of the forces of production within one country clashing with the conditions in foreign countries. The most general prerequisite of the development of the forces of production is the territory in which the group lives. The territory comprises all the internal conditions of production; it is their ultimate source and governs all outside influences. A territory is the positive base of a distinct, independent national life.

Expatriated peoples lack this positive base. In the course of their adaptation to the natural and historical environment of the nations among whom they dwell, they tend to lose their distinctive national traits and merge with the surrounding social milieu. That such peoples nevertheless exist as distinct national entities demonstrates that objective forces do not permit them to adapt themselves to the surrounding social milieu or, at best, hinder the process of their adaptation. Two diametrically opposed forces operate in the life of landless peoples: (1) the urge to *assimilate,* which is a result of the group's desire to adapt itself to the environment, and (2) the tendency to *isolate* the group and make it inaccessible to the environmental pressure. The second factor operates as a negative element in the national development of expatriated peoples.

The national cohesion of territorial groups is based upon their national wealth, that is, upon their territories and the material conditions of production therein. A territorial nation possesses its own national economy within which the development of the forces of production takes place— it thus constitutes a complete economic unit. In the course of its development, a nation's forces of production may be hampered by the resistance of adverse conditions. The nation is then faced by a conflict arising from the need to expand the field of opportunities which determines its production. This necessitates an invasion of foreign territories, in which case, the national policies assume an aggressive character. When, however, the forces of production of a given group suffer from the intrusion of foreign economic interests, that group is faced by a national conflict that arises from the need to guard the integrity of its national territory. The policies of such a nation are defensive (protective) in character.

The *class struggle* is the concrete expression of the social conflicts that arise because the development of the forces of production disturbs the mode of economic relations of production. The *national struggle,* however, is an expression of the conflict between the developing forces of production and the existing conditions of production. But whereas social conflicts—such as the class struggle—take place within the socio-economic organism, national conflicts transcend the bounds of the territorial economic unit. Of course I am not speaking of completely isolated economic units, for such do not exist, but we do have to recognize the existence of *relatively* independent economic units. The increasing economic interdependence of the capitalist system makes it possible to speak of even a world economy.

There is a marked distinction between national and social conflicts. The class struggle—the concrete expression of social conflicts—grows out of the economic exploitation of one class by another. Competition within the bounds of a definite group is of importance only to the individuals concerned and does not provoke any social conflicts; competition between individuals of a social group is a social phenomenon but not a social problem. National struggles grow out of competition between national groups, and the exploitation of one national group by another is merely an incidental phenomenon that creates no crucial social problem. Only in one case does national exploitation attain the importance of an acute social problem, namely, when two national groups live together in one economic unit but constitute two distinct classes. Such a relationship exists in India, for instance, where the British residents form the class of bureaucrats and capitalists while the natives form the class of peasants and workers.

From a social point of view, national competition under capitalism is very different from individual competition. Individual competition aids in the development of the forces of production, sharpens the inner contradictions, and undermines the foundations of capitalist society. National competition, on the other hand, is a hindrance to individual competition and acts in the same manner as a monopoly. In Czarist Russia, for example, the Jew could have held his ground in competition with the individual Russian; but since this was an economic struggle between two national groups, the Russian majority was in a position to eliminate the competition of the Jewish minority. National competition, like any factor that tends to paralyze the freedom of individual competition, hampers the development of a capitalist economy and defers its rise and ultimate decline. National competition is not merely a struggle between two groups; it is an endeavor of one national group to seize the material possessions of another national group and to replace the latter along all economic lines.

Effective national competition is possible only within the national economic territory. No nation can compete successfully unless it has a strategic base. When national competition takes place between a nation living on its own territory and one that is expatriated, the former endeavors to expel the latter and to deprive it of the use of its economic resources. Since the expatriated nation has no basic possessions of its own, it cannot exist unless it is allowed to use the material possessions of the majority nation.

In order to penetrate the economic sphere of the native population, the expatriated nationality endeavors to adapt itself to the conditions prevailing in its new home. The native inhabitants, however, do not allow their economic strongholds to pass into the hands of newly arrived immigrants, who are therefore forced to become "useful" by turning to economic fields as of yet unoccupied. They are tolerated as long as they are active in economic functions that no one has assumed previously. But when the development of the forces of production reaches a stage wherein the native population can itself perform those same economic functions, the foreign nationality becomes "superfluous," and a movement is begun to rid the country of its "foreigners." Since these "foreigners" have no national material possessions to use in the competitive struggle with the native population, they are forced to yield their economic positions, thereby losing their livelihood. In short, the landless nationality can more or less withstand exploitation, bad as it may be, but as soon as it is replaced by national competition, the landless nationality loses its economic position.

At no time is the foreign group allowed to enter into agriculture and other basic industries. Even when it is being exploited, the foreign group is tolerated only in commerce and in the last levels of production. As soon as the native population is ready to occupy those positions, the foreign nationality is entirely isolated from any possible access to the economy. A national struggle thus comes into being. The Jews are the classic example of an expatriated group. The Jewish nation in the *Galut* has no material possessions of its own, and is helpless in the national competitive struggle.

In analyzing the Jewish problem we must bear in mind the fact that the national struggle is closely allied with the social one. There is no struggle that is equally in the interest of all classes of a nation. Every class has national interests different from those of other classes. National movements do not transcend class divisions; they merely represent the interests of one of several classes within the nation. A national conflict develops not because the development of the forces of production of the whole nation conflicts with the conditions of production, but because the developing needs of one or more classes clash with the conditions of production of its national group. Hence the great variety of types of nationalism and national ideologies. Since the Jewish nation has no peasantry, my analysis of its national problem deals with urban classes: the upper, middle, and petty bourgeoisie; the masses who are being proletarized; and the proletariat.

The upper bourgeoisie, because it is not confined to the home market, is not national in any true sense, but highly cosmopolitan. The Jewish bourgeoisie finds its interests best served by assimilation; and were it not for the "poor *Ostjuden,*" the Jewish upper bourgeoisie would not be disturbed by the Jewish problem. The continuous stream of immigration of East European Jews and the frequent pogroms remind West European upper bourgeoisie only too often of the miserable lot of their brethren. The East European Jewish bourgeoisie is, of course, more directly affected by the status of Jewry. The West European upper bourgeoisie, however, considers the entire problem to be a gratuitous and unpleasant burden. And yet it cannot find a safe retreat away from our East European masses. Since the Jewish upper bourgeoisie would like above all to lose its individuality and be assimilated completely by the native bourgeoisie, it is very much affected by anti-Semitism. It fears everything which tends to spread anti-Semitism. If anti-Semitism were the hobby of only a few psychopathic and feeble-minded individuals, it would not be dangerous. But anti-Semitism is very popular among the masses, and very frequently its propaganda is tied up closely with the social unrest of the lowest elements of the working class. This creates a dangerous cumulation of Judaeophobia.

Anti-Semitism is becoming a dangerous political movement. It flourishes because of the national competition between the Jewish and non-Jewish petty bourgeoisie and between the Jewish and non-Jewish proletarized and unemployed masses. Anti-Semitism menaces both the poor, helpless Jews and the all-powerful Rothschilds. The latter, however, understand very well where the source of trouble lies: the poverty-ridden Jewish masses are at fault. The Jewish plutocracy abhors these masses, but anti-Semitism reminds it of its kinship to them. Two souls reside within the breast of the Jewish upper bourgeoisie—the soul of a proud European and of an unwilling guardian of his Eastern coreligionists. Were there no anti-Semitism, the misery and poverty of the Jewish emigrants would be of little concern to the Jewish upper bourgeoisie. It is impossible, however, to leave them in some West European city (on their way to a place of refuge) in the care of the local government, for that would arouse anti-Semitic ire. Therefore, despite themselves and their efforts to ignore the Jewish problem, the Jewish aristocrats must turn philanthropists. They must provide shelter for the Jewish emigrants and must make collections for pogrom-ridden Jewry. Everywhere the Jewish upper bourgeoisie is engaged in the search for a solution to the Jewish problem and a means of being delivered of the Jewish masses. This is the sole form in which the Jewish problem presents itself to the Jewish upper bourgeoisie.

The middle bourgeoisie is bound more closely to the Jewish masses. The economic interests of a middle and petty bourgeoisie depend on the market which the mass of the people affords, the market which is coextensive with the national language and cultural institutions. Therefore, in the case of territorial nations, the middle and petty bourgeoisie are the chief supporters of all types of "cultural" nationalism. Since this section of the Jewish bourgeoisie has no territory and market, it falls under the influence of assimilatory forces. On the other hand, because of the intense national competition in which the middle and lower bourgeoisie are involved, the isolating factor of anti-Semitism is felt in every branch of activity. Anti-Semitism is at the root of all the discriminatory laws against Jews in politically backward countries and of the social boycott in the bourgeois-democratic countries. The boycott, becoming more organized and more intensive, overtakes the Jewish bourgeoisie everywhere: in trade, industry, social life, and even in the press. With the growth of capitalism there is a corresponding growth of political democracy on the one hand, and of national competition on the other. Those who see in the growth of political democracy the elimination of discriminatory laws against the Jews and the corresponding lessening of the acute form of Judaeophobia (such as pogroms) see merely one side of the process. They fail to recognize the continual sharpening of national competition in bourgeois society, whose growth is parallel to that of democracy. This process strengthens the hostility and makes for a stronger and more efficiently organized boycott against the Jews. The Jewish middle and petty bourgeoisie, with no market of their own, are powerless against this menace. In the white-collar class the discrimination against the Jewish physician, engineer, and journalist forces them to face the Jewish problem. Jewish misery is closer to them than to the upper bourgeoisie. Their nationalism, however, is of a specifically middle and petty bourgeois character. Lacking any means of support in their struggle for a market, they tend to speak of an independent political existence and of a Jewish state where they would play a leading political role. They feel the effects of state anti-Semitism very strongly and therefore strive to protect Jewish civil and national rights. Since they are directly affected by the poverty and degeneration of the Jewish masses, they tend to advocate a Jewish national policy.

But as long as they succeed in retaining their middle-class position, as long as the boycott and the isolation brought about by anti-Semitism have not yet undermined their material well-being, the center of gravity of their political interests continues to be in the *Galut*. Their personal needs remain outside the Jewish national sphere, for the conflict between their economic interests and the conditions of production restricting Jewish life has not yet reached a peak. In other words, as long as the Jewish middle bourgeoisie retains its economic position it is relatively unconcerned with the Jewish problem. True, the Jewish problem is a cause of certain discomforts to the middle class, but the class is not sufficiently hard pressed to desire a radical change in its condition. Its energy can be utilized to a certain extent in behalf of the rehabilitation of Jewish life, but the middle class as a whole can never be the base for a movement of Jewish emancipation.

II

For the purpose of this discussion we may consider the Jewish petty bourgeoisie and the proletarized masses as one group. As a result of historical circumstances, this group constitutes a large majority of the Jewish people. To us proletarian Zionists this class is doubly significant. First, the Jewish proletariat has become socially differentiated from the larger group only recently. (To understand the Jewish proletariat it is necessary to analyze properly the petty bourgeoisie, which still serves as its reservoir of manpower.) Second, the heterogeneous mass of emigrating petty bourgeoisie and proletarians-to-be is the main source of human material for future Jewish rehabilitation.

National competition, which is characterized by economic isolation and government boycott—both organized and unorganized—weighs heavily on the back of the Jewish petty bourgeoisie, which suffers much more acutely than the petty bourgeoisie of any other nation and is forced to enter the ranks of the proletariat. However, the extent to which Jews can become members of the established working class is quite insufficient. Capitalist economy requires a large reserve of unemployed labor. To this reserve the Jewish petty bourgeoisie supplies a larger percentage than the petty bourgeoisie of other peoples.

Should we divide world production into two groups, one engaged in creating the means of production and the other in producing consumer goods, we would find that Jewish capital is invested mainly in the production of consumer goods. Because of the effects of national rivalry among the masses who are in search of jobs, Jewish labor finds employment almost exclusively at the hands of the small Jewish industrialist. Hatred of Jews on the part of non-Jewish employers and workers practically excludes Jewish labor from non-Jewish workshops.

Aside from the intentional boycott, both organized and unorganized, there are other factors that contribute to the Jewish worker's inability to face the competition of the non-Jewish worker. The Jewish proletarized elements are mainly city-bred, while their non-Jewish rivals hail from an agricultural environment. The latter have a number of advantages over the former. They are stronger physically, and their standard of living is lower. The Jewish worker, steeped in the traditions of a nonworker's life, requires much more comfort and luxury; therefore he adapts himself more quickly to the class conflict and enters the struggle with his employer more readily than the non-Jewish worker. In addition, for historical reasons, the Jewish worker is not as well prepared technically as the non-Jewish city-bred worker. These factors, however, are insignificant in comparison with that of national competition between the Jewish and non-Jewish worker. National competition is found even in the well-developed capitalist countries such as America, England, and South Africa—wherever the Jewish immigrants encounter masses of non-Jewish immigrants who are better adapted to obtain employment. As a result Jewish labor gains employment mainly from the Jewish middle bourgeoisie.

As soon as the national conflicts and national competition grow intense, a conscious anti-Jewish boycott is undertaken, resulting in immigration restrictions. In both England and America there is ample evidence of growing anti-Semitism with all its reactionary characteristics and consequences. Since Jewish capital becomes the sole employer of Jewish labor, the growing need for proletarization among the Jewish masses cannot be satisfied.

Jewish capital is mainly invested in the production of consumer goods. This type of production is usually characterized by seasonal employment, sweat-shop conditions, and piece-work. The exclusion of Jewish labor from the heavy industries is so prevalent that non-Jewish workers consider these as their own special field of employment. The encounters between the Jewish and non-Jewish workers at Bialystok are ample proof of this state of affairs.

The national problem of the declining Jewish petty bourgeoisie consists in its search for a market which should free it from the horrible economic isolation that characterizes it at present. In the case of this group the national question is very acute. To solve it, the Jewish petty bourgeoisie is forced to abandon its native lands and to migrate to new countries, but even there it finds no satisfactory solution. Misery overtakes the bourgeoisie; poverty is its lot in the new country. It therefore enters the labor market and is transformed into a part of the working masses. In the labor market, too, it must face national competition. Consequently, the proletarized Jewish petty bourgeoisie can penetrate only the final levels of production. A national struggle thus arises based on need and the impossibility of satisfying it.

The national question of the petty bourgeoisie, then, is the quest for a national market and the conservation of the associated cultural institutions such as language, national education, etc. Concretely, the problem of the Jewish petty bourgeoisie is that of emigration: the quest of an expatriated nation for a place of economic security. The Jewish problem migrates with the Jews. Thus a universal Jewish problem is created that involves not only Jewish philanthropists but also the political powers of the civilized nations.

The existence of an impoverished petty bourgeoisie constitutes a great danger. It represents the decaying remnants of a previous economic order. Being socially and psychologically disorganized, they constitute a "mob" whose activities will be characterized mainly by chaos and reaction. Wherever they are given a chance to engage independently in the solution of a social problem, they inevitably produce undesirable and chaotic results. The progressive forces within a democratic country must always be alert lest these elements cause irreparable damage. But these "dregs of the capitalist order" also participate in the quest for a solution of the Jewish problem. Pogroms and other primitive forms of reaction are their method of solving the Jewish problem. This "solution" succeeds only in poisoning the entire surrounding political life. This mob is the same everywhere: in Baku and in London, in Kishinev and in New York, in New Orleans and in Berlin, in Tokyo and in Melbourne, in San Francisco and in Vienna. Everywhere its method is identical—pogroms and violence. It kills Jews in Russia, massacres Armenians in Caucasia, and lynches Negroes in America. This mob is the mainstay of all political charlatans and of all the reactionary forces of a moribund social order. These excesses which the dying regime sponsors are a permanent menace to law and order in democratic countries. But they are inevitable as long as migrations of petty bourgeois and proletarian masses continue and as long as national competition exists between them and the corresponding

Jewish classes. It is significant that these antisocial methods of solving the Jewish problem are employed by the most reactionary elements of society under the leadership of representatives of the middle bourgeoisie and the chauvinistic intelligentsia. The democratic governments, however, cannot afford such chaotic methods for the solution of any problem. For these interfere with the law and order that are so necessary for the proper development of capitalism. Open violence and public scandals are not in the interests of the ruling bourgeoisie. Both the bourgeoisie and the revolutionary proletariat are equally interested in a peaceful and systematic solution to the various problems, including the Jewish problem.

How then is the solution to the problem to be achieved? Those factors that tend to intensify the conflict did not exist in the feudal countries where Jews had been living for a long time. The complete social isolation of the Jews and the migrations common to Jews and non-Jews alike are recent and are closely bound up with the development of capitalism. Under these circumstances it is futile to resort to assimilation as a solution. It may sound paradoxical, but is true nevertheless, that in the Middle Ages the prospects for assimilation were not as utopian as they are under the present order. In the Middle Ages the isolation of the Jew was not as fundamental as it is at the present time. The Jews, though excluded from the basic economic processes of life, nevertheless had some economic foundation. They fulfilled a function that accelerated the development of the system of production of that society and were thus "useful." The then existing civilized world was their national market. Later, as capitalism developed, the Jews were eliminated, and wholesale expulsion took place. But this was not typical of every country where Jews lived and did not occur in all places at the same time.

Only in the first epoch of the newly developed industrial capitalism did the assimilating factor operate strongly in Jewish life. It was then that the industrial revolution caused the walls of the ghetto to collapse, and a wide field of free competition was opened to the Jews. The epoch of the decisive struggle between capitalism and feudalism was the golden era of Jewish assimilation. But this era of free competition that characterized the rise of capitalism was superseded by national competition. Assimilation then gave way to isolation.

All assimilationists are essentially utopians, for all the forces operating within Jewish life point in a diametrically opposed direction. Intensified national competition does not stimulate Jews to assimilate; on the contrary, it strengthens the bounds of national solidarity. It unites all the scattered parts of the Jewish nation into one isolated unit. Along with the development of the inner national forces, national competition evokes universal interest in the solution to the Jewish problem. All the processes operating within Jewish life arise from national competition against the Jews and are influenced by Jewish migration. Therefore, to obtain a correct perspective of the development and dynamics of Jewish life, it is necessary to make a thorough investigation of the tendencies of Jewish migration.

Emigration alone does not solve the Jewish problem. It leaves the Jew helpless in a strange country. For that reason Jewish immigration, and any other national immigration, tends toward compact settlements. This concentration alleviates the process of adaptation to the newly found environment, but at the same time it accelerates the rise of national competition in the countries into which the Jews have recently immigrated. If so large a number of Jewish immigrants had not settled in New York, Philadelphia, and Chicago, it is doubtful whether national competition against them would have come into existence; but the existence of the Jews as such would have become impossible. The outward contradictions of Jewish immigration—the clash between the habits brought along from the old country and the conditions in the new country—necessitate concentration.

Such concentration, however, contains a double contradiction. Mass concentration aims at facilitating the process of adaptation to the new environment, but results in the segregation of the newly arrived group and hinders the process of adaptation. Upon his arrival, the immigrant seeks to enter the first levels of production. Through their concentration in the large cities, the Jews retain their former economic traditions and are condemned to the final levels of production—the manufacturing of consumer goods. Thus the need of the Jews to develop their forces of production and to become proletarized remains unsatisfied.

The contradictions inherent in this process lead to decentralization of the concentrated mass of immigrants. Jews settle in more or less compact masses not in one place but in many, thus aggravating the problem. Instead of remaining localized, the contradictions appear in numerous places. The Jewish problem thus becomes more acute and evolves into a world problem. As a result of these two fundamental contradictions, the Jewish petty bourgeoisie and working masses are confronted by two needs. The impossibility of penetrating into the higher levels of production creates the need for concentrated immigration to an undeveloped country. Instead of being limited to the final levels of production as is the case in all other countries, the Jews could in a short time assume the leading position in the economy of the new land. Jewish migration must be transformed from immigration into colonization. This means a territorial solution to the Jewish problem.

In order that the Jewish immigration may be diverted to colonization of undeveloped countries, it is not sufficient that the colonization should merely be useful to the Jews. It is also necessary that immigration to the previous centers becomes more difficult. This, in fact, is taking place. Because of national competition, immigration to the well-developed capitalist countries is being limited. At the same time, the need for Jewish emigration is steadily becoming greater, and it can no longer be satisfied by the old centers of absorption. New lands must be found, and the emigrants increasingly tend to go to semiagricultural countries. To avoid decentralization, there is need for organizational forces that would unite the Jewish masses and would systematize the spontaneous processes of migration. Left alone, Jewish migration will continue to be a confused and scattering process. A new and conscious element is required. The Jewish emigrating masses must be organized, and their movements—directed. That is the task of the conscious Jewish proletariat.

The dynamics of Jewish life operates as follows: (1) emigration of the petty bourgeoisie who turn to proletarization, (2) concentration of Jewish immigration, and (3) organized regulation of this immigration. The first two are the products of the spontaneous processes operating in Jewish life; the last is introduced by the organized Jewish proletariat. The capitalist economy has reached the stage where no revolutionary changes are possible without the participation of the working masses and especially of the organized sections of the proletariat. The emancipation of the Jewish people will either be brought about by Jewish labor or not be attained at all. But the labor movement has only one weapon at its command: class struggle. The class struggle must assume a political character if it is to lead to a better future. Proletarian Zionism is possible only if its aims can be achieved through the class struggle; Zionism can be realized only if proletarian Zionism can be realized.

III

Proletarian Zionism is a complex product of Jewish proletarian thought. After eliminating all incidental, temporary, or local factors and aberrations that inevitably complicate every fundamental social process, we could find an unusually strict consistency in the development of the Poale Zion. As in the case of every social movement, the evolution of Jewish proletarian thought is the result of a wide gap between the needs of the masses and the possibility of satisfying these needs. The main factors that give rise to this gap operate in two directions: (1) the *social* conflict between the developing forces of production of the Jewish proletariat and the economic relationships in which it lives, and (2) the *national* conflict between the developing forces of production of the Jewish proletariat and the sum total of the conditions of production. The Jewish proletariat therefore faces two tremendous tasks: the abolition of the capitalist system and the elimination of national oppression.

The social conflict is invariably clearer and much closer to the proletariat than the national conflict. The social conflict is embodied in the personal relations between employer and employee. That the capitalist economy makes the worker de facto master over the operation of the means of production gives the worker a powerful weapon of struggle at once. The obvious exploitation of the worker and the possibility of his laying down his tools and gaining concessions thereby present the economic side of the social conflict in bold relief. For this reason the worker grasps this phase of the conflict in its very early stages of development. The political aspect of this conflict is much more complicated and therefore harder to analyze and comprehend. The determining factors are more remote from the worker, and his encounter with them takes place at a relatively advanced stage of the economic struggle.

As a result of the economic law that operates in organic and social mechanics (a direct consequence of the more general law of conservation of energy), every gap between need and provision seeks its abridgement first within the framework of the conditions that caused it. Only gradually the realization of the necessity to change the conditions matures. The struggle's emphasis then shifts to new and more remote spheres. At the beginning of its struggle, the proletariat strives to attain liberation by means of economic conflict. Only at a more advanced stage does this struggle assume a political nature. The Jewish proletariat passed very rapidly through both stages of development of the social conflict. The economic struggle very easily transformed itself into a political struggle because of the harsh conditions prevailing under the Czarist regime.

The national conflict is infinitely more complex than the social one. In the national struggle the personal relations between the oppressed and oppressor do not play such an important role. In spite of the personal character of national encounters, it is clear at first sight that national oppression is of an impersonal nature. The objective and impersonal characteristics of class exploitation appear to the proletariat only at a late stage in the development of proletarian thought. National oppression, on the other hand, immediately makes its impersonal nature manifest to the observer. The oppressed Jew is not faced by a particular non-Jewish individual who is directly responsible for his sufferings. It is very clear to him that a whole social group oppresses him. He finds it difficult to analyze his social relations to this group, especially in the early period of the conflict. In addition, the mutual national relationships do not provide the oppressed group with any weapons for its struggle.

The stages in the development of national conflicts are therefore more numerous than those of social conflicts. The Jewish worker first tried to solve his national problem under the same conditions that had given rise to the problem. Gradually, however, he arrived at the revolutionary solution—the need for a radical change in the conditions of his national existence. We can understand now why some Jewish proletarian parties offer a highly advanced analysis of the social conflict but are very backward in their interpretation of the national problem. Such parties may have a large following, which only proves that the national conflict is not sufficiently advanced for the true analysis to win support. Such backward programs are doomed to extinction with the development of national conflict. It is not at all surprising to see such proletarian parties existing among Jews, especially when we remember that the Jewish problem is probably the most complicated of all. To find a correct solution requires the expenditure of much energy. For this reason the initial response of the Jewish proletarian parties to the national problem is often primitive and reactionary.

The proletariat must be considered from two different angles. First, the proletariat produces social wealth; and second, it constitutes a class that carries on its own struggles with the nonproletarian classes. The worker, as such, is interested only in the raising of his wage level and in the general improvement of his work conditions. For this he needs, first of all, a secure place of work. As long as the worker still has to compete with others in the search for employment, he is part and parcel to the proletarizing masses and has not assumed as yet a definite proletarian class physiognomy. The worker becomes a full-fledged proletarian only after he has acquired the feeling of security in his place of work; only then is he ready to take up the struggle against capital for the betterment of his condition. His place of work becomes a strategic base for his struggle, in contrast to what it had been formerly—a *casus belli* among the workers themselves. At this stage of development there emerges proletarian solidarity. Workers' solidarity is of course not an absolute guarantee against competition for employment. The danger of dismissal is always imminent; every now and then the worker has to be able to defend his place in the face of competition of his fellow worker. Again he emerges as a potential member of the unemployed, with the interests that were peculiar to his former status during the transitional period of proletarization. Thus in dilatory fashion, sometimes falling, sometimes halting, often retreating, the proletarian slowly emerges purified by the sufferings of his bitter struggle for work and bread. The road travelled by the proletarian in the formation of his class consciousness is long and hard.

The worker who is bound by his economic insecurity to the work place so that he cannot use it as a strategic base, is not in a position to carry on independent political action and can play no historical role. He is not master of his own fate. But when we speak of the proletariat as a class, we must exclude workers' competition for employment and imply only unconditional class solidarity in the struggle against capital. The worker is concerned with the place of work only insofar as he has not succeeded in entirely severing his relations with the proletarizing masses, to which he formerly belonged and into which he may be thrust again at some future time. The interests of the proletariat as a class are related only to the strategic base—to those conditions under which it carries on its struggle against the bourgeoisie.

The development of the forces of production of the masses who are forced to proletarization compels them to find a place of work; the development of the forces of production of the proletariat demands a normal strategic base for an effective class struggle. The striving for a strategic base is neither less materialist nor less idealist than the struggle for a place of work, but the former concerns an entire stratum of society while the latter is merely in the interest of individuals or groups. In the sphere of interests connected with the search for a work place, there arises a personal as well as a national competition. The achievement of a strategic base eliminates both. Without a work place it is impossible to carry on a struggle; and as long as any group of workers is subject to national competition, it cannot carry on the class struggle successfully. Its strategic base is bound to remain weak.

Thus although the proletariat as a class is ideologically not concerned with national competition, national competition may nevertheless have an indirect but important bearing on its interests. With the petty bourgeoisie and the proletarizing masses this competition expresses itself concretely in the form of a national struggle. In the case of the proletariat the competition assumes the form of a national problem, which looms before the proletariat as well as before all classes of a nation. If the development of the forces of production of the proletariat (i.e. of its class struggle) is hampered by the abnormal conditions of its strategic base, then the national problem arises, and the national consciousness of the proletariat awakens.

In classes that retain a caste character, national consciousness and class consciousness exist and function independently of each other. For example, the feudal lords of Russia are "genuine Russian patriots" as well as members of the nobility. As Russians they have the "welfare of the nation" at heart, but as nobility they are ready to exploit the nation for their own ends. The middle and petty bourgeoisie and the impoverished masses characteristically have their class consciousness obliterated by their national consciousness. Class consciousness is, so to speak, excommunicated as a threat to "national unity." These classes are, then, *nationalistic*. Only with the proletariat is the national problem closely allied with the same strategic base, with the same imperatives of the class struggle upon which its class consciousness is built.

One characteristic of the relationship between class consciousness and national consciousness should be noted. Because the national interests of the proletariat have little in common with the national struggle of other classes, proletarian nationalism is not aggressive; but it is thoroughly negative—it fades away as soon as the need for normalizing the strategic base is gone. That does not imply, however, a lack of positive content. No other class is as capable of providing a real national program such as the proletariat offers. There are all sorts of misunderstandings with regard to the nationalism of the proletariat. Some who fail to see its positive content consider it reactionary. Others, who see clearly the causes which have given rise to it, are apologetic; they consider a Jewish national program to be a tragic necessity. "Unfortunately, we are forced to carry through a national program. We would like to assimilate, but we are forced to remain Jews"—such for example is the tone of the propaganda of the Z.S.

But these errors are merely the result of immature thought. The proletariat welcomes everything that aids in the development of its forces of production and opposes everything that hampers that development. Therefore the obfuscation of class and national consciousness is equally odious to the proletariat. The proletarian is not ashamed of the tasks incumbent upon him as a class-conscious worker, and he is equally unashamed of his national obligations. With pride we declare, "We are Social Democrats, and we are Jews." Our national consciousness is negative in that it is emancipatory. If we were the proletariat of a free nation, which neither oppresses nor is oppressed, we would not be interested in any problems of national life. Even now, when under the pressure of national conflicts we have acquired national consciousness, spiritual culture concerns us less than social and economic problems. Ours is a realistic nationalism, free from any "spiritual" admixture.

For the Jewish proletariat the national problem arises because the development of its forces of production disturbs the conditions of its strategic base, which is unsatisfactory both politically and economically. The economic struggle of the Jewish worker is successful during the busy season when his employers are forced to yield under pressure in order not to lose valuable time. Once the season is over, the employers are in a position to take back all the concessions they had previously granted. At the beginning of the new season, the fruits of the economic struggle have vanished, and the worker once more has to take up the struggle in order to regain the same uncertain victory. The Jewish strategic base is even less satisfactory politically. Since the Jewish worker is employed almost wholly in the production of consumer goods and performs no important function in any of the primary levels of production, he does not hold in his grasp even a single fundamental thread of the economy of the land in which he lives. His influence upon the general mode of life is thus very limited. He is incapable of paralyzing the economic organism in a single stroke as can the railroad or other workers who are more advantageously situated in the economic structure.

The Jewish worker is not exploited by *gross Kapital;* his exploiter is the small capitalist whose role in production is negligible. When the Jewish worker does go on strike against the industry which exploits him, he does not appreciably disturb the equilibrium of the country. He is not even strong enough to obtain his just demands without the support of the other more fortunate workers of the surrounding nationalities. He cannot obtain even the most minor concession when his national needs do not coincide with those of workers of another nationality. This helplessness engenders within him the sense of proletarian solidarity and brings him closer to revolutionary ideals. Class antagonism within Jewish life is comparatively minor. First, the concentration of capital is small. Then too the Jewish middle class, which is oppressed even more than the middle class of any other nationality (such as the Armenian), constitutes itself as an opposition group. Politically it offers the proletariat some support, unreliable though it may be. Under these conditions, the Jewish proletariat is doomed to trail behind the mighty political labor movements of the country.

The Jewish proletariat is in need of revolution more than any other. It is hoping most ardently for the good which is expected to come with the growth of democracy in society. The terrible national oppression, the exploitation on the part of petty Jewish capitalists, and the comparatively high cultural level and restlessness of the city-bred Jewish proletarian— the son of the "people of the book"—these generate an overwhelming revolutionary energy and an exalted spirit of self-sacrifice. This revolutionary zeal, hampered by the limitations of the strategic base, very frequently assumes grotesque forms. A disease of surplus energy is the tragedy of the Jewish proletariat and is the source of its sufferings. A chained Prometheus who in helpless rage tears the feathers of the vulture that preys on him—that is the symbol of the Jewish proletariat.

IV

In its efforts to solve the problems connected with the national conflict, the Jewish proletariat has undergone definite stages of thought and activity. Its reactions have become steadily more complex, more coordinated, and more revolutionary. At first the Jewish worker attempted to solve his national problem in the framework of the conditions that had given rise to it. Only at a later stage did he realize the need for a radical change in the conditions themselves. Each one of the stages through which the proletariat passed was of significance, for each was anticipating the following, more revolutionary stage. It is the Jewish proletariat that has developed the most coordinated program for the solution of the national problem, namely the program of the Jewish Social Democratic Workers Party, Poale Zion.

Our ultimate aim, our maximum program, is socialism—the socialization of the means of production. The only way to achieve this is through the class struggle of the Jews within the ranks of worldwide social democracy (on this I shall not dwell).

Our immediate aim, our minimum program, is Zionism. The necessity for a territory in the case of the Jews results from the unsatisfactory economic strategic base of the Jewish proletariat. The anomalous state of the Jewish people will disappear as soon as the conditions of production prevailing in Jewish life are done away with. Only when the Jews find themselves in the primary levels of production will their proletariat hold in its hands the fate of the economy of the country. When Jews participate in those sectors of economic life wherein the social fabric of the whole country is woven, then will the organization of the Jewish proletariat become free and not rely on the proletariat of the neighboring peoples. The Jewish workers' class struggle will no longer be directed against a powerless bourgeoisie, as in the *Galut,* but against a mighty bourgeoisie which organizes the production of the country. The class struggle will enable the proletariat to wield the necessary social, economic, and political influence.

Our point of departure is the development of the class struggle of the Jewish proletariat. Our point of view excludes a general program of the Jewish people *as a whole.* The anomalies of the entire Jewish nation are of interest to us only as an objective explanation of the contradictions in the life of the Jewish proletariat. The subjective motivation of our program flows solely from the class interests of the Jewish proletariat. We defend our own interests, that is, the interests of the Jewish worker. We also defend our cultural and economic needs wherever we are. We fight for the political, national, and the ordinary human rights of the

Jewish worker. For that we advance national demands along with the general demands of the Social Democratic minimum program. The national demands enter automatically into our minimum program.

We will consider the Jewish question fully solved and its anomalies wholly removed (insofar as it is possible within the framework of bourgeois society) only when territorial autonomy for the Jewish people shall have been attained and the entire nation shall constitute a relatively unified national economic organism. But colonizing a territory is a prolonged process, during which we must also defend our needs in the *Galut*. We must assume that a large part of the Jewish people, including a part of the proletariat, will always remain in the *Galut* as an ordinary national minority. For that reason we include in our program, along with territorial demands, the demand for the maximum protection of our national needs in the *Galut*. Explicitly, this means national political autonomy for all Jews in *Galut*.

National autonomy is not a radical solution of the Jewish problem and, therefore, cannot remove the anomalies of the Jewish economic strategic base. However, it provides the Jewish proletariat with the necessary political forums, and places the proletariat in the political arena face to face with the Jewish bourgeoisie. But even if it is incapable of making a radical change and cannot give the Jewish proletariat an efficient weapon in the struggle against the prevailing form of capitalism, we must still remember that national political autonomy is the maximum obtainable in the *Galut*. The shortcomings of national political autonomy emanate from the abnormal conditions of *Galut* life.

National political autonomy, even with all the democratic guarantees possible, remains only a mere palliative. Without territorial autonomy it will not lessen the national oppression of the Jewish people, will not change the Jewish social structure, and will not set great forces in motion. Jews, however, will be granted a normal representation which will serve to make an end to shameful backdoor politics. It will be a powerful unifying force among the Jewish masses, will provide them with a proper financial apparatus, and most important, it will provide them with a political education that will teach them even in the *Galut* to create and shape their own destiny. This achievement is small in comparison with what can be obtained in an autonomous territory, but is important when compared with what exists at present. We know how limited our civil equality will be in practice, yet we demand legal civil equality. We know that our national equality in the *Galut* will in reality be very circumscribed; nevertheless, we demand full national equality without any legal limitations. Life itself will see to it that we do not gain too much, so we must do everything within our power to get the optimum out of national equality.

An examination of the growth of democracy will reveal the stages in the attainment of national political autonomy. Just as socialism will result from processes implicit in the concentration of capital and will be established by means of class struggle, just as the fall of autocracy will result from processes inherent in the capitalist development of Russian society and will be precipitated by the class struggle—so will the realization of national political autonomy result from processes inherent in the development of society along nationality lines, and will come about through the class struggle of the proletariat and its allies. However, our most important national demand is territorial autonomy, which is being realized by means of processes inherent in Jewish immigration. In the course of its migration, the Jewish people does not degenerate nor resurrect itself—it merely transforms itself.

V

The most general law governing migration in the capitalist era, as propounded by Marx, says that *the direction of migratory labor depends upon the direction of migratory capital.* In order to deduce the real facts concerning general and Jewish migration, it will be necessary to describe the social relationships between the entrepreneur and the laborer. Language is the medium of contact, constituting a national bond. In small-scale industries, the entrepreneur and the laborers are in close propinquity; for there the entrepreneur not only organizes and distributes the jobs but frequently also works shoulder to shoulder with the employees. Mutual understanding of questions pertaining to the functioning of the industry thus develops another national bond. But in large industrial establishments, a complex hierarchy of managers and officials separates the entrepreneur capitalist from the laborers. Therefore in large-scale production there is no necessary national tie between entrepreneur and worker.

Similarly, in the field of distribution the language is merely a means of communication between the seller and the buyer. The wholesale merchant is separated from the consumer by brokers and other intermediaries. To him, therefore, language and other national ties are of little significance. The retailer, however, is closely allied with the consumer by language and national customs. Large industry and business are international, while petty industry (and a part of middle industry) bears a clearly defined national character. The latter's sphere of activities is determined by the national market, and its sphere of exploitation reaches only the workers within the national boundaries. (As far as Jewish industry is concerned, this particular analysis has to be modified, for the Jews find themselves in a foreign economy. They do not use their national language in business but generally assume the language of the land. However, wherever they live in compact masses, Jews do not assume the foreign language very readily.) The small merchant is very close to the consumer and is therefore liable to national boycott, but the large capitalist can very easily hide his nationality under a hierarchy of intermediaries.

This fundamental fact—the existence of national ties between the entrepreneur, worker, and consumer in petty industry and their absence in large industry—is even more obvious during the migration of capital and labor. *Capital and labor of petty industry always migrate together and retain their national character in their new domicile.* The migration of labor is never directed to countries with a large labor reserve in the peasantry. Countries such as Germany, France, and Italy will never be countries of immigration as long as their capitalist development follows the present trend.

In determining the direction of migration we must also consider the differences between the level of economic development and of cultural and political development. In the European democratic countries, all parts of the population enjoy the benefits of a high cultural and political level of life, regardless of sharp economic differences. If we want to apply to the phenomenon of mass migration the law according to which migration tends in the direction of least resistance, we must determine the resistances and all factors connected with them. We then arrive at the following important conclusions: Of two countries acceptable for immigration, the country that promises higher economic level affords the line of least resistance. Of two countries with identical economic levels, the country that promises higher cultural and political levels affords the line of least resistance.

The causes of emigration may lie in a prolonged economic depression or oppression. In the capitalist era, the proletarizing masses emigrate because of persistent economic pressure. The landless peasant masses migrate to new countries where pools of unused capital accumulate because of the absence of reserve labor forces. Accumulation of capital is possible only in places where there are good prospects for its development. A country's cultural and political standards are of great importance in determining the influx of capital. For that reason the ruined peasant population of Europe will not migrate into politically backward countries. *The migration of European peasantry is tending and will continue in the direction of the democratic countries of the New World.*

The outstanding national character of the lower middle class is evident in the process of immigration. The peasants concentrate into national blocs in their newly found homes. Italians, Germans, and other nationalities make up independent settlements. Along with the Italian peasants, who constitute a mass of small consumers, there immigrate also Italian petty merchants, artisans, and professionals. This is the case with every national group of immigrants. Only international investment capital, the transfer of which gives direction to immigration, is perfectly free of any national character. (One other group bearing no national character in immigration includes the dregs of society such as professional thieves, white slave traffickers, and gamblers. International hooliganism knows no nation or fatherland. Its favorite centers of immigration are the harbor cities, the gold and diamond districts, and all places where it is possible to fish in troubled waters.)

Of an entirely different character is the immigration of the urban small industrial population. In this case, the migration of wage labor depends on the small capitalist. The urban small industrial population follows the entrepreneurs of its nation. No matter how acute the need for proletarization becomes, it will not be fulfilled unless conditions force the small capitalist to emigrate. On the surface it would seem that economic ruin is sufficient to cause the emigration of small capitalists; but this is erroneous, for a ruined capitalist loses his class status. In order for capitalists to emigrate, there must be a constant economic threat or continual persecution. In the case of Jewish emigration, pogroms, civil persecution, and general insecurity play a decisive role. If the new country of refuge is economically suitable, if Jewish capital may be utilized to advantage and production enhanced, emigration of the impoverished masses increases and the success of the first pioneers of Jewish capital brings additional numbers of Jewish entrepreneurs and workers. Mass immigration is thus precipitated and gains impetus from new pogroms and persecutions. (It must be noted that for small capital the cultural and political development of the country is of much less significance than it is for large capitalist ventures.)

Until recently, international capital was directed to the newly developing countries. The large flow of capital into those countries accelerated the development of the forces of production, exploited natural resources, and created a demand for labor. For that reason an intensive migration of the proletarizing peasantry of many nations has been directed toward the new countries. Since a developing economy ruled by international capital created a need for consumer and service goods, there was room for Jewish immigration. Jews followed the general stream of world migration. This situation was the case until recently. Lately, new tendencies began to appear. The natural resources, for the development of which a great deal of capital has been expended, became limited. Wage reductions became common, and capitalists' profits diminished. International capital began to look for new investment channels and turned to financing agricultural projects. At the same time, workers who had been too compactly settled were unable to find employment. Thus a break occurred in world immigration, and even larger groups of immigrants turned to agrarian countries.

It is necessary to point out two characteristics of agricultural colonization in undeveloped countries. These characteristics arise because colonization takes place on the initiative of government institutions that encourage loans in order to improve conditions in the grain trade and to provide livestock and machinery on a long-term credit basis. Italian, German, and Slavic peasants who formerly immigrated into the United States, Australia, and South Africa as unskilled workers, at present go to Argentina, Brazil, and Canada where they become independent homesteaders on government lands, with an inventory for which they can pay on the installment plan. Even though these homesteaders appear to be independent, they find themselves in the clutches of investment capital. Because of long-term credit, loans from international financiers do not seem so oppressive and do not ruin the farmers. In agrarian countries the farmers cannot grow products to meet their household needs; they must grow crops for the market. They must pay their debts and must therefore exchange their products for money. The new countries dump large quantities of grain on the world market, and the resulting competition eliminates those elements that cannot maintain the proper standard of farming.

On the other hand, long-term credit helps the farmer to entrench himself in his holdings and keeps him from proletarization. In countries predominantly agricultural there is no place for large individual farms because of lack of laborers. Instead of offering one's services to a landowner, one has the opportunity to acquire land himself. Even the intensification of agriculture does not tend to ruin the farmers, because they cooperate in the introduction of machines, new methods of fertilization, and land irrigation—in which the government is of great help. Along with the farmer, there enter into the land small merchants of the same nationality, who satisfy the limited needs of the farming population.

Since the stream of world migration has turned in another direction, Jewish migration must also find new channels. But are predominantly agricultural countries adapted to Jewish immigration? To answer this we must first distinguish between spontaneous immigration and planned colonization. It is clear that spontaneous, unregulated Jewish immigration cannot direct itself to new countries in order to serve commercial and industrial functions or to take up agriculture. The former task is impossible because in those countries there is no place for small capital. Small-scale production and small commerce do not reach the world market. If the Jewish masses do not find a local market for their products, they have no good reason for immigrating into those countries. It is true that the Jews can make a determined attempt to engage in farming, but such attempts are doomed to failure. Jewish farmers would have to compete in the world market and would surely lose. As city-bred people, the Jews are unable to compete with Italian and other peasants who have an agricultural background. The geographical location is unimportant. Jewish workers may live in Africa and the Italians in America—they will still compete in the world market.

For this reason all attempts at Jewish land-colonization to date have been a failure and have borne merely a philanthropic character. Equally unsuccessful will be the attempts at planned colonization in such lands. The organization of such colonization must assume from its very inception the character of a large-scale financial enterprise. It will have to compete in the world market and will swiftly be led to bankruptcy. If, on the other hand, it should attempt to engage in large-scale manufacturing, it will fail either because of comparatively low productivity or because of the relatively higher price of Jewish labor. Territorialism, if it is to continue being a revolutionary movement within the Jewish people, must find support in the spontaneous processes of Jewish life. Territorialism does not signify a mere spontaneous migration of Jews but a spontaneously concentrated immigration. The analysis of territorialism may be considered as complete only when one can point to a designated land for immigration. Territorialism apart from a particular territory is utopian.

The above-mentioned determined laws of the processes of immigration and emigration have led us to the conclusion that Jewish immigration is being excluded from countries of wide land-colonization and from countries of large industrial investments. The worldwide stream of immigration increasingly tends toward agricultural countries that offer free land to immigrants. In this era of capitalist competition, the Jews cannot turn to farming at once. The economic activities of the Jewish immigrants tend to lose their industrial and commercial character and be transferred from the final levels of the process of production to the primary levels— to the basic industries and farming. This transfer, however, cannot occur at once. That is why Jewish migration differs from the general stream of migration and must seek entirely different channels. Everything that tends to isolate Jewish life helps to make Jews more nationally conscious:

Jewish immigration assumes a national character, which finds expression in the spread of a national ideology of emigration.

The need for emigration of the Jewish nation is merely one of the forces leading to its rehabilitation. When planned immigration will assume a national character it will fuse with our other aspirations for rebirth. Abstract territorialism is an incomplete ideology of national emancipation; its complete and synthetic form is Zionism.

Jewish immigration is slowly tending to divert itself to a country where small Jewish capital and labor may be utilized in such forms of production as will serve as a transition from an urban to an agricultural economy and from the production of consumer goods to more basic forms of industry. The country into which Jews immigrate will not be highly industrial nor predominantly agricultural but rather semiagricultural. Jews alone will migrate there, separated from the general stream of immigration. This country will have no attraction for immigrants from other nations, and will be the only one available to the Jews. Of all countries available for all immigrants, this land will provide the line of greatest resistance. It will be a country of low cultural and political development. Big capital will hardly find use for itself there, while Jewish small and middle capital will find a market for its products in both this country and its environs. *The land of spontaneously concentrated Jewish immigration will be Palestine.*

The immigration of the Jews into Palestine will differ considerably from their previous wanderings. Formerly, they had to adapt themselves to the needs of the native population; their primary function was to satisfy the natives' consumer needs or, as in the case of the United States, the needs of a mixed population that consisted more of immigrants than of natives.

In Palestine, Jewish immigrants for the first time will not only aim to satisfy the needs of the native population, but will also produce for the external market of the surrounding Mediterranean countries and in time even for the world market. Until now Jews have always been dependent on the native populations in the *Galut*. The organization of Jewish labor was not self-sufficient and was determined by the nature of the relationships that existed among the native population. The Jewish welfare in the *Galut* was always dependent upon the "usefulness" of the Jews to the ruling nationality. The needs of the natives, their ability to pay, and the rivalry between Jewish merchants and professionals and the corresponding groups of the native population—all helped bring about a narrowed field for Jewish economy in the *Galut*. Aside from these limitations the Jews, both in their old places of residence and in the new lands of immigration, began to be displaced and become pauperized—they became superfluous. Compulsory isolation became their fate; national oppression and persecutions took place. The chief cause for this one-sided dependence on the native population lay in the expatriation of the Jewish people.

With the migration to Palestine the situation will change radically. The welfare and functions of Jewish immigrants in Palestine will depend not on the native population but on the foreign market, which will for a long time be able to absorb the products of Palestine because of the favorable location of the Mediterranean. Jewish labor will encounter national competition neither on the part of the native population nor on the part of the new immigrants. In Palestine, the Jews will perform the functions which serve as a transition from the production of consumer goods to the creation of the means of production. As to the question of how many Jewish immigrants Palestine can absorb, it is easy to see that this depends on the degree of capitalist development in the neighboring countries.

If, for instance, Egypt becomes a land with increasing exports, it is evident that the imports to Egypt will grow as well. Since the Jewish settlers in Palestine will be interested in the neighboring foreign market, large-scale capitalist enterprises will develop there. The tendencies of Jewish immigration will be affected by those of the world market insofar as they affect the southeastern shores of the Mediterranean. I do not assert that Jewish immigration to Palestine will always progress uniformly; from time to time it may fluctuate. And because of economic crises or political complications a temporary exodus from Palestine may take place. *But the general tendency will undoubtedly be a continual growth of Jewish immigration into Palestine.* Those who think that such a radical transformation of Jewish life as territorialism implies can occur without a bitter struggle, without cruelty and injustices, without suffering for innocent and guilty alike, are utopian. Such revolutions are not recorded in ink with high sounding phrases; they are written in sweat, tears, and blood.

We have investigated the tendency toward the concentration of Jewish immigration and toward the formation of a relatively economically independent Jewish community in Palestine. The masses of the Jews in the *Galut* who do not take a farseeing view of their emigration needs, will join in our Zionist endeavors because of their immediate needs. The greater the interest of the surrounding nations in the radical solution of the Jewish problem and the greater the national consciousness and organization of the Jews in the *Galut* in response to oppression and isolation, the more energetically will organized Zionism impress itself upon this spontaneous process and the more desirable will its results be.

The broadening and consolidation of Jewish economic and cultural positions in Palestine will proceed at a rapid pace along with the above-mentioned processes. Parallel with the growth of economic independence will come the growth of political independence. The ideal of political autonomy for the Jews will be consummated by *political territorial autonomy in Palestine,* which is the ultimate aim of Zionism. For proletarian Zionists, this is also a step toward socialism.

VI

Because proletarian Zionism has recognized the *spontaneous concentration of Jewish immigration in Palestine,* it has completely shaken off all former utopian concepts concerning the realization of territorial autonomy. Immigration to Palestine rises above those measures with which utopians usually approach the question of Palestine. Some of us may revere Palestine as our former fatherland. Others may consider it a proper center of immigration because of its geographic proximity to centers of Jewish population. Still others may imagine that the ideology of the movement of national emancipation includes a special preference for Palestine, or on the other hand, that Zionism is guided by purely practical calculations. All these differences of opinion have no bearing on our analysis.

Our Palestinism is not a matter of principle, because it has nothing to do with old traditions. Nor is it purely practical, for we do not recognize the existence of other fit territories to choose from. The trend of thought of the practical adherents of Palestine is as follows: a territory is needed; Palestine is a possible territory; it is the best territory under the circumstances; therefore—Palestine. Our line of thought, however, is: there are migratory processes inherent in Jewish life; Palestine is the future land for the spontaneous waves of immigration; consequently we will have territorial autonomy in Palestine. The practical adherents of Palestine assert that theoretically they are territorialists and practically for Palestine. With us, however, theoretical territorialism is not to be distinguished from concrete territorialism, for concentrated Jewish immigration will direct itself toward Palestine and not toward any other territory. We do not claim that Palestine is the sole or best territory, but merely indicate that it is the place where territorial autonomy will be obtained. Our Palestinism is neither theoretical nor practical, but rather prognostic.

Thus we have liquidated the "search for a territory." We entrust this task to the inherent processes of Jewish immigration. Our task is not to find a territory, but to obtain territorial political autonomy in Palestine.

The task of the Territorialist movement is to regulate spontaneous processes, especially the immigration processes, which finally lead to territorial autonomy. As a matter of fact we have two territorial movements—bourgeois Zionism and proletarian Zionism. What then is the role of each in Jewish life?

In every spontaneous process, it is necessary to distinguish between two factors—creative and liberating ones—even though the distinction is difficult. The development and accumulation of the forces of production, the creation of new combinations of material forces, the growth of capitalism—these are the creative factors in the evolution of modern society. The creation of free conditions for the development of the productive forces, the growth of democracy—these are the liberating factors of modern social evolution. Both factors are spontaneous, even though they are subject to regulation. The bourgeoisie regulates the creative factors of the spontaneous process; the proletariat regulates the liberating factors. The development of capitalism is being carried on by the bourgeoisie, but it is the struggle of the proletariat that brings about the growth of democracy.

The bourgeoisie's sphere of activity cannot be precisely delimited from that of the proletariat. The bourgeoisie is partly interested in and aids in the process of the growth of democracy but its role is insignificant in comparison with that of the proletariat. On the other hand, in whatever concerns the development of the forces of production and the capitalist evolution of society, the organizing role belongs to the bourgeoisie. Although the proletariat is interested in the development of the forces of production, its sphere of activity lies outside of it, and it puts forth no particular demands therein. When the dictatorship of the proletariat is attained, labor will organize all work. Until then the proletariat does not interfere, as a class, in the regulation of the creative factors. Thus it is not the task of the proletariat to be concerned with digging canals or building railroads. Here the proletariat puts forth no demands, because these are the creative factors of capitalist evolution. But whenever it does interfere in the technical organization of work, it is for the sake of obtaining better working and living conditions. In the case of colonization, one finds an identical situation. Colonization methods do not concern the proletariat in the capitalist era, for they are part of the creative sphere of capitalist activity, of the organization of production. The proletariat, however, may demand some regulation of the property relationships and other legal arrangements in the colonies, for these are in its proper sphere—that of liberation.

When we pass to those spontaneous processes in which territorialism is realized, we must again distinguish between creative and liberating factors and thus clarify the respective roles of the bourgeoisie and the proletariat. The creative elements in the process consist in accumulation of capital and labor in Palestine, in exploitation of the natural resources of the land, in technological development, and in the general development of the forces of production. To regulate all these is mainly the task of bourgeois Zionism. Immigration into Palestine must be properly guided, and colonization must be supervised. To regulate the spontaneous Jewish immigration to Palestine means to facilitate the entry of capital and labor, and to utilize those forces in the most economical and rational manner possible. This must be the realistic direction of the activity of the Zionist Congress.

The Jewish proletariat lives in the *Galut,* and there it struggles for its daily needs. Among these needs is the freedom of immigration to Palestine—the inviolability of the right of entry there. Objective processes lead the Jewish proletariat to Palestine, where it must struggle bitterly. It would be easier to attain freedom in Palestine if life in *Galut* were more bearable. The stronger our political power in Palestine, the more respected will our rights be in *Galut.* This is an integration of *Galut* and Zion. The maximum we can obtain in the *Galut* is national political autonomy, while in Palestine the maximum is territorial and political autonomy. Which shall we obtain first does not matter. National political autonomy in *Galut* is not only one of the means by which territorial autonomy in Palestine can be obtained but is also an independent goal. These two aims are united by the historical process which unfolds itself simultaneously in all its breadth in *Galut* and Palestine.

Utopianism suffers because it strives to ignore historical processes. By means of human endeavor it wishes to create something not inherent in social life. Fatalism, on the other hand, assumes that effective participation of the human will in these historical processes is impossible, and thus it drifts passively with the stream. Utopianism knows of no historical processes. Utopians fear to mention the phrase "historical processes," for they see in the so-called historical process fatalism and passivity. Fatalists, on the other hand, fear the conscious interference with the historical process as a dangerous artificiality. They forget that history is made by men who follow definite and conscious aims. Utopians forget that the results of human activity coincide with human aims and purposes only when those are well adapted to the historical necessities of social life.

We ask, "What role can our will, our consciousness, play in the historical processes of Jewish life?" To the conscious intervention of human will there must be added another factor—organization. Organization is not a mere sum of individual efforts, but a collective social force. Along with historical social tendencies we must introduce planning. Regulating historical processes means facilitating and accelerating their progress, conserving social energy, and obtaining optimal results from the labor put forth.

4
The Jubilee of the
Jewish Labor Movement
(1912)

It will be twenty-five years in July since Jewish workers in Russia went out on their first mass strike and the Jewish Labor movement began to assume a more or less planned and conscious character. This was the first important step of the Jewish Labor movement not only because of the extent and the duration of the strike (all workers in Bialystok's mills were on strike for two months), but also because of its wonderful organization. These first steps toward organization of Jewish labor date back to 1887, exactly ten years before the rise of the Bund.

Broadly speaking, the Jewish Labor movement is not as young as is commonly thought. In two years we shall celebrate the fiftieth anniversary of the first-known Jewish trade union, the Women's Tailors Association in Mohilev, organized in 1864. (This association was described by S. Tatichev in the journal *Promishlenost i Zdorovie* [May 1903], by Sarah Rabinovitch in "The Organization of the Jewish Proletariat" [1903], and by S.A. Margolin in *Voskhod* [May 1906].) The whole period between the organization of this labor association and the rise of the Bund has not yet been thoroughly investigated; I hope the reader will bear with me while I try to acquaint him with at least the most important events.

The Jewish Labor movement in Russia is fifty years younger than the Russian Labor movement, yet has had interesting aspects from its very beginning. The above-mentioned Women's Tailors Association functioned not only as a regular fraternal organization, offering financial aid or sick and death benefits to its members, but also led the struggle of the workers against the employers. Naturally the employers were very much averse to the association, which had a great influence among the workers, and reported it to the authorities. Consequently, the association's leaders suffered severely at the hands of the police. The strikes waged by the association against the employers were important not only because of the number of workers involved and the size of the plants, but also because of the nature of their demands. The great majority of Jewish workers were employed by small industrialists. It is no wonder that the first steps toward labor organization were made in the manual trades rather than in the large factories.

The first traces of economic struggle in Jewish industry appeared in the seventies. In 1875 a very interesting correspondence from southwest Russia was published in *Vpered* (an illegal journal of the celebrated Russian revolutionary socialist, P. Lavrov). It includes descriptions of some of the unorganized strikes of Jewish workers in the tobacco factories of Vilna and other cities. Due to the "conspiracy" laws, the exact dates of the strikes are not given nor are the letters signed. We know now, however, that they came from the pen of one of the first Jewish socialists, A. Zundelevitch.

One finds very little information about the Jewish weavers of Bialystok in the first issue of the illegal *Bialystok Worker* (April 1899). In its leading article we find: "Who of the older weavers does not remember the terrible strikes that took place some decades ago? The 'rebels,' as they were then called, threw a scare into the manufacturers and the master weavers." The writer tells us that during those strikes the workers quite often invoked terrorism, broke factory windows, and were responsible for similar disorders. Most of the strikes were of a defensive nature. They were called to combat oppressive measures instituted by the employers such as wage cuts, lengthening of the work day, fining the workers excessively, and harsh treatment of employees.

The *Rabochia delo* (nos. 4-5, pt. I, p. 34) gives a description of a huge aggressive strike. It took place during the Russo-Turkish war of 1877–78. The manufacturers were doing a booming business filling army orders and sending exports to Rumania. The workers demanded higher wages; after a three-day strike they won. All Bialystok workers participated in the strike—Jews (about 1,500), Germans, and Poles—involving a total of 15,000 workers.

All the above conflicts, however, belong to the prehistory of the Jewish Labor movement, because the element of class consciousness and planned organization was lacking. In that distant past the movement was groping blindly. Even the Mohilev Women's Tailors Association had a strong religious character. Like all the associations of that period it had, for example, its own *Sefer Tora* (biblical scroll) and met in the synagogue, but employers were rigidly excluded from membership.

With regard to the economic struggle, the history of the Jewish Labor movement may be divided into short periods:

1. The early period, with which we have already dealt, and in which the socialist ideology and the economic struggle of the workers existed in separate spheres. Both were weak and divided, with no point of

contact between them. The workers occasionally went on strike but had no conception at all of socialism or class struggle. The few Jewish socialists of that time (with the exception of Zundelevitch) had not yet begun to think in terms of class struggle. Socialism had not yet found the path to Jewish workers and the latter did not know how to proceed toward a class-conscious organization. This period lasted from the 1860s to about 1889.

2. The preparation period for a broad organization started in the Russian Pale of Settlement with the general strike of the Jewish weavers in Bialystok in 1887, and with the founding of the first small strike fund in Vilna in 1888. We can therefore consider 1887 as the beginning of the organized Jewish Labor movement in the Pale. In the next decade the workers and the socialists sought and found each other.

3. The economic and political organization began with the founding of the General Jewish Workers' Alliance of Lithuania, Poland, and Russia—the Bund—in September 1897, and continued until 1901-1902. A new Jewish Labor movement then appeared on the scene— the Poale Zion or Socialist Zionists. The Bund ceased to rely solely on the economic struggle of the Jewish workers and assumed an outspoken political character.

4. The period of political splits can be divided into two subperiods: from 1901/1902 to the Revolution of 1905, and from the Revolution to 1907.

5. The fifth period begins now, and it is not up to the historian to consider it; that is left to the party spokesman and publicist.

All this concerns the Jewish workers in Russia only. In the remaining countries with Jewish communities, the course of events was naturally different. It is interesting to note, however, that at the time that a broad movement bearing a clear-cut mass character began in Russia, a similar manifestation appeared in other *Galut* countries. The first large strike of Jewish tailors in New York occurred in 1886, and in 1889 ten thousand Jewish tailors went out on strike for the first time in London. The Polish socialists began to organize the Jewish proletariat of Galicia early in the 1890s. In 1894 in Amsterdam, the first general strike of Jewish diamond workers broke out and resulted in the organization of the powerful Diamond Workers Union.

Although we have treated the beginnings of Jewish labor struggles in Russia before those in other countries, the almost simultaneous rise of broad mass movements in the other large *Galut* centers must be kept in mind. There is good reason for this development: the 1880s and 1890s were a period of worldwide economic recovery which contrasted markedly with the terrible crisis of the late 1870s. Parallel with this upward swing was the growth of socialism throughout the world. In America (Chicago) huge labor disorders broke out during 1886, and in Europe the Socialist International was revived in 1889. Deeply significant events also took place in Jewish life: a powerful anti-Semitic agitation developed, and emigration from Russia, Galicia, and Rumania to America, England, and Holland rose tremendously. The 1880s and 1890s were a period of blind groping, of universal uncertainty and dissatisfaction. Due to the common need for emigration, a living bond tended to unify the Jewish masses of the different countries.

Worldwide horizons spread before them, and the national idea began to manifest itself. The fruit of proletarian thought from different countries was carried over imperceptible, spiritual paths from one end of the world to the other. Socialist ideas were brought from tyrannized Russia to free England and America. Filled with a new content there, they returned through London, Koenigsberg, and Vienna to the ghettos of Galicia and Russia. A worker who had just gone on strike in New York could exchange his new impressions with a friend who would soon be striking in Bialystok or Vilna. His head full of vague longings, the Jewish worker set out on the long road. At all points en route, through Austria, Germany, France, England, and Holland, he came in contact with comrades from all countries, weaving a spiritual thread between East and West. The seed of revolutionary thought was thus carried to the four corners of the world. The flow of migration spread the Jewish Labor movement everywhere.

For that reason the years 1886 (the first mass strike in New York), 1887 (Bialystok), and 1889 (London) bring back glorious memories not only for each country with Jewish communities, but also for the whole world—wherever there are exploited people and wherever Jewish workers struggle for a better life. If the self-appointed leaders of the Jewish Labor movement had even the slightest conception of their own history, they would have now celebrated, throughout the world, the twenty-fifth anniversary of the Jewish class-conscious proletarian struggle in Russia.

In order that the reader may see why the Bialystok strike had the importance I ascribe to it, I shall outline the course of its event. During the Russo-Turkish war of 1877, wages among the weavers rose greatly because of favorable market conditions and the pressure of a successful strike. This was a golden era; they earned 10–15 rubles a week. Taking into consideration the low cost of living, this was a tremendous gain. (Living quarters cost 1½ rubles a month; a pound of meat was 4 or 5 kopeks.) Naturally there had to come an end to this golden era. A host of new workers were attracted to the trade; and on top of this, the manufacturers' booming business slumped after the war. Competition between the workers and the inexperience of the new hands forced wages down to such a low level, that in 1885–86 the weavers had to adapt themselves to a starvation wage of from 1 to 3 rubles a week, working from 14 to 16 hours a day. At the same time rent and food prices rose. The workers had no choice but to go out on strike. The strike was only against the master weavers, because their workers received the lowest wages, much less than even the factory weavers. All the two thousand Jewish workers who were employed by master weavers walked out.

The strike was organized on the following lines. The strike committee found it impossible to stop the whole trade at once, as it would have been difficult to raise the necessary funds for the support of such a large army of strikers. They therefore carried out a piece-meal stoppage. At any one time workers from only certain workshops were to stop, and the others who remained at work were to support the strikers. The discipline was exemplary; the complicated plan worked excellently. Workshops were stopped one after the other. As one group won and returned to work, others struck. A link in this strike chain lasted only a few days at the most, and the workers won everywhere. The walk-out began in July 1887. The governor of Grodno made a trip to Bialystok. He assembled all the workers and attempted to talk them into stopping the strike, but to no avail. The strike was won in September.

The socialist intelligentsia had no relationship whatsoever to the strike. Besides, it was not carrying on any socialist agitation in Bialystok at the time. In Vilna likewise there was still not the necessary connection between the socialist propaganda of the intellectuals on the one hand and the economic struggle of the working masses on the other. Socialist propaganda in Vilna had been carried on since 1885, but the correct approach to the workers had not been found. It was only during 1893 and 1894 that the mutual search for each other by both parts of the socialist movement—the intellectuals and the workers—ended. During these early years of groping both sides made considerable progress. There is record of only one strike of Jewish workers in Bialystok in 1887, four strikes in 1888, three in 1892, seven in 1893, and in 1894—nine strikes. (There were only several small strikes in Vilna and also a strike of brush makers in Vilkovisk.) Socialist agitation was already bearing some fruit; witness the celebration of May first as early as 1892 by some Jewish workers in Vilna.

During 1893 and 1894 almost all the socialists perceived the necessity of leading the economic struggle of the worker so as to educate him through his daily needs. In this way the problem of bringing socialism to the working masses was finally solved. This rapprochement on the basis of the economic struggle brought new strength to the Jewish Labor movement, enlarging and enriching it. For the first six or seven years

TABLE 4.1
Jewish Strikes, 1895–1904

Year	Number of Strikes (Jewish)	Approximate Number of Striking Jewish Workers
1895	83	4,700
1896	92	3,300
1897	150	23,800
1898	179	11,000
1899	223	18,600
1900	277	16,000
1901	453	22,000
1902	455	28,000
1903	340	41,000
1904	166	8,000
Total	2,418	176,400

the movement had almost exclusively an economic and cultural character. Only between 1900 and 1902 did the Jewish worker step into the political struggle.

The extent of the economic struggle in Lithuania and Poland is depicted in Table 4.1, which shows how many Jewish workers struck between 1895 and 1904. If we calculate the average size of the strikes for each year, we will see that the largest occurred in 1897—160 men per strike. The Bund was organized toward the end of that year of militant struggle. Going further, we discover that the smallest strikes (averages of 58, 49, and 62 men per strike) occurred between 1900 and 1902. In these years the Jewish Labor movement began to split; Poale Zionists appeared and were expelled by the Bund from its organizations. This shows that the history of the Jewish labor parties has an interesting relationship to the development of the Jewish struggle on the economic front.

I close with the following observation: This year we have a fourfold celebration. It is thirty-five years since the Jewish workers spontaneously took their first, not as yet conscious, step; twenty-five years since their first planned movement; fifteen years since the founding of the first Jewish labor party—the Bund; and five years since the founding of the World Confederation of the Jewish Socialist Labor Party, Poale Zion. Four historic years in the formation of Jewish proletarian revolutionary activity—1877, 1887, 1897, 1907! At each step the movement is ten years older, ten years riper in its consciousness. In each decade it takes a step forward to a new, broader perspective. From a chaotic state to the first spark of consciousness, and from a strong organization to worldwide unity—that is the development of the Jewish proletariat.

5
Anti-Zionist Front
(1911)

The social barometer of present *Galut* life forecasts stormy days. The soaring of commodity prices, the exorbitant military budgets, the feverish and unsuccessful efforts of diplomacy to check the growing war spirit, the constant rise of tax levies and interest rates, and the vacillating stock exchange—all these indicate that we are approaching the end of the industrial prosperity that prevailed during the last few years. No capitalist maneuvers can check the impending crisis. A new act in the drama of history is about to be staged. It seems as if the greatest upheaval confronts those regions densely populated by Jews, i.e. Eastern Europe and North America.

No sober person regards the coming events as the final conflicts or believes that this new chapter of history will usher in the millenium. The final victory of *Ahura-Mazda* over *Angra Mainyu* is still a long way off. The will to freedom of the various peoples is not yet sufficiently powerful for them to gain mastery over their oppressors. On the contrary, the impending period of enthusiasm and messianic hope will end in disillusionment and despair. That will be a welcome yet tragic phase in the development and decay of the capitalist order. Like one of those stormy waves which precedes the final overpowering ninth wave, this period will leave deep scars on the old world. Herein lies the historical value of the impending events.

The tension which embraces the social strata of all nations leads to the alliance of groups having common interests. The alliances proceed along the horizontal and vertical class lines. What regroupings can we expect within Jewish life? What changes in the social psychology of Jews will these processes call forth? To the thinking person these questions are very pertinent.

I

In periods of turbulent social change, the Jewish people, being landless and the weakest among the conflicting elements, is hardest hit. It brings the greatest sacrifices to the altar of progress. Therefore, the alignment of forces within Jewry assumes a distinct and peculiar form. Among other nations, the alliances usually proceed along class lines. The ruling classes unite and build one reactionary bloc whereas the suppressed groups form a revolutionary one. These blocs are not always internally harmonious, but they exhibit a tendency toward class unity. Even today this trend is manifest in many countries.

Among the Jewish people, however, the grouping does not occur on a class basis but on the basis of varying national aspirations. Within it the chief struggle is not between the proletariat and the bourgeoisie, or between the urban and agrarian populations, but between Zionists and *Galut* champions of all classes. The concentration of anti-Zionist forces usually precedes Zionist consolidation. This does not imply that there is no class struggle within the Jewish people. On the contrary, the class struggle within it is more intense and involves the masses to a greater extent than within other nations. But the class struggle in Jewish life has meager social content. Its historical horizons are limited. The class struggle of the Jews is primarily on the economic front.

We lack the political class struggle. for the Jewish people is now divorced from state functions and political rule as a unit. Under the prevailing conditions in *Galut* it is impossible to engage in this struggle. Instead, each class, guided by its own interests, participates in the political struggle of the people among whom its members reside. Although in its struggle against the general bourgeoisie the Jewish proletariat cannot avoid a clash with the Jewish bourgeoisie, that struggle is not for dominance within Jewish life, for there is no one to divest of or invest with power. In Jewish life, only the *economic* class antagonism finds full play; the political conflicts go off on a tangent.

I admit that with the achievement of national autonomy in *Galut* we shall gain a base for a political class struggle within Jewish life. But even this base will be narrow and limited in its social aspects. Our autonomous *Galut* life will never be a substitute for a Jewish national home. No wonder then that among Jews there is no conflict between class ideologies. The classes of our people possess different psychologies and opposing ideals, and their class psychologies are derived not from Jewish life but from the surrounding environment. These ideals (contrary to the views of our nationalists) are not abstractions, nor are they a product of rationalization; they are living and creative, for they have their origin in our everyday life. However, it is not from Jewish life that we derive our socialism, radicalism, liberalism, and clericalism. Our differing social ideologies are mere reflections of the life of our neighbors.

Within the Jewish people class struggle does not exist in its usual forms; we have among us a struggle between national factions. Once this struggle took place between the champions of Haskalah and Orthodoxy, then between Zionism and assimilation, and now between Zionism and "Galutism." It is unnecessary to point out that assimilation· has lost its ideological grounds today. Only tattered remnants remain of its former ideological garb and these are clumsily patched on to other ancient but seemingly progressive ideologies. Fifteen or twenty years ago the enemies of Zion (irrespective of class) negated the principle of Jewish nationality. Today, however, Zionism faces an enemy under whose banner various ideologies are united, the majority of which contain national aspirations. The hodge-podge of Yiddish culturists, the autonomists, the Social Democrats, and the various shades of bourgeois radicals, the staunch nationalist Sejmists, as well as the hazy Territorialists, who suffer from an anachronistic hatred for Palestine—all join hands to form the anti-Zionist front. Contemporary events have produced a mass of facts which point to the unquestionable consolidation of these forces. I believe that the coming era of social unrest will tend to strengthen this anti-Zionist front.

II

When Zionism appeared as a modern, positive force (Hibat Zion and Herzlism), two ideologies were current in Jewish life. One was the Orthodox ideology which accepted messianism literally and pinned its hopes for national salvation on the miraculous; the other was the Haskalah ideology which preached the adaptation of the Jew to universal culture. We have long since learned to distinguish between assimilation as an established fact and assimilation as an ideological rationalization. Assimilation as a fact, or as a genuine process, affects all Jewish groups. Assimilation *ad perfectio* as an ideology, however, is a comfortable and profitable "philosophy" for those apostates who have no sincere interest in the Jewish nation. Paradoxical as it may seem, assimilationists often display a profound interest in the Jewish people; in most cases, however, their inquiries seek but a justification for their rationalization. I am not speaking of individuals, for it is possible for an assimilated Jew to be a bitter enemy of assimilationist ideology, and for a Jew who has preserved all the customs and characteristics of his people, to be the most fervid devotee of assimilationist ideology. Assimilation is considered here purely from the viewpoint of a possible solution to the Jewish problem.

Prior to Zionism, assimilation, as advanced by the Haskalah champions in their fierce struggle with orthodoxy, was the only ideology of the upper classes of the Jews who came in constant contact with the analogous groups of other nations. This was in direct conformity with the time-honored tactics of the Jewish *shtadlan*. The first assimilationists really believed themselves to be the representatives of the Jewish people, its champions before the rulers and aristocracy of our neighboring nations. The Jewish masses kept aloof from this ideology and would have none of its politics. The Haskalah movement rendered valuable service to the Jewish people. It prepared the ground for the later modern movements in Jewish life. But Zionism, having awakened the dormant hopes of the Jewish masses, made surprising and violent inroads into the idyllic Haskalah philosophy. Simultaneously, the rise of a Jewish migration movement and the later development of organized Jewish labor began to undermine the already weakened foundations of assimilation. Assimilation, which until now had monopolized "modernism," "Europeanism," and "progress," suddenly clashed with mighty cultural forces within Jewish life. The "celestial light of the Haskalah" began to fade with the dawn of Zionism, the Labor movement, and the era of migration.

Zionism translated into terms of everyday creativity that which the people had until recently conceived of as a transcendent heavenly promise. Zionism illuminated the past and future of the Jewish people. The Labor movement drew the Jewish masses close to the cause of human emancipation, binding their hopes and struggles with those of humanity. The dynamic forces of Jewish immigration wrought their effect upon the minds of the most lethargic. How impotent was the artificial culture of the Haskalah intelligentsia compared to the dynamic and vital culture of the masses! At the beginning of the Russian Revolution the assimilationist ideology collapsed and its essence—the ties with the *Galut*—was inherited by other movements. The former indifference to the Jewish people gave way to the unique *Galut* nationalism, which, as early as 1905, gained a stronghold on Russian and Galician Jewry. *Galut* nationalism also crossed the Atlantic to America.

It is important that we differentiate between the three types of *Galut* nationalism. The first type was the inconsistent assimilationism, which, though employing the term *nation,* actually did not aspire to the full content of nationalism. Such was the "autonomism" advanced by the Bundist intelligentsia in the first stages of its development (1897-1908), and such is the current lip-service nationalism of the Jewish intelligentsia. The second type was the inconsistent nationalism that fell just short of Zionism. This was the *Galut* nationalism of the past two or three years which paraded under the slogans "Yiddish culture and autonomy." (Dubnov's "spiritual nationalism" with its profound attempt to establish a base for the national idealization of the *Galut* was likewise an inconsistent Zionism.) The third type was an abstract territorialism that attempted to solve the Jewish problem solely by immigration. Despite the great antipathy of the Territorialists toward the *Galut,* their very soul is bound to it. Only boycotts, pogroms, and persecutions torment them in the *Galut.* Their analysis of the Jewish problems fails to take into account the national, historic, and even economic factors; it merely considers the geographic ones. One who would solve the Jewish problem with a "tract of land"—somewhere near the Antipodes—has not yet broken with the *Galut.*

The identification of the Jewish masses with the cause of universal progress brought about Zionism and "Galutism," the latter adorned with the gay mantle of nationalism. The united front of the "Galutists" in the revolutionary period was in reality the first concentrated effort to form an anti-Zionist front. But the inherent chaos of the capitalist system on the one hand, and the Jewish dispersion on the other, hindered the development of an anti-Zionist front. This alignment is not an absolute fusion; it never was and never can be such—though its general tendencies lead in that direction.

I shall first consider the anti-Zionist alliance in the political field. Both before and during the Russian Revolution, proletarian and bourgeois *Galut* champions formed an alliance. The Bund conceived its greatest mission to be the attack on Zionism by any and every method, not excluding libel. The assimilated Jewish bourgeoisie rendered moral and material support to their proletarian allies and recognized the Bund as the "sole representative" of the Jewish Labor movement. During the elections to the second Duma an unsuccessful attempt was made to form a bloc of these same elements, disregarding all class differences. These mutual sympathies are felt even now. The Groupists, "empowered" by the Kovna Conference, pretend to be the sole representatives. Hence, the "sole representatives" of all classes united. . . .

In Galicia, where political life is aflame almost exclusively at elections, we saw (in 1907 and particularly in 1911) the solidarity of assimilationists and Hasidim with the Social Democrats. On these two occasions the Galician Bundists enthusiastically joined this smart set in a coalition directed against the Zionists. As a result of preelection agreements, an even firmer anti-Zionist front was forged in the shape of an alliance between the Galician Bundists and the Jewish section of the Polish Socialist Party, the strongest opponents of the Jewish national renaissance movement.

The anti-Zionist front is far less noticeable in Jewish communal activities. And yet, it is an undeniable fact that such institutions as the ICA, the Haskalah societies, and the loan and the immigrant information bureaus are centers around which the most diverse elements make common cause. In this field we find a silent, bitter struggle for supremacy between the anti-Zionist elements, who until now reigned supreme, and the Zionists, who are beginning to make their influence felt. The leaders of these institutions, the philanthropists and key men, as well as the officials and employees, are imbued with the *Galut* ideology. They think of community problems as if the fate of the Jewish masses were eternally and inextricably bound up with the *Galut* and moreover, as if the organization of *Galut* Jewry were the sole concern of our best minds. In this field, too, we note a silent "class collaboration."

The forms of the anti-Zionist alliance on the literary front are most amusing. A gentlemen's agreement seems to unite the non-Zionist bourgeoisie with the proletarian elements, and not long ago they conducted with rare avidity a joint struggle against Zionism in all its implications. It is significant to note that to this very day these class enemies have avoided attacking each other. The ideological attack of the Bund on the Jewish bourgeoisie was aimed only at Zionism, as if Zionism were synonymous with the bourgeoisie. But the most laughable feature of all was the lusty applause with which the bourgeois assimilationists greeted this identification. Barbs aimed against the bourgeoisie in general, including the assimilationists, crept into the Bund's systematic attack on Zionism. But the bourgeois colleagues of Jewish labor's "sole representative" indulgently accepted the Bund's demonstrations, well realizing that these attacks were merely a matter of form and only a sop to world socialism. At no time did the assimilationists and *Galut* nationalists of the bourgeois camp attack their proletarian allies. They were content to repulse mildly the attacks of the Bund. Certain publications follow these tactics even now.

It is noteworthy that the anti-Zionist alliance meets its most formidable obstacle to inner harmony on the literary front. Politics is a matter of action, literature of talk. In practice, the Bund may engage in activities which have no bearing on the class struggle; however, our "sole representative" does talk a good class struggle. The *Galut* nationalists are willing to place their press—with but few restrictions—at the disposal of their orthodox (Marxist) brethren; and the latter, despite their collaboration in other fields, dare not accept the offer. Freedom of the press would indeed have surpassed itself with such a motley crew gathered under one literary roof.

The Jewish people is small in numbers and exerts but little sociopolitical influence. Therefore, its various social processes appear trivial. The anti-Zionist manifestations, which I have pointed out, do not seem sufficiently important to command our attention. But one must remember that history wends its way through a road littered with the seemingly insignificant. Neither can we ignore the influence that the anti-Zionist intelligentsia exerts on our people and our future. The intelligentsia has appropriated to itself the Jewish labor and immigration movements. It rules the *kehilot* and the Jewish communal institutions. It obtrudes itself at the first sign of the organization of mutual aid, and is successful because it is united and because its proletarian allies, who make holy vows of class struggle, practice class collaboration. The anti-Zionist intelligentsia does not fear, and even welcomes, the various class elements. It tolerates freedom of speech in order to obtain unity of action. These tactics boldly reveal that both allies are busy bolstering their positions in Jewish life. The fact that our *Galut* life is not a resplendent one by no means minimizes the historical significance of these phenomena.

III

How can we explain the deep hatred between Zionism and the so-called "Galutism" in Russia and Galicia? It is very naive to assume that the ceaseless attacks on Zionism by the Bundists, or the brutal attack by the united front of the bourgeoisie, Hasidim, and Social Democrats in Galicia, drew their sustenance from theoretical differences. The bloodshed in the streets of Drohobich is the strongest refutation of such an innocent interpretation of the struggle in Jewish life. It is clear that that was a struggle for supremacy, a bitter conflict for material interests. It is equally clear that this was not merely a struggle of class interests. The struggle for and against Zionism may be compared to the struggle between the free-thinkers and clericals of Europe; the iconoclasm of the radical bourgeoisie and of the conscious proletariat are no more identical than are the interests of the anti-Zionist allies.

There is no people in the world whose members are so efficient, alert, stubborn, and adaptable in their struggle for personal existence as the Jewish people. Likewise, there is no nation so weak and spineless, infirm, and supine in its struggle for national development as the Jewish nation. One of the contradictions in the Jewish *Galut* life is the extraordinary strength of the individual and the unparalleled weakness of the group. Our people is not capable of harnessing the individual energy of its talented members for collective creation. Assimilation in its various nuances finds support among those individuals who are unconsciously dominated by careerism, and who anxiously seek to assure their own future even at the price of breaking their bond with their unfortunate and landless people. On the other hand, it is clear that the Jewish people as a whole, which is being deserted by irresponsible individuals seeking only personal success, needs strength and unity in order to become independent. Zionism in all its shades is postulated upon the collective fate of the Jews. *The paths to individual success and national welfare lie in different directions. This situation gives rise to the conflicting, antithetical, material interests within Jewish life.*

Assimilation was unaffected by the antagonism between the individual and the group interests. But when Zionism called upon the individual to sacrifice personal interests for the sake of the national renaissance, the assimilationists instinctively felt the danger of Zionist agitation. To defend the rights of individual careerism, assimilation armed itself with a well-equipped arsenal of bogeys—depicting Zionism as "reaction," "chauvinism," "narrow-mindedness," etc. Indeed, Zionism was based on and drew its nourishment from the conflicting interests of the individual and the group; *Galut* nationalism unconsciously attempted to reconcile the interests of the individual and the group.

The individual on whom benign fortune smiles warmly does not desire to leave his well-established *Galut* domicile. *Galut* is his home and the non-Jewish environment—his fatherland. But the Jewish people, as a historic organism, as a material and spiritual tradition, as a mode of living and as a cultural, psychological type has its effect upon every individual. True, the Jewish people does not have a very strong material tradition. We have few petrified relics of the collective efforts of earlier generations. We do not possess the power of the soil, the magnetic force of the black earth. Instead, we have many cultural traditions—our thought processes, temperament, and intellectual inheritance. These traditions rarely allow an individual to escape from their tenacious grasp. With all his careeristic strivings the Jew remains within the fold. This is the source of the inner contradiction of assimilation. On the other hand, the Jewish community must fortify itself and become rooted in the surrounding environment, tying itself organically to the soil of the neighboring peoples. A whole people cannot live as if in a hostelry. A neglect of this truth caused the inner contradiction of General Zionism.

Formerly, assimilation offered a more subtle way of solving the above contradiction. As soon as the theoreticians of assimilation were convinced of the impossibility of obtaining security for themselves by purely individual endeavor, they instinctively began to seek those paths the masses were following in their inevitable attempts to become rooted in the *Galut.* The assimilationists who fell heir to the influence of the old custodians of the Jewish people, of the plutocracy and communal leaders, found open before them (in this period of transition) all doors to the Jewish masses, to their institutions and organizations. The older generation ruled the *kehilot,* the Jewish charities, and educational institutions. Their descendants gained control of the modern societies, mutual aid organizations, and workers' associations. These new rulers have demonstrated their ability to exploit the hereditary habits of the Jews in order to strengthen their own positions. As the "sole representatives" of Jewry, or of their own class, they received the recognition of the corresponding groups of the neighboring peoples.

Without any original desire to serve the Jewish people, these leaders returned to the fold thanks to the failure of their personal, careerist assimilationism. These talented and active intellectuals were to a certain extent valuable. They organized charity, cheap credit, education, statistical surveys and emigration bureaus, and led strikes and political labor demonstrations. They monopolized Jewish communal affairs almost completely, in keeping with the historical principle of "priority rights." All of these activities had one aim—*to obtain the recognition of the neighboring peoples, and to achieve personal integration in the Galut through the medium of the Jewish people.* Thus, our "Galutistic" intelligentsia, which in spirit remained indifferent to the fate of the people whom it served, brought no sacrifices for the sake of the group. Personal ambitions were thus happily harmonized with service to the community.

The services which this intelligentsia rendered the Jewish people were not fundamental but superficial, for they were confined to the limits of the *Galut.* These services satisfied only the most temporary needs. Hence certain groups and individuals profited thereby, while the basic problems of the people remained unsolved. All this activity on the part of both the bourgeoisie and the proletarian intelligentsia was and remains opportunist, because it arose out of personal and transient rather than national and fundamental needs. Since these activities brought some amelioration, the "Galutistic" intelligentsia boasted to the outside world of the partial confidence in them displayed by the Jewish masses. They were responsible for the unpleasant atmosphere of loud self-advertising and partisan mud-slinging. That was the cause for their ideological shallowness, their avoidance of all organic unity with Jewish life, their fanatical falsification of all positive values of the Jewish people, their fear of facing the naked truth. Their chief concern was to be the "only representative" of the Jewish people to the mighty, enticing, outside world. Therefore they maintained that "within the Jewish people, under our care, peace must reign."

This extremely vapid and negative ideology enabled the intelligentsia to abandon their former assimilationism. The demise of assimilation did not drive them to tears, called forth no memories, since it did not shatter their personal careers. (The tears shed at the Sixth Zionist Congress over the question of Uganda vs. Zion for the territory of the Jewish people is a superb example of the collective feelings of Zionists.) With characteristic shrewdness, the intelligentsia turned from assimilationism and cosmopolitanism to a distorted *Galut* nationalism even before the 1905 Revolution. Zionism, on the other hand, underwent quite a different evolution. It was created by the section of the Jewish intelligentsia that was most sensitive to the terrible blows of social and state anti-Semitism. These Zionists were unable to link the happiness of their people with personal careerism. They renounced the *Galut,* seeing in it the chief source of Jewish suffering and sterility. But the Zionist intelligentsia swung to the other extreme and turned a deaf ear to the positive everyday realities of Jewish life.

Highly inspired by the ideals of our national rehabilitation in Palestine, Zionism's vision was far too lofty to see the needs of the passing moment. During the first twenty years, Zionists did not think of capturing and fortifying our positions in the *Galut* and did not deem it necessary to combine their personal interests with general interests. The Zionists viewed the economic struggle of the workers, the fight for civil rights, the development of the Yiddish language, and intradiasporic migrations as futile. Since the basic work was to be done there, in the historical home of the Jewish people, of what avail were temporary efforts in the *Galut?* Meanwhile the anti-Zionist elements gained control of the communal institutions. Their extreme intellectual poverty was offset by their great sense of practicality and organizational prowess; despite its courageous and penetrating thought, Zionism proved itself organizationally impotent.

Every social upheaval had its repercussions among the Jewish people—bringing new hopes, grave dangers, and alluring prospects. Zionism banked on the dangers and worries of the *Galut,* while "Galutism" fortified itself with bright prospects and hopes. At first Zionism tried to ignore these hopes and prospects and with a sickly joy grasped at everything that was tragic and horrible in Jewish life, to obscure the bright spots. Anti-Zionists, on the other hand, underestimated the gravity of the situation, and met the upheaval smilingly, with a soothing self-deception; it was not courage but vacuity that closed their eyes to the depths of the cavern. None in the Jewish community called out: "With head held high are we going to meet our fate!"

Zionism grumbled and waged an ideological battle, while its enemies built strongholds in Jewish life. In those dark yet important years, the most active and mature elements deserted Zionism one after another. A new form of *Galut* nationalism arose from the bosom of Zionism, more profound and genuine than the wordy nationalism of the semiassimilator. Even workers who theoretically remained loyal to Zionism deserted it, to unite their immediate tasks with the ideal of vitalizing the nation in its land of residence. Finally, after this fermentation had carried off the most radical and sober, the headquarters of the Zionist army began to fight for positions in the *Galut*. The Helsingfors Program in Russia and the formation of the Jewish National Party in Austria initiated a new trend in Zionist politics. Thus Zionism at last began to strengthen Jewish *Galut* positions.

Zionism became synthesized and integrated. It encompassed every need of Jewry in the *Galut* and in Palestine, in the present and in the future. But most Zionists were so psychologically unprepared for these tasks that only lately have they undertaken them in practice. Unfavorable circumstances undoubtedly contributed to this backwardness, particularly in Russia. Besides, the most important communal positions were already in the hands of the enemies of the *real* renaissance of the Jewish people. It was difficult for Zionists (if we exclude the Poale Zion who have long since understood the question and developed their tactics accordingly) to become accustomed to the thought that Zionism was facing a *struggle for power* within Jewish life.

Zionism must take over all that has been usurped by its enemies to the detriment of the people. The positions that the anti-Zionist intelligentsia had held were not taken away from Zionism; they simply never were under Zionist control. It is noteworthy that where Zionism strives to penetrate into Jewish life, it is received warmly by the masses. It was so in the elections to the first and second Duma, and in Galicia a year or two earlier. To date Zionism has failed to utilize the potent sympathies for it that lie dormant in the Jewish masses. On the threshold of a new era in universal and Jewish history, when the Jewish people faces new dangers and contemplates glorious visions, we pose these questions: How can we overcome the organizational weakness of Zionism? How can we develop the maximum of activity among the masses so sympathetic to the ideal of rebirth in our national home? The answer is: *A national front against the anti-Zionist front.*

6
Jewish Anti-Semitism*

It is a well-known and tragic fact that many a Jewish worker who has slaved away for years in a growing Jewish industry awakes one fine morning to find himself ruthlessly displaced by a non-Jew from the very factory to which he has given so much of his sweat and blood. This problem becomes particularly acute when the industrialist introduces modern methods of production, that is, when he substitutes machine labor for hand labor. It has become almost axiomatic that Jewish workers are not privileged to work at the machines but are doomed to manual labor.

As early as ten years ago our movement (the Poale Zion) called attention to this phenomenon in Jewish life. Another faction, which to this very day considers itself the "sole representaitve" of the Jewish Labor movement (the Bund), mocked the Poale Zion and heaped ridicule upon our ideas and actions. But contemporary life has demonstrated the correctness of our view and has forced our opponents to take cognizance of the real conditions. Now, when the elimination of Jewish workers has reached the stage of a veritable epidemic, when the tragic news of the dismissal of Jewish weavers, spatsmakers, and tobacco workers has become an open secret, they awake from their slumber and evince interest in this tragedy of Jewish labor. It is natural that those who only now have recognized this malignant condition are puzzled and bewildered. They neither analyze the symptoms of the disease nor propose a cure.

What accounts for this state of affairs? To date, numerous theories have been advanced. Our optimists, who seek to minimize Jewish tragedies, have attributed this plight to insignificant and incidental causes. The optimists maintain that this abnormality has its origin in the fact that Jews lack craftsmanship, that they are unaccustomed to physical labor. They conclude that were the Jewish workers to receive a good vocational training, there would remain no obstacle in the effort to penetrate the primary levels of production. Those publicists and "community leaders" who uphold this view have not the least understanding of the history of the Jewish working-class, nor of the laws of capitalist development. It is erroneous to assume that Jews are excluded from factories because of lack of proper training. Are the peasant boys and girls who make up the bulk of the workers in the large factories better trained or more skilled? On the contrary, modern industry demands unskilled labor power; only the foremen and the technical experts need have special training. Second, the Jewish workers did not become workers overnight. For hundreds of years a working class existed in the Jewish ghetto. Moreover, Jewish craftsmen had their own guilds with their trade rules just like the workers of other peoples. The Jewish shoemaker, tailor, bookbinder, or upholsterer received the same training as did his German contemporary. In the course of centuries, Jewish workers developed their own labor traditions and techniques. That these traditions and techniques were more adapted to ghetto life than to the outside world, that the Jewish weaver has for centuries specialized in making a *talis* and not a shawl, the Jewish capmaker a *yarmulke* and not an officer's cap—all this does not prove that the Jewish laborer has no tradition nor historical past. For if our "community leaders" should speak less and investigate more, they would discover that even in Western Europe today it is claimed that the modern manual worker does not adapt himself easily to factory work, and that no amount of vocational training in the most advanced country can fully prepare him for modern industry.

A second reason frequently given is that the Sabbath hinders the Jews from penetrating into the large industries. Our optimists who cling to the Sabbath theory fail to understand that, for the Jews, the Sabbath is not only a religious tradition but a deeply-rooted socioeconomic institution. The Sabbath should be an advantage rather than a disadvantage to the Jewish worker; for the Jewish employer is also accustomed to rest on Sabbath, and were he not to entertain any particular hatred for the Jewish worker, he would certainly employ him. The fact that the foreman and the expert are in most cases imported non-Jews, for whose sake the employer is "forced" to keep his factory open on the Sabbath, provides no valid excuse: the foreman is not the owner, and there are many Jewish workers who *would* work on Saturday. In many instances Jewish workers have agreed to work on Saturday but were refused employment.

A third reason commonly advanced is that the Jewish worker is culturally on a higher level than his non-Jewish competitor. The Jewish worker demands better pay and better working conditions, and most important, the Jewish worker is a frequent striker. The Jewish industrialist who fears the strike of the Jewish worker refuses to employ him. This assertion is true. The Jewish worker, his non-Jewish comrade, and the employer, are equally aware of it.

In the five-year period from 1900 to 1904, the numbers of striking workers per thousand were: 55 in Germany, 70 in Belgium, 75 in England, 150 in France, and 130 in Russia. Among Jewish workers in Russia—

240 of every 1,000 struck. Are we, then, to conclude that the big Jewish industrialist is justified in his fears? No. For the majority of the Jewish strikes occur in small shops and not in large factories. The following figures illustrate this clearly: in small workshops, 17.5 percent were lockouts; in small and middle-sized factories, 50 percent of the strikes were provoked by the employers; and in large factories (employing 200 workers or more), 67.5 percent of all strikes were forced by the employers, and only 25 percent were called by the workers.

The Jewish striker meets with a smaller measure of success in the large factories than in the small workshops. The manual workers had a complete victory in 72.7 percent of all strikes and suffered a complete loss in 7.9 percent. The Jewish workers in the small factories (employing from 20 to 50 workers) scored a victory in 68.7 percent of the strikes and suffered a loss in 14.9 percent; in the middle-sized factories (employing from 51 to 200 workers) they scored a complete victory in 56.9 percent and suffered a complete loss in 20.7 percent; and *in the large factories (employing 200 workers and over), they scored a complete victory in 27.6 percent and suffered a complete loss in 41.7 percent of all the strikes.*[1]

These figures prove that the complaints of the big industrialists against the audacity of the Jewish worker are groundless, for in most cases the employers were the aggressors. If anyone has a right to complain it is the small owner, for in his workshop the Jewish worker is truly a frequent striker. In this respect the big Jewish capitalist might consider himself fortunate. Nevertheless, *the small owner continues to employ the Jew, even though the latter is a striker.* The small owner may make frequent use of the police; he may suffer financial losses; but he does not replace the Jewish worker with a non-Jew. Who, then, is responsible for the expulsion of the Jewish worker from Jewish industry? It is the big capitalist, the "lord manufacturer." In order to pacify the Jewish community, the big capitalist rationalizes his refusal to employ Jewish workers by claiming that the Jewish worker is a chronic striker.

If we wish to investigate the real causes of the displacement of Jewish workers, we must consider the problem in its two parts: *isolation* and *discrimination.* We must give due consideration to the fact that historically the Jewish worker has been torn away from nature (agriculture), from the natural resources (mines, quarries, and forests), and from those industries that produce the means of production and the transportation facilities (metallurgy, manufacture of machinery, steamships and railroads). The Jews have been removed for centuries from the basic branches of production upon which the economic structure depends. They are concentrated in the final levels of production—those branches that are far from the core of our economic structure (the production of consumer goods). This phenomenon cannot be attributed to anti-Jewish discrimination. Jews were not forced out of metallurgy into locksmithing. They were not transformed from railroad men to teamsters, from farmers to tailors, cobblers, and cigar makers. They were not forced out of forestry and thrust into the match industry. True, the Jews have not engaged in basic industries since their dispersion, but neither the Sabbath nor the economic struggle of the Jewish worker is responsible for this state of affairs. Its root lies in the unique history of *Galut* Jewry.

Our severance from nature and the basic industries is the chief characteristic of the Jewish economic life in *Galut*. Under the capitalist economy, however, we note the additional anomaly that even in those branches of production in which they have long been engaged, the Jews are restricted from entering the more developed forms of industry. This second phenomenon is not an historical one, and the two-thousand-year-old wandering of the Jew, which is responsible for the first anomaly, is not at all responsible for the second. These phenomena are often confused. We shall differentiate between them by calling the first *isolation* and the second *discrimination*.

We already know the cause of our isolation. What, however, is the cause of our discrimination? It may be attributed to the assimilationist tendency of the Jewish bourgeoisie: The Jewish manufacturer who is about to become a big capitalist wants to sever, as soon as possible, his relations with the Jewish community from which he emerged. He does it for two reasons—to conquer the Gentile market and be on the same footing with the Gentile manufacturer. His Jewishness is in this respect a disadvantage, since his competitors refuse to recognize him as an equal. He is thus eager to display his *goyish* (Gentile) patriotism. Second, to the extent that he is traditionally bound up with his people, he seeks to govern them. He utilizes his influence in the *kehilah* and in the charitable institutions as a means of crushing the Jewish masses and public opinion. The fewer ties he has with the Jewish community, the less he fears its control. He is anxious to employ Gentile workers and managers and, as much as possible, restrict his commercial intercourse to Gentiles, in order to identify himself with his Gentile competitor and rid himself of Jewish public control. To the Jews he offers charity and faith; yet in his business he prefers to associate with Gentiles or with Jewish assimilationists of his own kind.

Upon introducing steampower into his factory (the symbol of large-scale production), the Jewish employer substitutes the Gentile for the Jewish worker. Being an enemy of *Jewish* labor, he is particularly angry when the latter protests or strikes. Hence, he justifies his acts with the Sabbath excuse or the pretext of the inexperience or physical weakness of the Jewish worker. But these are not his real motives. The truth is that he wants to rid himself of the Jews and the Jewish environment. And when our "sole representative" (the Bund) and its bourgeois allies take the contentions of the Jewish capitalists seriously, it only proves how shortsighted they are and how superficially they interpret Jewish reality.

We have noted two diseases: isolation and discrimination. Two types of treatment are possible: one is in the form of a palliative, the other a radical and lasting cure. Marx often quoted William Petty: "The land is the mother, and labor is the father of wealth." As long as the Jewish people lives in the *Galut,* it will not have a "mother." The remedy will come only with an economic revolution, when the Jewish people will have its own land, its own territory. Palliatives are of little help in the *Galut. The only cure for isolation is Zionism.* Such is not the case with regard to discrimination. Our enemies want to rob us of positions which we have won with our sweat and blood, to expel us from those fields into which we have penetrated. This we must firmly oppose. Since we possessed the power to win our economic positions, we must be strong enough to retain them regardless of our present weakness. *We must strike at the anti-Semitism of the Jewish capitalists.*

Let us pause awhile and ask ourselves: What is our aim? Do we wish to render only temporary relief to the Jewish workers, or do we wish to make their continued displacement impossible? Do we want first aid for the unfortunate, or are we interested in finding a radical solution? At the present time the masses are so depressed that they long for even a modicum of relief. Therefore, the agitation for first aid, for weak and even demoralizing palliatives—and we certainly have an overabundance of palliatives—finds fertile soil among the masses. The bourgeois nationalists prescribe philanthropic remedies and the Bundist guardians deliver social sermons. The *Galut* nationalists reproach the Jewish industrialists for being "bad Jews," having no pity on the poor Jewish workers. They appeal to the national conscience of the capitalist. The Jewish "communal leader" often succeeds in arousing the capitalist's pity to the extent of bringing about reemployment of a few Jewish workers. The Bundists don a *kosher* proletarian mask and reproach the Gentile Polish workers for being "bad Marxists." They appeal to their sense of solidarity; they write humble letters to their Polish comrades, appealing to the latter's sense of class justice. The results are nil. The tactics, both of the *Galut* nationalists and of the Bundists, are as ridiculous as they are harmful.

An appeal to national pity and class philanthropy helps sometimes. Reproaches are temporarily effective. When the manufacturer succumbs to the newspaper sermons and the spark of Jewishness flares up within him, he sometimes consents to take back a few Jewish workers. In such instances, how does the worker feel toward his boss, who has become a man of "good" deeds? The boss is a "great and pious Jew" and the worker will have to pay bitterly and dearly for his boss's justice. The worker is no longer a proud, dignified man, but an uninvited beggar. The boss's pity is a strong weapon with which to break the spirit and resistance of the Jewish worker. Socialist pity, likewise, may occasionally be of help. Through such pity the Jewish weavers in Bialystok persuaded their Gentile comrades to permit them to work. But do not for a moment imagine that all Jewish workers were accorded this right. No. The class compassion of the Polish workers led them to introduce a system of *numerus clausus* for the Jews. Previously we were blessed with a *numerus clausus* in schools, and now, class solidarity as conceived by the Bundists has blessed us with a *numerus clausus* in the factories. What a remarkable victory!

One who is overjoyed at our great victory in Bialystok, one who can humble himself by appealing to the class consciousness of his comrades (as did the shoemakers in Warsaw), is not fit to defend his honor and has lost all courage to struggle for his interests. Such demoralization has been introduced into the ranks of the working masses by our "sole representative," the Bund. *We must understand once and for all that one who has no national dignity can have no class dignity.*

Notes

*This essay was written not long before World War I and was never completed (ed.).

1. During the same period government statistics show that there were only 481 strikes in European Russia, affecting 1,030 factories. Belgium in the same period registered 487 strikes; and Switzerland, in the course of 40 years (1861–1900), had 1,001 strikes. In general, the Jewish striker was not less successful than the non-Jewish. Whereas only 7.5 percent of the strikes in Belgium were won completely, 9 percent in Austria, 3 percent in France, 30 percent in England, 49.5 percent in Germany, and 26 percent in European Russia—the Jewish workers in the Pale won 63.5 percent of their strikes completely, achieved partial victory in 22.5 percent, and suffered complete defeat in only 14 percent of the strikes. The intensity of the economic conflict between the Jewish employer and the Jewish worker, too, is greater than among the non-Jews, as is evident from a comparison of the "resistance coefficients" of the strikers. Thus, for example, in the aforementioned five-year period the number of strike days per striking worker in European Russia was 4.7, compared with 9.5 days for the Jews in the Pale. The power of resistance of the Jews was twice as great as that of the non-Jews.

7
Difficulties of Poale Zionism
(1913)

I

"How difficult it is to be a Poale Zionist!" exclaimed an old party comrade at a jubilee celebration of the Warsaw organization. "How much easier to be a Bundist, or a member of the Polish Socialist Party! In those organizations one is little perturbed by questions that provoke thought or study. How difficult and responsible, however, are the burdens of a Poale Zionist!" We can fully appreciate the complaints of our devoted comrade, who, though paying for his party convictions with a life-sentence in Siberia, still remains a devoted Poale Zionist. In spite of all difficulties we firmly adhere to our principles. Wherein lies the power of this mission, which, while so complicated and so difficult, is yet so dear to us all?

There is a law of nature known as the law of the economy of energy. Each creature strives to achieve the maximum results with the minimum of effort. This law operates in both the organic and inorganic worlds. The growth of plants, the expansion of roots, the movements of microscopic creatures, the instincts of the animal world, the conscious as well as the unconscious life of man—all are influenced by this law of nature. This law is felt in human culture, industry, science, morals, and art, in the ever-changing conflicts of social thought and in national and class struggles. In brief, *humanity strives to achieve in all its endeavors the greatest results with the least exertion.*

This tendency to economize energy is in itself not a simple but rather a complicated affair. There is no absolute measure of economy, for its degree always depends on given circumstances. Thus, theoretically speaking, the shortest distance between any two points is a straight line. Yet this does not take into account the practical complications of a given situation. Imagine for a moment that between two given distances there is a mountain or a lake; it soon becomes evident that the straight line is by no means the shortest or the easiest way. To avoid unnecessary difficulties one would have to go in a round-about route or construct a tunnel or a bridge. In other words, the simplest is not always the true or correct path. Human life, both individual and group, is so complex that a simple solution is often impossible.

Nevertheless, under this law man strives first of all to achieve his goal in as simple a manner as possible. He first attempts to follow the short, the straight way. But life's realities often force him to adapt himself to complicated conditions by employing new and rational means. Such is the case in the history of the individual and the group. In the past men sought to conquer distance by the simplest means of transportation—horse, camel, or sail. Now it is very difficult during one's short lifetime to master the techniques of transportation, which have become complicated as a result of the introduction of railways, steamships, automobiles, and aeroplanes. *The development of human culture finds expression not through simplification but through differentiation and refinement of the mental and physical faculties.* Simplicity of thought and social tactics are often a sign of primitiveness.

There is another aspect to this problem. The law of the economy of energy refers not only to the exertion of the least amount of energy, but also to the achievement of the maximum results. In its most elementary and abstract expression, the simplest form of action is inaction, the simplest form of thinking is nonthinking. Thus we would conserve all energy. But man's ideal is the attainment of the maximum amount of productivity with the minimum of effort. Marx clearly points out both aspects of this law in his thesis that the history of humanity depends on the development of the forces of production.

It is indeed difficult to be a Poale Zionist, for Poale Zion's thoughts and practices are more complicated and possess finer and more varied nuances than the thoughts and practices of other Jewish parties. Nevertheless, within Jewish life today, with its intricate *Galut* problems and its striving for renaissance, the Poale Zion program offers the maximum results with the minimum of effort. The Bund demands less spiritual and physical effort on the part of the Jewish proletariat, but it is also satisfied with more limited objectives.

We desire to revitalize Jewish life, Jewish labor, and Jewish energy in all fields of endeavor. We cannot be content merely with the results obtainable in the *Galut.* But even in our *Galut* work, our program for the Jewish proletariat opens a much greater vista than the programs of the other Jewish parties. According to the Socialist-Territorialist, the Jewish problem can be solved solely by a program based on emigration. To the Bundist, the *Galut* problem is somewhat broader, but its program and activities are limited only to the most direct forms of struggle with the bourgeoisie and the state. Hence, while the Socialist-Territorialists perform constructive work only in the fields of emigration and the Bund among Jewish workers on the strike, the Poale Zion endeavors to do constructive work along all economic, cultural, and political fronts.

It becomes obvious that the complexity of our program does not in any way hinder its practicality. Though the Socialist-Territorialists speak of the need for regulation of Jewish emigration, they let the practical work be conducted by the bourgeois territorialists and assimilationists. The Poale Zionists do not limit themselves to propaganda and have already, in the course of their short existence, achieved something through their own institutions (e.g. the Palestine Workers' Fund and the Information Bureau in Jaffa). Though the Bundists constantly propagandize on behalf of the Yiddish language, literature, and schools, they have done very little for Jewish culture, science, and education in comparison with the youthful Poale Zion Party.

This clearly demonstrates that of all programs of the Jewish parties— both bourgeois and proletarian—the Poale Zion program presents the most inclusive solution to the Jewish problem. Therefore, it is indeed difficult to be a Poale Zionist—for Poale Zion theory and practice demand of the Jewish worker the greatest exertion of his spiritual and physical faculties. And yet this exertion is a bare minimum in comparison with the all-embracing program of Jewish life toward whose attainment the Poale Zionists strive.

II

Primitive minds presuppose that truth is simple. Complicated and well-founded thoughts puzzle the uneducated man. The question of the so-called consistency of the programs and tactics of social movements is complicated. The undeveloped and insufficiently conscious Jewish worker assumes that *consistency* means one of two things: here or there, *Galut* or Zion. He cannot comprehend the integration of the two.

In socialist thought, too, the question of consistency arises. Thus, for example, the anarchists, who desire to simplify the tactics of the Labor movement, accuse scientific socialism of inconsistency. The anarchists would indeed be right in their criticism were socialism to preach *social revolution* on one day and *social reformism* the next. Actually socialism integrates in its program both the struggle for social revolution and for immediate reform. Thus, scientific socialism is more complex than anarchism, and though the common mind may not fully comprehend it, it is, nevertheless, consistent. Socialism then has to bridge the gap between reform and revolution, just as Poale Zionism has to integrate the *Galut* and Zion. The whole is greater than any of its parts. Since socialism is a basic element of Poale Zionism the difficulties of socialism are also the difficulties of Poale Zionism.

Scientific socialism demands that our ideals be based on the objective forces operating in society. It is not sufficient that individuals or even the masses feel a need for something; it is essential that these needs and desires, expressed as vital elements of a party program, be in harmony with historic trends. The objective forces which form the basis for an ideal also create the "historic necessity" for this ideal. The prime difficulty of the Poale Zion program is that it demands of the Jewish worker who supports it to be thoroughly convinced that the social program of the *Galut* and the national program of Palestine are not only beautiful ideals but also objective possibilities.

We can now fully comprehend the demands that scientific socialism makes of each Poale Zionist. First, he must become acquainted with the conditions of our present-day social life and must study the essence of the historic necessity of socialism. Second, he must fully comprehend the nature and solution of the economic and cultural problems of the Jewish working class. Third, he must orient himself to the problem of nationalism in our own times and particularly in the Jewish national problem. One should not err in concluding that every Poale Zionist must necessarily be a great theoretician. Not every Poale Zionist need thoroughly master the socialist, the Poale Zion, or anti-Poale Zion literature; nor need he necessarily be an expert in all questions pertaining to the Socialist movement of each nation and the Poale Zion movement of each country.

Through active participation in the Socialist Party, the worker acquires what is commonly termed a socialist consciousness which is of greater value than his mastery of books. This is in reality the essence of socialist education. The very fact that the masses participate in socialist work in increasing numbers is sufficient proof of its historic necessity. The course of the historic necessity of socialism cannot be charted with mathematical accuracy. Human knowledge is as yet not sufficiently developed to be able to foresee historic developments with mathematical precision. It is not correct to assume that Marx, or for that matter any other thinker, has succeeded in proving beyond any doubts the historic necessity of socialism. Theories can illustrate and interpret—not prove historic necessity. But that which theory cannot do, life can. His daily experiences rather than books will convince the worker that the struggle between himself and the capitalist becomes ever fiercer.

In a similar manner, our education aims to develop a Poale Zion consciousness. That consciousness, even more than our literature, will solve the theoretical difficulties of our program. Poale Zion literature can illustrate and interpret our program; it cannot prove its merits. The fact, however, that our movement grows and develops is in itself sufficient proof of its historic necessity. The steady growth of national consciousness among the Jewish masses, the gradual rise of respect for the Jewish personality, the growth of the movement for Jewish national rights, the growing Jewish Labor movement in Palestine—all these are the objective facts, the *real* factors that find their theoretical expression in the Poale Zion program. Our program is more difficult than that of other parties which content themselves with a narrower perspective. Our task, however, is not impossible to achieve; for our theory is based on the needs of Jewish life, and on the living experiences of the organized Jewish proletariat. Like socialism, Poale Zionism will solve its *theoretical* difficulties only through its *practice*.

8
The Aims of Yiddish Philology
(1913)

Of all the sciences, philology plays the greatest role in the national revival of oppressed peoples. Philology is not a hollow theory for scholars and sedentary academics but a practical guide for the people. It does encompass certain theoretical and historical components such as the history of the language and culture with which it is concerned and the general principles of language development. Yet its purpose and its educational importance lie with the practical life of the people. The first objective of every awakening people is the mastery of its own language in order that it be used all the more productively in its national creativity. As long as a people remains illiterate in its own language there can be no national culture. National culture comprises not only the poetic works of literary masters but primarily and foremostly the skill to correctly speak and write the mother tongue.

At the beginning of a national and cultural renaissance—during the genesis of national culture—there is chaos. The folk language is divided into countless dialects. People of different localities speak differently and everybody writes as he pleases, each writer fashioning his own words according to his own understanding. Only philology can bring an end to this havoc. Philology ascertains the root of each word and traces its history and the development of its meaning. Science thus allows general and clear principles to replace personal whims and inventions. A general dictionary and a general grammar are established and the folk school, literature, and the press see to it that they become mandatory. As long as a nation lacks a national philology it remains far from modern national culture.

Unlike general linguistics, which is a general science, philology is a national science. It presupposes that its object-language entails cultural and historical value at least with respect to the past. Usually philology transcends this limitation and operates on the premise that its object-language has a national significance for the future. Whoever does not believe in the survival of the Yiddish language can be a Yiddish linguist, but not a Yiddish philologist. Linguistics is concerned only with the forms of the language while philology extends to its cultural productivity.

These are not all the tasks of Yiddish philology. At present, however, we are concerned with elementaries, and the elementaries of national culture entail the correctness of speech and writing. It is therefore no surprise that national philology is so highly prized amongst oppressed peoples. Each nation counts amongst its national heroes not only political freedom-fighters and great poets and thinkers, but also those philologists who laid the first stones in the foundation of a national linguistic science. Cultural revivals begin almost universally with the establishment of literary, philological, and ethnographic institutions. One need only take note of the esteem in which literary and philological societies are held by the Finns, Latvians, Estonians, Slovenes, Czechs, Slovaks, Flemings, Catalans, Ukrainians, and other awakening peoples. The few exceptions consist of the Jews and several other small and luckless nations. It is one of the signs of our national impoverishment that amongst us Jews there are still no institutions dedicated to national philology.

It cannot be said that Yiddish philology is poor or that there is no Yiddish philology at all. On the contrary, there is an entire body of books, brochures, articles, and notices on Yiddish language, literature, and folklore. But this corpus of research has almost no national significance. Our people know nothing of it, and it is useless to our intelligentsia. Why? First, it is almost entirely written in foreign languages. Second, it has neither order nor central theme, dealing as it does scatteredly and chaotically with isolated problems and details such as the question of the diminutive forms in Yiddish grammar or the history of this or that book. Third, nearly all the existing works on Yiddish are purely academic. They are remote from life and do not strive toward practical educational goals. The field of cultural education is handled for us by the daily press, which ponders over the question whether Yiddish is a folk language, a national language, an ugly jargon or a cultural medium worthy of our use. The majority of the authors who deal with Yiddish are assimilationists, alien to the Jewish nation. In their scientific writings they continually seek to demonstrate that Yiddish is a bona fide German dialect and that the Jews are the bearers of German culture in the Slavic lands.

We do not know for sure the age of the Yiddish language, but Yiddish is no exception; it is impossible to determine with assuredness when any language was born. In any event, Yiddish is probably no younger than 600 or 700 years. It is older than the period during which German Jews began to settle in Galicia under the Galician King Daniel and in Poland under Duke Boleslav (thirteenth-fourteenth centuries). Old Yiddish manuscripts which survived date back to the thirteenth century. Avé-

Lallemant, comparing Yiddish with the German thieves' language of the Middle Ages, concludes that Yiddish is 800 years old. Our language and our literature are far from being young. The study of Yiddish is itself 400 years old. Martin Luther, Johann Agricola and other early sixteenth-century theologians made occasional remarks regarding Yiddish. The well-known Hebrew scholar and founder of Aramaic science, Sebastian Muenster, afforded Yiddish a prominent position in his Hebrew dictionary of 1523. In 1609 the brilliant Christian linguist Johann Buxtorf the Elder published an explicit description of Yiddish. When we take into account that the philology of many nations (e.g. the Estonians, Latvians, Ukrainians, and the Serbs) is not older than 70 or 80 years, and that of other nations younger still, we have all the more reason to be ashamed that our national science has not yet acquired a respectable position.

The scientific investigation of our language suffers considerably from the deep-rooted prejudices of our intelligentsia against Yiddish. To this day there are many who consider the very idea of Yiddish philology to be funny. Just such ignorant claims as "Yiddish is a dirty jargon" or "Yiddish is a corrupted German dialect without a grammar and without any cultural importance" were voiced 80 or 100 years ago by the reactionary people-hating pseudointellectuals amongst the Greeks, Serbs, and to some extent even today amongst the Ukrainians, Catalans, and others. But life has undone the endeavors of the folk-hating zealots. Modern Greek, Serbian, and other folk languages are liberating themselves more and more from cultural enslavement and are progressing rapidly on the road toward national creativity. It is beneath the dignity of a scientifically trained philologist to engage in dispute with the anti-Yiddish arguments enumerated above. Whoever has the vaguest notion of linguistic science knows very well that any language spoken and understood by millions of people must have an internal order and a systematic structure. Otherwise, quite simply, nobody would understand it. What is called "grammar" may be written down or not, but the language nevertheless has its rules, its philological law. The cultural value of a language is wholly independent of whether its grammar has yet been written. Every living language of a living people is a living organism, a free individuality with its own laws and caprices. Simple and lucid as the structure of a language may be, it is at the same time inexhaustible. No scientifically trained person will boast that he knows the entirety of a language. Yiddish has a straightforward structure, and yet the task of Yiddish philology is infinitely broad and endlessly deep because Yiddish, too, is a unique living organism, unbound in its creative freedom.

The Yiddish philologist encounters great difficulty in consequence of Yiddish belonging to the category of mixed languages. A truly pure language does not exist. Hebrew has many Aramaic, Greek, and Persian elements, and Russian includes numerous Turkish and Finnish words. There are, however, languages whose mixed structure is immediately conspicuous such as English—a mixture of Celtic, Germanic, and Romance elements, Japanese—a mixture of native and Chinese elements, or Persian—a mixture of native and Arabic elements. An extreme example of a language mixture is provided by Turkish (Osmanli). Inherently an agglutinative language without inflections of the Ural-Altaic group, Turkish is combined with completely alien inflecting languages—the Indo-European Persian and the Semitic Arabic. Yet this union is harmonious throughout and highly organic and productive. There are many beautiful and powerful languages that are more mixed than Yiddish, yet nobody will call them "jargon."

Yiddish consists mostly of Germanic words and forms. In addition, it has many Semitic (Hebrew and Aramaic) words, an especially Semitic syntax and style, as well as Slavic (Polish and Ukrainian) elements. Finally, one finds in Yiddish a small but fascinating element—the handful of Old French, Italian and Portuguese words, such as *tsholnt* (a baked Jewish dish served on the Sabbath), *fatsheyle* (kerchief), and *bentshn* (to bless). It is evident from Old Yiddish writings that the Romance element was once far more extensive in it than it is today. There is almost no doubt that these words are remnants of the Romance languages our grandfathers spoke before turning to Yiddish.

Just as in other mixed languages, the several elements emerge in Yiddish as an autonomous organic compound. It is not a language mixture or a hodge podge but a language, albeit a mixed one. As soon as German, Hebrew, and Slavic elements enter the folk language, they cease to be German, Hebrew, and Slavic. They lose their erstwhile status and assume a new one; they become Yiddish: Their pronunciation is fitted to its phonetics, their declension—to its morphology, and their position in the sentence—to its syntax. Yiddish frequently fuses elements of diverse origins, as from Hebrew and German (e.g. *bagazlen* [to rob], *unterkhasmenen* [to sign]) or Hebrew and Slavic (e.g. *tsvuak* [hypocrite], *kolboynik* [jack of all trades; wicked fellow]).

The elements of multiple linguistic origin within Yiddish are by no means mutually contradictory. They perform complementary functions in the language and combine with each other as organically as the functions of a living organism. One of the goals of Yiddish philology is to determine the functions performed by the Hebrew, German, and Slavic elements in Yiddish. The usual view, that Hebrew words express more lofty and abstract concepts, and Germanic words everyday matters, is incorrect. We have *got* (God) and *gedank* (idea)—Germanic words for higher concepts, and *mekhutn* (in-law) and *mishpokhe* (family)—Hebraic words for everyday matters. Many erotic terms also originated in Hebrew. The difference might be formulated thus: The ideas and relations of life are generally derived from German. The phenomena that arose in the realm of intimate Jewish existence are for the most part derived from Hebrew, while the forms and feelings of daily life in the narrow family environment, as well as many uncouth personal characterizations, are Slavic in origin. A single concept may acquire divergent nuances depending on the genetic descent of the word used to express it. Let us take, as an example, three of the words for "God" in Yiddish. *Got* (God) is a universal concept and is expressed by a Germanic word. *Reboyne sheloylem* (master of the universe), of Hebraic descent, conveys only the relationship between God and the people of Israel. Finally, *gotenyu-tatenyu* (dear little God, dear little father), derived from Slavic, discloses an intimate, almost childish relationship with the almighty power. There are, of course, numerous important exceptions to the stated rule. In general, though, the Germanic words stem from the contact of Jews with the European world, the Hebrew and Aramaic words from Jewish communal life, the *kheyder* (traditional Jewish primary school) and the yeshiva, Slavic words from intimate contacts with peasants, housekeepers, and Gentiles employed to perform tasks on the Sabbath. In as much as the three elements—Germanic, Hebraic, and Slavic—provide different functions in the language, the mixed nature of Yiddish is no hindrance to its development. On the contrary, our language is thereby enriched with words, and its potential expressive power is enhanced.

As was said before, most words and forms in Yiddish are Germanic. Consequently, every high school student thinks that "Yiddish is corrupt German." Whoever makes this claim is unfortunately ignorant of what German is. Yiddish does not derive from the German that is studied in school for examinations. That German—the language of Schiller and Goethe—is not the stepfather of Yiddish but its stepbrother, and indeed its younger stepbrother. It is older than the German our "intellectual" deems acceptable and in fact three or four hundred years older. Both derive from Middle High German and both are "corrupt." Yiddish was "corrupted" by Hebrew and Slavic impact, modern German by Latin and French. Yiddish was "corrupted" in the marketplace and the yeshiva, German in the universities and the bureaucratic chancelleries. Modern Yiddish contains many Old Germanic words which have long been lost in literary German. Frequently a word or a grammatical form which our ignorant "intellectual" considers corrupt German is in fact an Old Germanic form preserved from extinction in Yiddish.

A sweeping task of our philology entails the enrichment of the Yiddish language. The problem is not that Yiddish is poor. On the contrary, this language must be very rich in expressive capability, because it is fused from three exceedingly rich language families. This wealth, increased by the liveliness of Jewish temperament, is continually manifest in Yiddish. The poverty from which it suffers results from social and psychological causes. Wandering about on the streets for generations, dragging along at fairs, it was not privileged to be bred in chancelleries and refined in universities. For this reason, Yiddish is poor in scientific ideas and lacks a sophisticated legal and political terminology. Most significantly, Yiddish was severed from nature as were its people, hence the dearth in names of minerals, plants, and animals.

The paramount tasks of Yiddish philology can alternatively be formulated as the nationalization and humanization of the language. Nationalizing Yiddish entails purifying the language thoroughly and enriching it extensively, to the point where it can express all aspects of Jewish creativity. Humanizing Yiddish entails turning it into a means for incorporating into the Jewish nation all the cultural values of modern panhuman development. Our great writers saw the need to enrich and to cultivate the common folk language without even having recourse to the methods of scientific philology. Mendele Moykher Sforim is the Columbus of the Yiddish language, and Yitskhok Leybush Peretz is its Napoleon. Mendele discovered Yiddish and Peretz conquered European worlds on its behalf. The unexpected blossoming of Yiddish poetry and literary criticism unearthed innumerable paths of expressive possibility, demonstrating to us that this language can become a rich and powerful cultural and educational means of our people.

Scientific philology must contribute with its methodology by introducing order into the chaotic process of creativity. Mendele nationalized Yiddish; his first literary grandchild, Sholem Aleichem, wondrously popularized it, and Peretz humanized it. The three great writers divided amongst them the historical task. Let science too have a part in the heritage. Mendele discovered the language, so let us explore it. Peretz brought to it new nations, so let us create an order among them. Philology must excavate the homeless layers of folk creativity by searching out the treasures of our national creativeness scattered across the libraries of Western Europe. Old Yiddish literature had its classical works such as the *Shmuel-bukh,* the *Mayse-bukh,* and the *Seyfer Mides,* which served as models for long generations and were even translated into other languages. The people possess masses of witticism, jokes, songs, stories, and riddles—a folklore that philology must research and cultivate. The methods of philology will enrich the language by enabling the nation to become acquainted with its literary past and to learn to benefit from its latent wealth. But this is a task that individuals cannot take upon themselves. Individuals can work on single branches, since it is they who have the initiative. But only a societal institution can organize the work of philology in its entire breadth. Only when we have united our people's strengths, when there is an authoritative national organization for philological purposes, will Yiddish philology be able to befittingly fulfill its aims.

Note

This essay is dedicated to the luminous memory of the noble Yiddish scholar, the prematurely deceased and unjustly forgotten, Dr. Philip Mansch of Lemberg (1838-1890).

9
Hebraismus Militans
(1913)

Hebraists are at war. Against whom is obvious. For more than 120 years they have battled against Yiddish-speaking Jewry. It will soon be 125 years since Mendelsohn's disciple, David Friedlander, came out with his impassioned proclamation against Yiddish, in 1788. No measures were spared against the despised *mame loshn* (mother tongue)! Thus Euchel, editor of *Hameasef* and one of the first Hebraists, thrashed the *mame loshn* in trashy satire; Tuvia Feder tried the same precisely 100 years ago, through mudslinging and pasquanade. His good friends and disciples in Germany, Bohemia, Poland, and Russia treacherously resorted to that old Jewish stratagem of informing the nobles.

The case against Yiddish is so old and well known that in the past 125 years the militant Hebraists have not presented one new agrument. Meanwhile Yiddish, together with its people, came a long way, changing its appearance, casting off the caftan for the work shirt, sprucing up with collar and gloves, and stepping out in tails and decolletage. In the last century Yiddish also changed its battle stations and tactics. Previously diffident and fearful, wanting only to be left to itself, harming no one, Yiddish begged to gasp its last breath in peace. Lately, however, the servant girl rose up against the mistress, declaring herself a national language and sovereign of the people's spirit. But the Hebraists are still up to their old tricks. Ahad Haam battles with pasquanades, more refined though they may be. But in this Tuvia Feder was certainly more skillful. Mr. Frug hurls satiric insults and others try to stifle the "Jargon" through ponderous sermons. Denunciations occur as well. Teachers at the Jaffa Hebrew gymnasium know their business as well as did their grandfathers in Prague and Breslau.

Gentlemen Hebraists! Best to change your ways. Your old methods, as you plainly see, just do not work. On the contrary, the "loathsome Jargon" became more "harmful," more "impudent," more "loathsome." Is not a new unheard of strategy due? Because while you resort to your old *hosannas*, Jargon will—"heaven forbid"—occupy newer, more dangerous positions. Yiddish will also—"heaven forbid"—seize its place in the modern folk school.

Quickly! Pay heed to Mr. Jabotinsky's warning: "If Jargon becomes the language of instruction in Jewish folk schools, this will be the end of Hebrew." Take no consolation in the fact that Yiddish, during all its 700 or 800 years of existence, was the language of the *heder*, of yeshiva *pilpul*—and nonetheless nothing ever happened to Hebrew. Nor can you rely on the internal historical value of Hebrew which, for the two thousand years since the Jews ceased instructing their children in the tongue of the prophets, kept it from dying. No, one dare not rely on Hebrew's history or vitality. You should do nothing but follow and act according to Mr. Jabotinsky's plan. Follow these plans and adopt resolutions; that is how you will save Hebrew. Think of new strategies—the ghosts of Wessely, Euchel, and Friedlander have waited anxiously for 125 years for this new tactic, the almighty resolution.

Hebraists wage war against whom? With verve and devotion they wage war against . . . Hebrew. Not Jargon, but *loshn kodesh* (the holy tongue) and modern Hebrew are the real targets of their arrows. In the process the Hebraists make an ugly laughingstock of themselves, turning the people's hearts from the very language before which the Hebraists bow. The masses do not grasp fine distinctions. Even those most conscious are only human and not strangers to anger and grief. When the Hebraists holler in the name of Hebrew it is natural for their audience to assume that they have the sanction of *loshn kodesh* to speak in its name. We must therefore protest that the Hebraists dig a grave for Hebrew with their own hands, through their deeds and calumnies. We are left with but one consolation: Hebrew has already withstood much distress as its zealots besmirch its integrity. Yet Hebrew remains refined and august and strikes even deeper roots in the new styles of Jewishness that emerge. Hebrew will also overcome this nuisance known as Hebraism.

What the Hebraists have given us that is positive is the idea of a language revivified. Hebrew has begun to live again in the mouths of a new generation, exhibiting further evidence of its vitality. Indeed, this is to the credit of the Hebraists—But which ones? And where has this success been achieved? Hebrew has been revived in Palestine, although not entirely. This has been accomplished, *not* by those Hebraists who fight *mame loshn* here and heap scorn on *loshn kodesh*, but by those who practice what they preach. Since the new *yishuv* in Eretz Israel began, conditions there became favorable to the revival of Hebrew. Till now, everything that is being done in Palestine bears the mark of a more or less artificially made and maintained experiment. It is also possible to experiment with Hebrew. I believe in this kind of experimentation, but should we experiment here in the *Galut*? This is just inappropriate for Zionists and those dead set against the *Galut*. After all, it is they who claim that no national accomplishment in the *Galut* is durable. If so, what is there to Mr. Jabotinsky's latest plans for Hebrew publishing houses, a new children literature in Hebrew, and folk schools with Hebrew as the language of instruction—in the *Galut*?

Since it is possible to obtain a few teachers for a progressive *heder* and some rubles for a publishing house, would not good sense dictate directing the work and money of the Hebraists to Palestine, where they could do some good and the effort would not be wasted? Or perhaps Mr. Jabotinsky imagined when he was in Palestine that all Jews there already spoke Hebrew, that no Jewish children attended missionary schools, and that there was nothing left to do? But the *Galut* Hebraists are determined to conduct their experiments here—their anti-*Galut* notions notwithstanding. Mr. Jabotinsky is among their most intelligent journalists. When an intelligent man spites his own good sense, what is there left to say?

10
National Helplessness versus National Self-Help

(1915)

The most important question facing the Jewish worker at the present phase of history is: How can our nation be insured against the recurrence of the horrible persecutions and tragic events which so often befall it in the various countries? Each nation has its troubles. The Italians are not assured against earthquakes; the Chinese—against floods; the Indians— against failure of crops, cholera, and pests. Nature is responsible for these catastrophes. Human knowledge, however, can combat these blind elements of nature. Other nations suffer from continual oppression: Ireland and India are under the yoke of Great Britain, and Russia is under the yoke of the Czar. These peoples suffer because they are not sufficiently conscious of their nationality nor are they internally united. They therefore cannot successfully revolt against their oppressors.

Some nations are being ruined by the World War, although they do not want war and are not to be blamed for it. Among these nations are the Serbians, Belgians, Poles, Latvians, and Armenians. Nevertheless, they find a double consolation in their sufferings. They are neither alone, nor deserted or persecuted; they have someone to come to their aid. A great many nations came to the support of the Serbians and Belgians, and Russia pretended to come to the aid of the Armenians. Of greater importance is the fact that these nations may sooner or later expect to receive recompense for their sacrifices. *They struggle for their own national cause.* Should they lose in the struggle, the loss is not permanent; for they remain on their own soil and can always wait for the opportunity to arise and regain their rights.

The Galut condition of the Jewish nation is not only tragic but hopeless. Our Galut tragedy is not temporary but permanent. We do not fight for a Jewish cause; we suffer for foreign interests. We do not possess our own land, and are neglected by this colossal world which has its own troubles. We have no side to join in a war; the world is hostile toward us and wishes to wipe us out. Under the best conditions, the world is indifferent to us. Our fate is always determined by the fate of other nations. How can we escape from this extraordinary condition? Are we absolutely helpless, or can we extricate ourselves? The Jewish workers receive various answers to this question. Some Jewish Socialists place their entire faith in assimilation; others, in the progress of humanity. We Socialist-Zionists are convinced that our freedom depends primarily upon the *national self-help of the Jewish masses*. The latest, most dreadful of all catastrophes befalling the Jews, the World War, substantiated our viewpoint.

Death and suicide are the most radical reliefs from disease. Similarly, assimilation is the most radical solution to the Jewish problem. If there were no Jews, there would be no suffering from the Jewish tragedy. Nevertheless, no medical expert would advise his patient to take poison for a cure. No honest statesman or idealist ever attempted to solve, for example, the Polish question by suggesting that the Polish people should cease to exist. And how would the Belgians in their present plight look upon anyone who gave them the excellent advice to assimilate with the Germans, and cease to exist as an independent nation? Only to us Jews have self-appointed "physicians" had the audacity, the shamelessness, to preach national suicide. It is beneath the honor and dignity of our great heroic and martyred people to take the assimilationist-utopianists seriously. The Jewish nation *lives* and *will* live! Other nations may love or hate us, but they will never succeed in wiping us out, either by persecution or by assimilation.

Nevertheless, were assimilation possible, we might have considered it. The truth is that assimilation is nothing more than a harmful illusion. The Jewish masses become assimilated to some degree only. At most, they accept the external characteristics of the neighboring nations: the clothes, the language, certain foods and habits. But inwardly, in their spirit, they remain strange to their neighbors' culture. Even the most assimilated Jews cannot intermingle with their neighbors, and always lead a distinct Jewish life. As long as other nations exist, the Jewish nation will also exist. A part of the Jewish intelligentsia and upper bourgeoisie strenuously attempts to commit national suicide, but the Jewish masses, the Jewish working class, will not yield to the notion that the Jew disappear among foreign nations and alien cultures.

"Human progress" is a beautiful idea yet we must always be aware that progress does not create man, but man creates progress. Progress is not self-made but must be won, step by step, by the masses. True, there is such a thing as technical, scientific, and economic progress. We continually become wiser, keener, and more experienced in the control of nature. That alone, however, cannot make our character more humane, our feelings more refined, our motives, nobler. Political institutions do not of themselves become ennobled, and social justice does not just "happen."

Social and political rights grow only through bitter struggle. Oppression maintains itself as long as the oppressed have not the strength to throw off the yoke and institute a new *equilibrium*. The moral progress of mankind is nothing more than a result of this bitter struggle for this equilibrium. Whenever might and helplessness meet, oppression will be the inevitable result. The only defense the weak have is their own organized effort and their common struggle for their interests. The law, the police, and the courts of justice will at most come to the aid of the innocent, suffering *individual*, but not to the aid of the oppressed *group or nation*. Every law, every statute is passed and controlled by the powerful, who utilize technical progress for their own purposes. The laws and judicial practices can improve in favor of the oppressed classes and nations only by means of their own efforts.

The World War has clearly demonstrated that even the best of mankind will not cease to oppress the weak if the latter comes into conflict with its own interests. As proof we submit the example of the German Social Democratic Party, which consented to the military move of the Imperial Army in occupying neutral Luxemburg and Belgium. No one will deny that the German Social Democrats are good socialists. But when it seemed to them essential to violate the neutrality of weak neighbors, they did not hesitate in the least. The Belgian and French socialists acted similarly.

In short, the weaker element, be it class or nation, should not depend on the humaneness and justice of the stronger. The basic principle of socialism is that the emancipation of the working class must come through its own efforts and through its own struggle. What a fine thing it would be if the worker depended on the moral progress of the capitalist to cease exploiting him!

And a.e v'e not naive in assuming that the Jews will cease to suffer and will be guarded against all catastrophes when the nations shall have become more humane and shall no longer persecute weaker peoples? We Jews should trust no one but ourselves. *The emancipation of the Jewish people can be gained only by our own efforts.* The only solution to the Jewish problem is the creation of an equilibrium of power which will not permit other nations to persecute us so freely without being called to account. The uniqueness of the Jewish tragedy resides in the fact that Jews have no land of their own. For that reason Jewish interests and needs do not evoke respect.

Consider a tiny country like Montenegro, which has a quarter of a million poor, semibarbarian inhabitants, without any influence whatsoever on world civilization. Then consider the Jewish nation, a cultured people of over thirteen million, with a thousand-year-old culture, a people of great capitalists and great revolutionists, of Rothschilds, Poznanskys, and Schiffs, and of Marxes, Lassalles, and Gershonys; a nation which has statesmen, journalists, artists, poets, teachers, and social leaders everywhere; a people of great capabilities, exerting a powerful influence on civilization.

Whose interests will be taken into greater account—that of the thirteen million highly cultured Jews, or that of the quarter million Montenegrins? Whose voice will ring clearer in the international chorus of the movements for freedom? The answer is plain. The Montenegrins are in a better position to struggle for freedom than are the Jews. The interests of the Montenegrins will be taken into greater account for they do not depend upon assimilation and human progress, but on their own small forces and planned connections with the great powers of the world. This must also be the national political slogan of the Jewish worker: *organized national self-help. We must unite ourselves in the struggle for our own future.*

11
Two Currents in Poale Zionism
(1915)

Amidst today's nationalist passions each class-conscious worker and every socialist must pose this question: How do the two great ideas of liberation—*social liberation* of laboring humanity and *national liberation* of oppressed peoples—relate to each other? This is not the place to broach the full breadth of this matter. We simply wish to illustrate it through the concrete instance of the Jewish Labor movement.

There is a party in the Jewish proletariat that takes on both tasks simultaneously in very radical form. This is *Poale Zionism*, or proletarian Zionism, which wants to answer the social question through socialism and the Jewish question through Zionism. We define socialism as the socialization of the means of production of private property and the introduction of collective, socialized property in terms of land and capital. Further details regarding the future social order may be the free concern of every individual Poale Zionist: One may be a collectivist and believe that the land and means of production will belong to a great state, and another may be an anarchist and believe that the means of production will belong to voluntary unions of workers, without powers of political organizations and coercion.

With regard to this question I am an anarchist-socialist. I regard the politics of state and organized coercion as a means of protecting private property which will perforce be abolished by a collective organization of labor. I am a Marxist without the *Zukunftsstaat*. Be that as it may, I regard the differences between socialists and anarchists as *Zukunftsmusik*, as a question for the far off future, not a question that warrants the split in today's labor movement. The complete split between socialists and anarchists is, I believe, the greatest misfortune of the socialist movement, the greatest obstacle to the progress of the revolutionary struggle. Socialism captured all the elements with *organizational abilities* and anarchism all the *militant individuals* with *spirited drive*. Consequently both movements became one-sided and incapable of toppling capitalism. Thanks to this infelicitous split both sides were constrained to accomodate themselves to exisiting conditions, and are equally to blame in that we are now further away from the social revolution than we were prior to the First International.

Equally unimportant for Poale Zionism are the philosophical differences between various revolutionaries. One may be a materialist, the other a Kantian, one a Marxist, the second an empiriocriticist. I myself am an empiriocriticist, believing neither in materialism nor idealism, rejecting all religions whether in obvious or disguised forms. I find every metaphysic laughable even when it hides behind the most innocent "scientific" masks. In other words I am a Marxist without "matter." But this has no direct bearing on the social movement and as far as I am concerned, all philosophical questions may be quietly left in abeyance until after the social revolution. It is therefore possible for socialists, anarchists, syndicalists and Wobblies, materialists, Kantians, empiriorealists, revolutionaries à la Marx, Kropotkin, and Isaiah—to come together in one party. What is essential however is that they actively strive toward the abolition of capitalism and any form of private property in land and in the means of production.

The same freedom prevails among us regarding Zionism. Here too there are many tunes of *Zukunftsmusik* that have no bearing on the practical questions of the movement. One may think that the future Jewish colony in Eretz Israel will take the form of an independent state (*Judenstaat*), a second may envisage it as an economically, politically, and culturally autonomous society. One may envisage the territories of Eretz Israel limited only to Palestine, a second may have imperialist-expansionist dreams about "neighboring lands," including Mesopotamia, the Dark Mountains, the River Sambatyon with its Leviathan and Wild Bull. The essential thing is that a separate homeland must be found for the Jewish people in Eretz Israel. In sum, Poale Zionism aspires to socialism, i.e. the abolition of private property in the means of production and to Zionsim, i.e. the creation of a national home in Eretz Israel. All other philosophical issues and details about the future are declared private matters.

There are also many questions of general import which cannot be left freely to individuals as private matters. The first question is *how to link socialism and Zionism so that no contradiction exists between them and so that both great tasks support each other harmoniously.* The problem is that socialism can be only realized through class struggle and Zionism only through national struggle of the entire Jewish people. How do both lines come together? There are two distinguishable currents in the international Poale Zion movement: one calls itself Socialist and the other Social Democratic.

Socialist Poale Zionism handles the problem by bringing national unity into socialism. It wants to realize socialism without class struggle. Social Democratic Poale Zionism handles the problem by bringing class struggle into Zionism. It wants to realize Zionism together with the entire Jewish nation, but without renouncing the class struggle against the bourgeoisie for even a minute. Both currents therefore look differently upon socialism, Zionism, and work in the *Galut*. As stated above, I am not referring to philosophical differences regarding principles about the future. It is, on the contrary, a disagreement over practical working methods which on several occasions almost split the World Confederation of Poale Zion. Not so long ago it almost caused a split in the American Poale Zion movement, which was avoided only with great difficulty. The entire future of Poale Zionism and its influence on the broad working masses hangs on this disagreement.

I adhere to the Social Democratic tendency in Poale Zionism. Except for an incidental interruption (in 1904–1905) I have been in the ranks of Social Democratic Poale Zionism for fifteen years now. Socialist Poale Zionism, which was founded by N. Syrkin and afterwards by the Austrian Poale Zionists S. Kaplansky, L. Hazanovitch, and others, is just as old. The views of the Social Democrats received its clear and unambiguous formulations in the programs and literature of the Russian Poale Zionists, and this current has remained steadfast in its principles all these fifteen years. The socialist tendency on the other hand distinguishes itself in its vagueness, its constant vacillations, and the wide dissension within its own ranks.

I am thoroughly convinced that now—during this confused and tragic war period—the time has come for Poale Zionism in America to define itself conclusively. Its spiritual physiognomy must finally be defined so that the broad Jewish masses may decide once and for all whether they accept Zionism as part of their ideal. Winning the masses over to the Zionist ideal is now the most important task facing Poale Zionism in this country. Consequently the discussion must no longer remain within the narrow confines of the small party which exists here. The leaders of the party have done everything, to the point of excluding entire unions and party activists, in order to stifle discussion. We must therefore interest the wider public in this question. Only in this manner will we be able to force the conservative party leaders to listen to our complaints and to change their tactics—those tactics whose results have hitherto been most tragically fruitless.

Indeed fruitless. Just look around; see how bourgeois Zionism blossoms in this country and how weak and insignificant Poale Zionism is. In the shortest span of time the largest bourgeois institutions have declared themselves Zionist: The Independent Order of Brit Abraham, The International Order of Brit Shalom, The Galician Farband, The Rumanian Farband, etc., etc. Has anyone heard anything about the Workmen's Circle, the Cloakmakers' Union, or the Amalgamated etc. declaring themselves Poale Zionists? And let us not say that Poale Zionism disturbs the powerful *Forward* machine. Bourgeois Zionism certainly had its difficulties with the American Jewish Committee. But at the right moment for Zionism the influence of the American Jewish Committee disappeared into thin air. When will Poale Zionism's right moment come if not now during this period of world war and national reevaluation? And if Poale Zionism here is not fit enough to make the best of the moment, just what can it make the best of? Indeed, what can it do at all?

Many of my party comrades will be infuriated with me because of these questions. But there will also be some who will take their obligations more seriously and understand that only now, not later, is the time to pose these questions. Truth must stand above party deliberations and diplomatic niceties. And the truth is: *Lo zeh haderech.* This is not the way. Let each of my party comrades pose the question: Whence this amazing weakness of Poale Zionism here [in the U.S.A], even at this amazingly opportune moment? And let him not be content with such lame excuses as insufficient strength, insufficient funds, or insufficient work. There must also be a reason for our having insufficient strength or for our not having worked hard enough.

The reason is that Poale Zionism is not serious about socialism and does not have the Jewish worker at heart. Poale Zionism is alienated from the theory and practice of the class struggle and consequently the working class is indifferent to Zionism. Now is the time to change tactics. This is the demand of the Social Democratic current. More on that in future articles. The point of my articles is to show how Poale Zionism can become more of a force to be reckoned with. For now it is merely a club. And if this goal requires losing complacency, I shall not be discouraged. Nor shall I be afraid if my own comrades answer me through protests and boycott or if the opponents of Poale Zionism capitalize on our internal differences.

12

The Socialism of Poale Zion Here

(1915)

The organizational weakness of Poale Zion in this country derives from its superficial approach to socialism more than any other factor. It is socialist, but its socialism *is not tied to the class struggle*. The official party program speaks of class struggle, but not much and in diffuse form. The old program of 1905 stated: "As socialists we participate in everything that leads to the liberation of the working masses together with all socialist organizations, so long as they do not contradict our national aspirations." In the appended notes it says: "National solidarity . . . facilitates the class struggle" (?!) and "Poale Zionism strives, on the one hand, to inculcate class consciousness among the Jewish working masses, and, on the other, to awaken their national consciousness." In the new program of 1909 class struggle is discussed only in the following few words: "The party organizes the Jewish working class because of the professional and political struggle against capitalism."

But take for example B. Zuckerman's pamphlet *Der Poale Zionism*. Herein the word socialism is twisted and turned in all possible directions. Socialism is elevated to the sky as a holy ideal implanted in the hearts of all Jewish workers, but in the entire pamphlet *there is not a single word about class struggle*.

It would appear that there is no antagonism between labor and capital. I know that B. Zuckerman is familiar with the class struggle and can evaluate its significance. But he forgets it when he speaks of Poale Zionism. At such times he is only aware of abstract socialism and concrete Zion. Class struggle and Zionism are two different things to him. And such is the case with the Socialist current in general. How does it envisage the *actualization of socialism*? Regarding socialism world over, among all nations and the Jews of the Diaspora countries, they ignore it; it is not a very popular theme with the Socialist Labor Zionists.

Of course they have much to say about socialism in Eretz Israel. This is a kind of amazing socialism that is realized through peaceful means and solidary cooperation with the bourgeoisie. The means to achieve a socialist order in Eretz Israel are: the shekel, the Zionist congress, the bourgeois socialist national fund, various worker cooperatives such as the Ahvah and Franz Oppenheimer's "*Siedlungs Genossenschaften*," i.e. agrarian industrial cooperative colonies and garden towns. So, what about the class struggle? N. Syrkin answers us that we cannot afford a class struggle in the future *yishuv* in Eretz Israel. There, a Garden of Eden of social justice must be organized forthwith.

Thus while N. Syrkin was able to please the bourgeois Zionist delegates at the Zionist convention in Boston, I doubt that intelligent class-conscious workers can be pleased. But the entire thrust of American Poale Zion compels them to go hand in hand with bourgeois Zionism in order to win them over for the respectable plans for social colonization. Here there are two noteworthy theories that Socialist Poale Zion is working on. First, the idea that without the bourgeois Zionists little or nothing can be accomplished in Eretz Israel, and second, that Poale Zion must, therefore, strive "to bring the social spirit into the General Zionist movement."

Both theories virtually eliminate the need for the existence of a separate socialist Zionist party. If the working class alone can accomplish so little in Zionist colonization and if it must teach social justice to the capitalists, the simplest thing would be for the Poale Zionists to dissolve as a party and join bourgeois Zionism as a radical wing. Then there would eventually be no difference between Poale Zionism and Mizrahi: both are simply parts of the bourgeois Zionist whole, mere wings—Poale Zionism with a radical program and Mizrahi with an Orthodox one. We return happily to N. Syrkin's original ideas, which he developed fifteen and twelve years ago, that Zionist socialist parties must belong simultaneously to two different parties: For socialism they must work in the general socialist parties and for Zionism—in the Zionist organization.

Such is indeed the case. The Socialist Poale Zionists consider themselves part of General Zionism. They regard all of the bourgeois Zionist accomplishments as their own, they feel at one with General Zionism, identifying with its institutions. And what of the sublime theory of "bringing a social spirit into the General Zionist movement"? Pipe dreams. A Hebrew University in Jerusalem! A "golden book" of the National Fund, where all exploiters can perpetuate their names in the memory of the people! But let us pay closer attention to the theory of the "social spirit."

The Socialist Poale Zionists proudly point to some of the supposed success of their social preachings to their bourgeois kindred spirits. If we take them at their word, they carried out the following social reforms in the Zionist organization: First, the Zionist Congress adopted in principle Oppenheimer's plan for cooperative colonization, and for that created a separate fund and donated National Fund land for such colonies (the cooperative colony Merhavia and others). Second, workers' homes were built on National Fund land. Third, they worked to get the National Fund to renounce its previous tactics of supporting, with credit, private capitalist developers and of engaging nonorganized Arab strike breakers, instead of organized Jewish workers.

The Poale Zionists talk themselves into believing that *they* accomplished all this. But this is a great error. This was not accomplished by the Poale Zionists as an organization or as a party but by individual persons, social reformers among the Zionists like Franz Oppenheimer, Dr. Pasmanik, and the Poale Zionist S. Kaplansky. Social reformers such as these can be found everywhere and are by no means in need of a separate Poale Zion party. If there were no Poale Zion party or if they had no business at all with the Zionist Congress, the socialist spirit among the bourgeois Zionists would not be one whit less powerful than it is now.

If the National Fund and the Palestine Office take the demands of the workers into account, that has nothing at all to do with the Poale Zionists shouting hooray and singing Hatikvah [the national anthem] with the bosses. Nor is it because the Poale Zionists regard themselves as an organic part of the General Zionist movement, nor because they become inspired by the National Fund and the shekel. The real reason is very different. It is because of the fierce struggle which *the Jewish workers* wage to this day *in Eretz Israel*, with determination and enthusiasm, and which they will continue without concerning themselves with N. Syrkin's prophetic sermons about the class struggle in Eretz Israel.

Jewish workers in Eretz Israel struck, struggled, and withstood stiffnecked lockouts on the part of the bosses, organized into professional unions and cooperatives, created their own social-democratic press, and, last but not least, erected the military organization of settler-guardsmen, Hashomer. Hashomer struggles not only against these unorganized Arab peasants but also against the Jewish bosses with their small shops and petty-noble interests. If not for this intense and long-lasting struggle of the working masses in Eretz Israel, nothing would have helped, not Kaplansky's diplomatic speeches nor Syrkin's prophetic ideas.

And the joke of it is, that under the pretense of bringing the social spirit into bourgeois Zionism, the bourgeois spirit is brought into proletarian Zionism.

When the Zionist workingmen follow the leaders and think of the shekel, the National Fund and the Colonial Bank, the National Library in Jerusalem, the Polytechnic Institute in Haifa, and what not, as their own socialist (!) institutions, the most dangerous confusion arises in their class consciousness. The separation between capitalism and Poale Zionism disappears and the Poale Zionist learns to dance to the tune of the bourgeois Zionist. The clearest expressions of this are the countless fund raisers of all kinds which the bourgeois Zionists are fond of conducting on Mondays and Thursdays. Here the "kosher" Poale Zionist feels as if he is attending the most holy of ceremonies: He works with all the means at his disposal, to the point of exhaustion, collecting alms and becoming inspired, together with bourgeois Zionists, forgetting in the process socialism and class struggle.

No wonder that the organized and class conscious workers feel indifferent if not downright hostile to this kind of socialism. Such socialism, they feel, is a phrase without serious content. They understand that Socialist Poale Zionism is not consistent in its socialism. Nor is this at all denied by many socialists. I myself heard many Poale Zionists say we are first of all Zionists, then socialists; we are 85 percent Zionists and all told 15 percent socialists. As long as Poale Zionism regards itself as an organic part of General Zionism, as long as it continues to regard the bourgeois Zionist institutions and funds as its own; as long as its socialism is not tied to the theory and practice of a living class struggle, Poale Zionism will continue to remain a clubhouse without social impact and without influence on the broad Jewish working masses.

Not only the *Forward*, "cosmopolitanism," or assimilation are to blame. The Poale Zionists here are also to blame that Jewish workers are so unfamiliar with Zionism and the idea of the national liberation of the Jewish people. This is the bitter truth that I want to tell my comrades openly: This is also *your* fault; do not place all the blame on the opposition. Take a good look at yourselves, and if you will, hear me out.

Having heard me out perhaps you will see that when the worker does not want to place any trust in his boss this is a *healthy instinct*. The worker who keeps away from the kind of people who are close to his boss, is right. Workers who suffered sweatshop slavery, strikes, and hired gangsters will not trust you so long as you maintain and demonstrate solidarity with the bourgeois Zionists. Bourgeois Zionism is necessary for our people, but leave it for the middle class. Your task is proletarian Zionism, and you must nurture it not through flower- nor flag-day and not by Zionist conventions but wherever the worker suffers and struggles.

The two currents of Poale Zionism, about which I spoke in earlier articles (the Socialists and the Social Democrats), part company in their views of socialism, Zionism, work to be done in the *Galut*, and in the forms of party organization and discipline. The Social Democratic current prevails in Russia and to some extent in Austria and Eretz Israel. The Socialist prevails in America and to some extent in other countries. There is also a Social Democratic current here, *and through the good graces of both sides, both currents can peacefully and in solidarity work together in one party, as has hitherto been the case.*

The Social Democratic Poale Zionists are of the firm opinion that no socialism and no freedom movement are possible without class struggle. In this they concur with revolutionary socialists, anarchists, and syndicalists of all nations. They also recognize peaceful means as a tool of the Labor movement, namely parliamentary action and cooperative organization. But they absolutely insist that these peaceful means can, at best, facilitate the class struggle, serve an auxiliary function in the economic struggle, and direct political action. Peaceful means, however, must in no way supersede the direct struggle. And this is their view of Zionism as well. Within the Zionist movement a serious class struggle transpires and will continue so long as the working class has not freed itself from the capitalist yoke through social revolution. In order to interpret this further we must explain how the Social Democrats conceive of Zionism and the Jewish question in general. We can do this only in abridged form. For a detailed discussion the reader may refer to R. Kendzhersky's pamphlet *Di grundlagn fun Poale Zionism*, and my articles from 1905.

Neither the bourgeois Zionists nor the Socialist Poale Zionists have a clear answer for the following cardinal question: Does Zionism solve all the problems of Jewish life or only some of them? The bourgeois Zionists eschew any specific answer, but their whole psychology bears witness to the fact that they regard Zionism as the definitive answer to all Jewish questions. They want to destroy the *Galut* altogether and concentrate all Jewish life in Zion. The Socialist Poale Zionists are less resolute on that point but in general they tend toward the opinion that in Zion all the needs of the Jewish people will be met and their sufferings ended. The Social Democrats, on the other hand, regard Zionism as the answer to only one aspect of the Jewish question, namely the question of Jewish homelessness and uprootedness. There is an enormous number of Jewish questions and these questions change with the times. Some of them relate to the *Galut* because no matter the extent of the realization of Zionism, a large portion of the Jewish people and possibly the majority will forever remain dispersed among other nations. And these questions of the *Galut* find their solution in various ways outside Zionism.

The Jewish question is very complex and cannot be solved by means of one simple prescription such as the colonization of Eretz Israel. The task of proletarian Zionism is to struggle for healthy and productive living conditions for the Jewish people. The Jewish people lives an abnormal life, from which it suffers, in that it nowhere has an independent political home. We therefore strive to acquire for it such a home, and a host of historical, colonial, and practical reasons convince us that the only home our people can have is in Eretz Israel. That is by no means to say that we want all people to return home. This is neither possible nor entirely desirable. All peoples have their own homeland. Even the oppressed peoples have their own homes, though they may not be fully in charge there. But all peoples, upon leaving their own territories, have dispersed themselves throughout the world. The might of a nation has two aspects—being concentrated in the homeland, and the strength of its dispersal which carries it to all four corners of the world. If the Jewish people had a politically independent center in Eretz Israel and strong colonies throughout the world, it would become among the strongest and healthiest of nations.

In short, the Jewish question can be solved only by connecting healthy *Galut* life with a healthy center in the independent homeland. Zionism really solves only some Jewish questions. The rest are solved through national consolidation in the *Galut* per se. Without Zionism there is no healthy national development but neither so without the *Galut*. We want a secure Zion and a secure *Galut*—that is the catch-phrase of Social Democratic Poale Zionism.

Among the questions which Zionism as such can solve only partially is the Jewish workers' question. Through the creation of an independent homeland for the people, the condition of our workers also becomes more normal and the class struggle on the Jewish street will acquire healthier forms. In the countries of the *Galut* Jews are excluded from a number of important industries such as coal mining, metallurgy, the railroads, and also from agriculture. Jewish labor bears a specific character, concentrated as it is in the weakest industries such as the needle trades, shoe production, the tobacco industry. This robs the Jewish worker of the ability to spread out and exploit his revolutionary energies. His class struggle is consequently limited and insufficiently productive. These anomalies will disappear in Eretz Israel, where the Jewish worker will penetrate into all the hitherto excluded branches of production.

But exploitation itself, the struggle between capitalists and workers, will continue full blown in Eretz Israel as long as capitalism exists. It is dangerously utopian to think that Eretz Israel alone will be an exceptional country and that only there will the kind of colonization occur which can be free of capitalist foundations. This is the fantasy of many Socialist Poale Zionists. We, the Social Democrats, find that the workers' question in Eretz Israel can and will be solved through class struggle alone, and we therefore strive to organize the worker entirely apart from the bourgeoisie, even within the Zionist movement itself.

Proletarian Zionism has its own work and has no need to join the bourgeois Zionist institutions in order to carry out its own tasks. The Socialists argue that the worker cannot accomplish very much independently in Eretz Israel. That is true as long as proletarian Zionism does not have sufficient strength. And its strength will remain meager as long as it is wed to bourgeois Zionism. Standing on its own feet, proletarian Zionism will in the end draw to its ranks the great mass of organized Jewish workers and will then acquire sufficient strength to fulfill its own aims. Instead of the Socialists' theory that Poale Zionism must, so to speak, "bring the social spirit into the General Zionist movement," the Social Democrats propound quite a different theory: *The Poale Zionists must inculcate the national and socialist spirit into the Labor movement.* We regard Poale Zionism as part and parcel not of the General Zionist movement but of the International Labor movement.

We therefore have a different understanding of the kind of work to be done in countries of the *Galut*. The Socialist Poale Zionists delude themselves in speaking of the equal rights of Zion and the *Galut*, and of Hebrew and Yiddish. Actually, for them Zion is superior to the *Galut* and Hebrew superior to Yiddish. Nor am I speaking of die-hard Hebraists and *Galut* haters such as N. Syrkin. Even the official spokesmen of the Socialist Labor Zionists consider *Galut* work, at best, as a means and preparation for Zionism (this is explicitly stated for example in Zuckerman's pamphlet). Work in the *Galut* is a means, and not the most important means at that—simply one of many. The aim throughout remains Zion. It is of course understood that to means one can never accord the same respect as to ends. No wonder then that while the Socialist Poale Zionists give generously of themselves for National Fund work, for cooperatives in Eretz Israel, etc., they treat matters and activities relating to the *Galut* as after-thoughts. Even in the national radical schools—their most important accomplishment among *Galut* activities—they devote too much time to Hebrew literature.

For us Social Democrats, work in the *Galut* has no lesser value as an independent goal than work in Zion. *Galut* and Zion are each ends unto themselves, and both may use each other as means. A healthy *Galut* life, a healthy independent Eretz Israel, a healthy labor movement—

these are the ideals of the Social Democrats. And if Socialists admit to being 85 percent Zionist and 15 percent socialist, we rejoin: We are 100 percent socialist and 100 percent Zionist.

Note

"Here" and "this country" refer to the United States, where the article was written (ed.).

13
Healthy and Sick Socialism
(1916)

It is absurd to contend that nationalism alone is responsible for the present World War. It is a grave injustice to burden the national impulse with sole responsibility for this bloodshed, for this holocaust of wild passions and sufferings, for this destruction of cultural treasures. Yet it is equally absurd to ignore the harmfulness of present-day reactionary chauvinism. Only those whose minds are still dominated by the clichés of the old radical canonical code will seriously believe that it is nationalism that is guilty of bringing on the current catastrophe. It is argued that were there no nations and no nationalism, there would be no quarrels among the peoples and all would live in unity and peace. Therefore it is the sacred task of all radicals to vilify all nationalism and to strive for the abolition of all nations.

We might, if we wished, develop prettier notions. By following this logic of an intoned ABC of Marx, we can reason that inasmuch as the instinct of self-preservation drives human beings to compete with one another, and in this process the weaker are exploited by the stronger, it is the sacred duty of every friend of mankind to fight this instinct of self-preservation. The same profound scholastics have discovered an additional series of syllogisms against nationalism, syllogisms whose validity is on par with the one cited above. It is argued that since national sentiments are easily exploited for militaristic purposes, all national sentiments should therefore be rooted out from the human heart. To be consistent, all sentiments of heroism, courage, and ambition—which are frequently exploited for militaristic purposes and may consequently be harmful—should also be done away with. Similarly, since militarism makes use of iron, steel, copper, bread, and boots, these too should be branded as reactionary tools.

Some of the more profound philosophers of this type contend that territorial boundaries are responsible for all human conflicts. Nations may continue to exist as long as they do not possess definite, demarcated territories; boundaries should cease marring the face of the earth. When the boundaries of the various fatherlands disappear, there will be no more wars. A nation that possesses boundaries automatically desires to expand its frontiers and does not permit another nation to encroach upon its own. Proletarians have no fatherlands, but if they have one, their attachment to it must be uprooted. To this day the Jews have been an exceptional case among all the nations of the world. All nations have boundaries, and fight and suffer for their fatherlands; only the Jews, faring better, have no land for which to suffer. The Jewish people can proudly claim, with Sholom Aleichem's *Motl Paisie*, the cantor's son: "How lucky I am to be an orphan." There you have an easy solution to the woes of the world: Let all the nations become orphans; let there be indiscriminate assimilation; let all the nations of the world become landless like the Jews, instead of letting the Jews become a normal people on its own land.

Such was the philosophy which dominated pre-war socialist thought, with the force of a holy creed given to Moses directly from Mount Sinai. The World War smashed those ideas, and turned those social cosmopolitans into social patriots. They leaped from one absurdity to another, substituting one ABC for another. They dumped the ABC of the class struggle into the waste-bin and pulled out the crumpled ABC of the patriotic struggle instead. Karl Marx was replaced by the old Imperial Majesty and the verses of the *Communist Manifesto* were discarded for the tune of: "How Fine It Is to Be a Soldier." Instead of: "Proletarians of all lands, unite" the new slogan became: "Citizens of all lands, to arms against one another!"

The case of Gustave Herve is a typical illustration of this change. He who had always been in the extreme opposition at all the congresses of the Socialist International, who continually demanded that energetic steps be taken against militarism, that the general strike be used against war, that war declaration be met with barricades on the streets—was the one to change the name of his militant organ *The Social War* to that of *The Victory*. At these Socialist International congresses, little heed was paid to him; his fiery speeches were received with condescending smiles. He was too logical and too consistently unilateral. But theoretically it was impossible to dissent openly from his views. No one dared and no one could, for Herve was simply pushing the Socialists' absurdities to their logical conclusion.

Unlike his comrades, Herve had the courage to be absurd. He maintained that "the proletarians have no fatherland"; for it is not their fatherland, but that of the rich and mighty, of the capitalists. This was Herve's dictum, befitting a courageous man who speaks out honestly. It was the Socialists who said, "True, we have no fatherland, yet we must defend the fatherland," who were illogical. Herve lambasted this inconsistency, mocked this line of thought, and spent his days in jail for his anti-war propaganda, in a French jail, on whose walls was inscribed: "Liberty, Equality, and Fraternity." Today Herve is still the same open, brave, and courageous fighter. He does not conduct diplomatic negotiations with his own conscience. What his comrades murmur he proclaims to the world promptly.

On changing the name of his organ he announced:

> I can no more call my organ *The Social War*. For sixteen months this organ has openly and consistently advocated the sacredness of national unity, and is determined to continue this policy even after the war.
>
> I find it necessary to proclaim that we feel ourselves bound more closely to the clerical and reactionary French patriot who is willing to continue the war until Prussian militarism is destroyed, than to the so-called Socialists of Zimmerwald who are too willing to accept a "German Peace."
>
> We want no more social war, no more civil war. Today it is just war; tomorrow it must be unity among the French, so that justice and brotherhood may prevail at home and abroad.

Thus wrote Herve because he wished to be consistent, because his conduct was motivated by principles of sobriety, clarity, and intellectual honesty. It was the same in Germany. If Socialists may become loyal to the Kaiser, His Majesty can also become a Marxist! We actually heard how "Comrade" Wilhelm II declared himself in love with socialism. . . .

We have described the two maladies and have observed the symptoms. We have noted the heat generated by the chauvinists and the chauvinistic reaction among socialists, which resulted from their earlier oversimplified antinationalist stand. One who today demands that all national boundaries be abolished may tomorrow shout hurrah for the Kaiser and find joy in the Imperial cannons. Such men cannot adhere to a healthy socialism. Marx was quite correct in saying that proletarians have no fatherland. In his day (70 years ago), healthy, progressive nationalism had hardly yet pecked its way out from its bourgeois liberal shell. But since then, progressive nationalism has become a unique historical phenomenon. Nationalism is not the reactionary product manufactured by petty bourgeois agitators; it is the instinct of self-preservation in nations, their healthy urge for self-determination.

It is thus understood by international socialism. Mankind is divided into nations and classes. Nations existed before they were split into classes. Nations remain, while classes change. In the Middle Ages classes were different from what they are today. Then, the division was feudal— burghers and serfs; today the division is capitalist and proletarian. The nations underwent cultural modifications, but in essence they remained the same, like water changing into ice or steam, though retaining the same chemical elements. This instinct of self-preservation in nations cannot be destroyed. It is rank dilettantism and sheer nonsense to demand that nations lose their identity and shake off their loyalty to themselves. The national instinct of self-preservation latent in the socialist working class is a healthy nationalism. Only international socialism based upon a realistic approach to nationalism can liberate sick humanity in this capitalist era and cure society of its social and national conflicts.

14

The Economic Development
of the Jewish People

(1916)

The socioeconomic structure of the Jewish people differs radically from that of other nations. Ours is an anomalous, abnormal structure. Stubborn *Galut* champions have been wont to reject or ignore this truth. But recently their eyes, too, have opened; and although very few have been able to offer a satisfactory analysis of our economic abnormalities, no serious student of Jewish life can ignore them.

The case of the Jewish people is analogous to that of the patient who has complained of sundry aches and pains for a number of years, but whose physician has not been able to arrive at any satisfactory diagnosis. There was no doubt about the patient's illness, but in the course of the illness the body developed some measure of resistance to it. As the years progressed and new resistance was built up, the character of the disease changed, new symptoms appeared, and the physician found himself in a continuous state of bewilderment. Likewise, the Jewish nation has not been a passive patient awaiting his inevitable demise. Resistance to the disease has appeared at various times. There has always been the normal effort to regain organic equilibrium. It was not unnatural therefore that the diagnoses of our social "doctors" varied with the morphology of the disease.

Thirteen or fourteen years ago such a diagnosis, devised by a group of Jewish Socialists, appeared under the name of *nonproletarization*. Its major thesis was that the Jewish proletariat cannot be proletarized. The obvious contradiction contained in the proposition that "the Jewish proletariat cannot be proletarized" led the Poale Zion, who were the first to develop this theory, to be also the first to renounce it. The [Territorialist] Zionist-Socialists (the Z.S.) retained this illogical theory longest. Yet they too attempted to remove some of its crudities by converting it into the "nonindustrialization" theory. Jacob Lestschinsky, the leading economist of the Z.S., dedicated his book, *The Jewish Worker in Russia*, to the exposition of this theory. Its major thesis that "the Jewish worker cannot be industrialized" differed only slightly from its prototype. The book, like the principle around which it was built, was an indiscriminate mixture of sound ideas with grave errors.

It is absurd to assert that the Jewish worker cannot be "proletarized." His being a worker is evidence of the fact that he has ceased to be an "owner," that he has placed his labor power on the market, and has ipso facto become a member of the proletariat. Therefore the proposition that Jewish workers cannot achieve their own proletarization becomes an even greater absurdity when it comes from a Jewish Socialist Labor Party.

Nor is it less absurd to contend that Jewish labor cannot be industrialized. Jacob Lestschinsky complained (in the book mentioned above) that around 1897 there did not exist a single factory which employed 1,000 Jewish workers. However, the very handbook[1] of statistics on which he based his work told us of a tobacco factory in Grodno, in the years 1898–1899, in which 1,594 Jewish workers were employed. The same factory boasted a steam engine of 36 horsepower. Moreover, the literature of the general and Jewish Labor movements in Russia contains detailed accounts of numerous strikes conducted by Jewish workers in the Russian Pale of Settlement. The illegal literature of that period (1900–1905) records no less than 50 factories, each employing more than 100 Jewish workers. The following outstanding examples are also worthy of notice: a millinery factory in Warsaw with 1,000 Jewish employees, a tobacco factory employing 500 Jews, and a glassware factory in Polonoye with 400 Jewish workers.

America opened to the Jewish immigrant even greater opportunities for work than the most highly developed industries in Eastern Europe. No statistics are available concerning Jewish factories in the United States, but of this we are certain: Jewish labor in America, which is concentrated almost exclusively in the needle industry (in contradistinction to greater diversification of employment in Russia), has definitely assumed the proportions of mass·production that characterize big business. In Paterson, New Jersey, for example, there are large textile factories with an enormous number of Jewish workers. In Chicago, Rosenwald's clothing shops employ several thousand Jewish laborers. It remains true, however, that Jewish industries never attain the large-scale development achieved by non-Jewish industries. No Jewish factory, not even the largest, can compare with such gigantic enterprises as Krupp's iron works or Ford's automobile factories. The Jewish entrepreneur never dreams of industries on this scale, nor does the Jewish laborer have any access to them.

To be sure, the Jewish masses do become *proletarized*; Jewish labor does become industrialized. The process, however, is slow, and its development is limited and linear. Moreover, Jewish entrepreneurs seem to have a natural tendency to small-scale production. The economist S.O. Margolin calls this tendency the *individualization of industry.* A Jew, possessing meager means, often decides to become a boss "on his own" under circumstances in which a Gentile will never dare undertake such a venture. The Jew will often establish a business or a factory with negligible capital and thus become a "capitalist." The Gentile will more often choose to remain a "wage slave" for his entire life, even when his savings are larger than those of his Jewish fellow worker. The enterprising spirit of the Jew is irrepressible. He refuses to remain a proletarian. He will grab at the first opportunity to advance to a higher rung on the social ladder.

This desire to achieve "success" is a deeply ingrained characteristic of the Jewish laboring masses. Tailors, shoemakers, and cigarmakers eagerly await the opportunity to rid themselves of their tools, and to climb into the higher strata of insurance, dentistry, medicine, law, or into an independent business. This continuous exodus of thousands from the ranks of Jewish labor and the necessary influx of thousands to replace them, furnish the explanation for the instability of the Jewish laboring masses. These peculiar phenomena of Jewish labor have their roots in the general nature of our economic history.

It would be possible to formulate and explain clearly this uniqueness of the Jewish economic past and present through recourse to the literature of the Poale Zion in Russia before and during the last decade, but we will base our analysis on literature much older than that. Let us begin with a distinction made by Aristotle, whom Marx frequently quotes with much respect (a distinction that Marxists unfortunately have forgotten or neglected). Aristotle distinguishes between two modes of gaining a livelihood: first, the livelihood gained from nature; second, the livelihood gained from man. The farmer, mountaineer, and fisherman gain their livelihood from nature; the businessman, the banker, and the physician gain theirs from man. In terms of this distinction, it is obvious that Jews, in contradistinction to all other nations, *derive their livelihood exclusively from man.*

I carry the analysis a bit further by employing the economic theory of Otto Effertz. He classifies human production on the basis of the share of labor and land (or elements derived directly from land) in it. If we use the farmer as an illustration, there can be no doubt that his work in producing a crop is both difficult and important; nevertheless, the part played by the soil in the production of the crop is greater than that of the human labor involved. The farmer tills, fertilizes, plows, sows, and in the end harvests; but ultimately it is nature that provides the most important factors in the production of the crop. On the other hand, the human labor involved in the production of a garment far exceeds the contributions of nature. The sheep and wool are the products of nature; but from the moment the shears sever the wool from the sheep's back, and on through the long process of cleaning, spinning, dyeing, and weaving, it is human labor exclusively that brings a piece of cloth to its completion. Nor has labor finished its task before the tailor cuts the cloth and tailors it into a suit of clothes. In this long succession, the contribution of nature is negligible in proportion to the overwhelming demands put on human labor.

In terms of this second distinction we discover that in Jewish production, again in contradistinction to that of all other nations, the proportion of human labor far exceeds the natural elements involved. This analysis explains why Jewish economics is a "luft" economics and why Jewish life is a "luft" life. The term *luftmensch* was Max Nordau's contribution to our literature, and it expresses all too well the severance of Jewish labor from the soil. To be sure, no nation's economic life is founded on land alone. All economic life consists of both elements, land and labor. Indeed, the development of industry is invariably accompanied by an increase in the element of human labor, and a proportional decrease in the elements of nature in production. Although the elements of soil and nature are decreasing in the economic life of other peoples, they are absent from Jewish production, which is built exclusively on human labor.

Further, within the labor element in production we should distinguish between physical and mental labor. It is a commonplace that in Jewish economic life, occupations that require mental labor far outnumber those requiring physical labor. We must not overlook the fact that among other nations, too, the proportion of mental workers increases with the cultural development of the people. Yet in the case of no other nation is the proportion as high as among the Jews. The capitalist, or entrepreneur, contributes *mental labor* to his enterprise. His work is that of organizing and managing the business. The wage-earner's contribution consists chiefly of *physical labor*. The natural gravitation of the Jew toward the occupations that require mental labor exemplifies the entrepreneuring spirit which drives the Jewish laborer to become a small but independent businessman. This so-called economic individualism is deeply rooted in the landless history of the Jewish people.

To recapitulate: two important phenomena may be observed in Jewish economic production: (1) The preponderance of the element of *human labor* over the elements of nature; (2) the preponderance of *mental labor* over *physical labor*.

The products of human enterprise are generally divided into three kinds:

1. Production goods, e.g. machines, raw materials, tools.
2. Means of communication and transportation, e.g. railways, coaches, wagons, ships, telephone, telegraph.
3. Consumer goods, e.g. food, clothing, houses, furniture, dishes, books, pictures, musical instruments.

Within these classifications of human production further divisions may be made, using as a criterion the proximity of a product to or its remoteness from nature. The story of a pair of shoes begins with the farmer's raising and feeding the animal. Then come the slaughterer, the tanner, and the various other craftsmen of the leather industry whose task is to refine the leather to a specific degree. Finally, out of the hands of the shoemaker emerges the finished product.

Accordingly, we must distinguish in production the following levels:

1. The primary level includes the branches of production nearest nature, e.g. agriculture, gardening, ranching. Here the elements of soil and nature are preponderant over that of human labor.
2. The level of basic industry—mining, quarrying, forestry, etc. On this level there is an increase in the proportion of human labor.
3. The secondary-middle level, which is even further removed from nature. It includes the metal, building, and textile industries.
4. The tertiary-middle level includes the chemical industry, the lumber industry, the production of leather, paper, etc. It approaches the level of the consumer and is further removed from nature. The occupations of many Jews fall within this category.
5. The final level of production includes the needle trades, baking, printing, etc., and serves the consumer directly. On this level is the greatest concentration of traditional occupations of the Jew. Here the elements of soil and nature have vanished completely, and human labor is the only constituent.

In the light of this classification, let us see what information is obtainable from the following tables. In Table 14.1, which is based on the Russian Census of 1897 and the Austrian Census of 1900, Jewish occupations are arranged in the order of their remoteness from nature. The table also furnishes us with the percentages that the Jews constitute in relation to the total numbers employed in the various branches of production. Table 14.1 reveals the following information:

TABLE 14.1

Occupational Distribution of the Jews and Their Percentage in
the Total Population of Those Occupatons

Level of Production	In The Russian Pale		In Galicia	
	Jews	Per Cent	Jews	Per Cent
1. PRIMARY LEVEL OF PRODUCTION Agriculture, gardening, cattle raising, etc.	35,822	0.6	47,996	1.5
2. THE LEVEL OF BASIC INDUSTRY				
Mountaineering, Mining	1,006	1.8	1,053	8.3
Quarrying and Digging	5,187	12.5	696	10.6
Forestry	3,200	12.4	928	10.6
Total	9,393	7.7	2,677	9.5
3. THE SECONDARY-MIDDLE LEVEL				
Metal Industry	40,082	21.2	4,410	15.9
Textile Industry	33,200	19.0	1,421	14.7
Building Industary	37,136	18.9	3,110	13.0
Total	110,418	19.7	8,941	14.5
4. THE TERTIARY – MIDDLE LEVEL				
Lumber Industry	41,359	27.2	4,229	18.1
Chemical Industry	6,514	34.1	1,430	37.9
Leather and Paper	20,446	43.9	1,938	39.2
Total	68,319	31.3	7,597	23.7
5. FINAL LEVEL OF PRODUCTION				
Foods	44,797	34.8	11,036	48.9
Liquors and Tobacco	23,548	38.3	22,981	70.8
Clothing and Hygienics	244,534	48.1	20,298	35.2
Printing, Etc.	18,996	53.9	450	21.4
Jewelry	5,240	66.5	....	
Total	337,115	45.5	54,765	47.7

Sources: The Russian Census of 1897; the Austrian Census of 1900.

1. *Jewish occupations are remote from nature.* In Russia only 0.6 percent of those engaged in agriculture are Jews, and in Galicia only 1.5 percent.

2. *The percentage of Jews in any level of production varies directly according to its remoteness from nature.* On the level of basic industry, 8 to 9 percent of the laborers are Jews. On the secondary-middle level the percentage of Jews rises to between 15 and 20. In the tertiary-middle level it reaches 25 to 33 percent.

3. On the final level of production Jewish labor represents 50 percent of the total; i.e. the Jews have their highest representation in occupations that are at the greatest distance from nature.

4. The vast majority of non-Jews gain their livelihood from nature (in levels 1 and 2, i.e. agriculture and basic industry), whereas the

majority of Jews earn their living directly from other men. In Russia and Galicia 70-80 percent of non-Jews earn their livelihood directly from nature; a similar percentage of the Jews earn theirs from men.

These figures are based on official government statistics. They incorporate no Zionist theories and are not motivated by the remotest concern with Jewish problems. The above are the writer's own classifications. He was compelled to make them for two reasons: First, because occupations are classified differently in Russia and in Austria. Second, because the classifications of the government statisticians are too general; we find, for example, in these government statistics that large-scale metallurgy, which rightfully belongs in class 3, and small metal-work, like that of the blacksmith, locksmith, or tinsmith, which rightfully belongs in class 5, are all in one category. Were official statistics anything better than the indiscriminate jumble that they actually are, they would display the economic condition of the Jewish people much more clearly. Even the veil of official figures cannot obscure the prevailing law of Jewish economics, namely, that the concentration of Jewish labor in any occupation varies directly with the remoteness of that occupation from nature. It is as if an inexorable whip of history was driving the Jews further and further away from soil and nature, and higher and higher into the insubstantial ether of social stratification; it is as if history had conspired never to liberate the Jews from the shackles of economic landlessness.

The story told by the figures of Table 14.1 is that of a people far removed from the most important, most influential, and most stable branches of production—far removed from the occupations which are at the hub of history. Instead of concentrating on the vital center of economic life, the Jews are scattered on its periphery. Obviously, the fate of society does not to any extent rest on the needle or tobacco industries. This superficies of social life, which is made up of the give-and-take of finished goods, must draw its sustenance from labor in such central branches of production as agriculture, sheep raising, mining, railways, shipping, etc.

The moral of this story told by dry statistics is that as long as the Jewish people remains remote from nature and basic industry, Jewish economic life will remain stagnant, its culture will be at a low ebb, and the political welfare of the Jews will remain the plaything of chance. These figures force upon us the inevitable conclusion that in *international* socialism, in the class struggle, and in the revolution, the part played by *Jewish* socialism will be as insignificant as the Jewish needle and flatiron are when compared to the non-Jewish tractor, locomotive, or steamship. Such is the chronic malady of Jewish history. Those who seek to strengthen the attachment of the Jews to the rarefied economic stratosphere of the *Galut,* those who seek comfort for the Jewish people in exile songs and exile hopes, merely help to perpetuate our chronic malady.

From this analysis of the chronic economic ailment of the Jewish people in terms of current concepts of economic theory, let us now pass to an analysis of the same group of phenomena in Marxian terms. Marx divides modern capital into two categories: (1) *Constant capital,* which consists of the means of production such as land, factory buildings, raw materials, coal, machines, implements; (2) *variable capital,* which consists of human labor power. In the capital invested in any enterprise we must, therefore, according to Marx, distinguish between these two categories. The investment in rent, coal, machinery, freight, etc. is the constant part of the capital; the investment in salaries and wages is its variable portion. All capital, both constant and variable, is created by human labor. Let us not fail to observe immediately that, since the number of Jews in the production of buildings, machines, means of communication, and raw materials is negligible, the Jews as a whole participate but little in the production and in the distribution of *constant capital.* Jewish labor is invested in the production of variable capital, and here too Jews are subject to competition on the part of non-Jewish labor.

The next step in this analysis is the observation that both kinds of capital are in a process of continual expansion. The rate of growth of constant capital, however, is greater than that of variable capital. In a developing technological economy the amount of work done by machinery constantly increases at the expense of human labor. Workers are dropped as new machines are introduced into the process of production. This law, that *constant capital grows at the expense of variable capital,* is one of the most important generalizations in Marxian economic theory. Marx establishes the fact that the machine displaces the worker, and that constant capital displaces variable capital. Since Jewish labor is concentrated exclusively in the production of variable capital, we must conclude that *Jewish labor is being increasingly displaced by non-Jewish labor.*

This is the obviously logical conclusion to which we are driven by Marx's economic theories. The failure of Marx's followers to observe this can be attributed only to their complete failure to examine Jewish economic conditions in the light of scientific principles. The development of technology will inevitably throw Jewish workers out of employment. Jewish labor will inevitably remain technologically backward, because the machine is its most formidable enemy. And all this, in turn, can be explained only by the fact that the Jew is divorced from nature. Fortunately, the displacement of Jewish labor is a slow process rather than a sudden catastrophe. In Europe, Jewish weavers, shoemakers, cabinet makers, and cigar makers are being gradually displaced by non-Jewish labor. With the introduction of the power loom, Jewish weavers in Lodz and Bialystok have become almost entirely a thing of the past and non-Jewish labor operates the machines. The shoe industry in Warsaw and Odessa has passed through the same evolutionary process. The large tobacco factories in Russia are now almost entirely in the hands of Gentile labor.

The Jews are compelled to seek new work; and under this compulsion they migrate to the four corners of the earth, in search of opportunities to develop new industries. Even in the countries where Jews have most recently found a haven, they are relentlessly pursued by the spectre of displacement. In England, where Jews founded a large, modern needle industry, Jewish labor is being displaced by Gentile girls. In America too Jews are losing control of the needle trade, of which they were the founders. Gradually, step by step, they are being eased out of their jobs in the American needle industry by the influx of Italians, Poles, Lithuanians, and Syrians.

As we proceed, it becomes more obvious that the Jewish economic structure is malformed because of its remoteness from nature. The so-called Jewish malady is a result of historical conditions, and is therefore chronic. It is well known that an organism afflicted by a chronic malady may survive for a long time. This is just what has happened to the Jewish national organism: it has adapted itself to this chronic ailment that has tortured it for almost two thousand years. But the Marxian analysis has brought to light another, more disquieting, complication. It warns us that under modern capitalism, the process of displacement will continue to aggravate our condition. After two thousand years, our malady has ceased to be quiescent. It has become acute.

The landlessness of the Jewish people is the source of its malady and tragedy. We have no territory of our own, hence we are by necessity divorced from nature. Therefore, given the recently developed environment of capitalist production and competition, this abnormal circumstance quite naturally assumes proportions of an acute and dangerous nature.

Table 14.2 will furnish us with the data on the efforts the Jewish nation has made to combat this disease.

In Italy, where the number of Jews is very small, their economic, political, and cultural conditions compare favorably with those of their brethren in any part of the world. Jews frequently occupy positions of importance in the political and intellectual life of the land. The statistics in Table 14.2, however, tell us a different story. The economic structure of Italian Jewry is one of the most abnormal and unproductive. Agriculture

TABLE 14.2

Occupational Distribution of 100 Jews and 100 Non-Jews

Branches of Occupations	Italy 1901		Germany 1907		Austria 1900		Russian-Pale 1897		United States 1900	
	Jews	Non-Jews	Jews	Non-Jews	Jews	Non-Jews	Jews	Non-Jews	Jews	Non-Jews
1. Agriculture	0.3	53.3	1.3	33.1	12.8	58.1	2.5	53.0	10.0	35.7
2. Industry	8.7	22.4	21.9	37.4	27.5	22.3	36.2	14.6	48.4	24.4
3. Commerce and Transport	50.3	8.3	50.5	11.1	34.4	5.1	34.6	7.4	28.2	16.4
4. Servants	0.3	1.4	0.5	1.6	5.2	2.2	11.9	11.8	11.2	19.2
5. Professions, Social and Government	18.7	6.4	6.5	5.1	8.3	4.5	7.2	8.2	2.2	4.3
6. Unclassified	21.7	8.2	19.3	11.1	11.8	7.8	7.6	5.0		
Total	100.0	100.0	100.0	100.0	100.0	100.0	100.0	100.0	100.0	100.0

is something almost totally foreign to the Italian Jew. Less than 9 percent of the Jews are engaged in industry, and not as workers but as entrepreneurs. Half of the Italian Jews are merchants. *Almost all Italian Jews obtain their income from the exploitation of foreign labor, chiefly in the nonbasic industries.*

The situation in Germany is not much different. The number of Jews in Germany is twelve times the number in Italy. Their part in the political life of the country is less conspicuous. The economic picture of German Jewry shows a larger proportion of productivity. As many as 22 percent are engaged in industry. Nevertheless, the major contribution of the Jews to the economic life of Germany is still that of capital used for exploitation. Austria has twice as many Jews as Germany. Galicia, Bukovina, and Vienna are densely populated by Jews. Among these masses one observes an urge to return to productive, "natural" occupations. More than one-fourth of the Jews are engaged in industry, and in the majority of cases not as capitalists but rather as wage earners and small-scale owners. Almost 13 percent of the Jews of Austria are engaged in agriculture. In general, then, we have a picture of a substantial number of Jews who have penetrated into the primary and basic levels of production.

In Russia, too, we can discern a similar return to productive occupations. Whereas in all other countries of Europe the Jew lives chiefly by commerce rather than industry, in Russia there is a greater tendency to industrialization. This development has been taking place despite the enormous obstacles imposed by the government. Despite the government restrictions that forbid the Jew to live in rural areas outside of the Pale of Settlement, many Jews are forcing their way back to the soil, to nature. A slow, but fundamental, revolution has been taking place in Jewish life. We have been witnessing the slow transition of the Jewish masses from unproductive to productive occupations. Emigration is the culminating point of this process. American statistics tell us that productive work has become the basis of Jewish economic life, and the Jewish proletarian, the true representative of Jewry.

No statistics are available concerning Palestine and the Argentine, but there is all reason to believe that in these two countries Jewish work has become even more productive, closer to nature and more deeply rooted in the soil than in the United States. And there is further reason to believe that in Palestine, with its Jewish colonies and Jewish agriculture, the economic position of the Jews is still more secure and less subject to the whims of chance. For hundreds of years the Jewish masses have blindly searched for a way that will return them to nature, to the soil. At last we have found it. *Zionism is the way. Zionism is the logical, the natural consequence of the economic revolution* that has been going on within Jewish life for the past few hundred years. Even in the *Galut*, our people have been striving to turn to more "natural" and more productive occupations, but this radical change cannot come to its full fruition in the hostile atmosphere of the *Galut*.

Zionism is the only movement capable of introducing reason, order, and discipline into Jewish life. Zionism is the only answer to the economic and historic need of the Jewish people.

Note

1. Published by the Jewish Colonization Association (title not available, ed.).

15
The Terrorist and the Shomer
(1916)

A slightly built peasant, with an unkempt beard and humble gray eyes bespeaking ceaseless toil, was crouching on his prison bed. Hopeless, embittered, he was perhaps dreaming of the broad earth and of freedom. I shared his prison cell in southern Russia together with several Gentiles who had been arrested for political activities. Once he turned to me all of a sudden and asked: "Pray, esteemed one, will the two new prisoners be hanged?" "I don't know. Probably." The answer tore itself out of my burdened heart. "Why? They were fighting our cause. Is there not enough land for all? . . . The governor thrashed all of us. . . . We blessed them when they shot the governor. Why will they hang them and not us? Is that justice, esteemed one?" Again he became motionless, and I continued to knead the black prison bread into checkers.

"*They are our heroes!*" His frightened thoughts stopped there, his eyes opened wider, and the unimpressive figure of the village rebel seemed to shrink. "*They are our heroes!*" For the first time the peasant understood that strange word. Now he began to grasp the meaning of the word "hero," which he had heard somewhere but which had meant nothing to him.

"They are our heroes"—that naive and pious exclamation rings in my memory when I pour over the *Yizkor* book. Every line, every picture pulsates with this thought: "They are our heroes." One of those two heroes who was about to be hanged for defending the tortured peasants was a Jewish lad. He gave the ardor of his youth and his life for a strange people, an alien nation. He gave his life for freedom in a strange land. He was neither a deep thinker nor a theorist; he did not participate in any discussions at secret gatherings. A fugitive conspirator, he dropped his own name and gave himself Christian names—a different one in every town. To this day I have not learned his Jewish name; I only knew him from occasional meetings at which I discussed the Jewish problem with him. "Oh you chauvinist, you bourgeois—you do not realize that everything depends on the agrarian problem. Give the Russian his land and his freedom and you dispose of the Jewish problem."

This reply used to ring with pleasant firmness. He looked at me as a wealthy philanthropist looks upon an arrogant beggar who spurns his charity. His eyes gleamed with the silent reproach: "I want to offer my life for the cause of freedom, for the land, for the peasants and for you— and you, foolish chauvinist, don't want to accept my sacrifice!" No. I appreciated his sacrifice, and the sacrifice of hundreds of other Jewish youths like him who gave up their dreaming heads for others. But I was not satisfied. They were not *our* heroes. And many of that wonderful generation of enthusiasts died, surrendering their last breath to the Czar's hangmen. The rest became wiser: they gave up their desire for the welfare of the world and turned to material gains. The erstwhile revolutionists became careerists.

But the spirit of our Jewish youth was not entirely crushed in the pursuit of pleasure and of a career. Somewhere that idealism survived. In the depths of the people's hearts there smoldered that urge for great historical deeds. The national spirit glowed with holy ecstasy. And instead of *their* heroes came *our* heroes who gave their lives for the Jewish land and Jewish freedom. The condemned Jewish terrorist found a worthy heir in the Jewish Shomer (guard). The terrorist denied his Jewish name, and went to the gallows with a Christian stamp on his brow. The Shomer changed his ghetto name to a national name—one symbolic of our past history and future hopes. *Their Berl* and *Velvl* became *Anthony* and *Konstantin. Our* new heroes, the Palestinians, come with new names, with names of our own land and freedom—*Shmueli, Ahduti, Reuveni.* Today there are hundreds of them; tomorrow there will be thousands. Some of them have already devoted themselves wholeheartedly to fructify the Jewish land, to renew her with young blood and muscle so that green shoots of Jewish freedom might sprout from her bosom. The Shomrim were the first defenders of the Jewish strongholds in Palestine, the guards of the Jewish national treasure. Some of them fell while performing their voluntary duty. The Russian terrorist was ready to kill and be killed because in his zeal he intended to destroy the ancient structure of despotism, to batter down with his own head the towers of falsehood and darkness. The modern Jewish pioneer went to Palestine not to destroy but to build, not to kill and be killed but to enrich the soil with his peaceful, fruitful labor. However, under the brutal, stubborn conditions of the desolate land he was compelled to arm himself against his semibarbarous neighbors. Our heroes were the opposite of the terrorists. The Shomrim fell with full understanding of the cause they defended.

By the graves of the fallen Jewish workers and guards Jewish youth composed a new and glorious prayer—a prayer of freedom and hope, of pride and dignity, and this prayer was bequeathed to the world in the form of a book. This black-bound book of memories and deeds is known as *Yizkor*. This new *Yizkor* does not bewail the death of these martyrs, it does not wring its hands in the helpless sorrow of *El Malei Rahamin*. *Yizkor* commemorates the souls of the fallen as only a comrade can. The authors of *Yizkor* are not mourners and orphans but warriors who pronounce a solemn oath at the graves of their fallen comrades.

And on Sunday, the living workers and Shomrim will assemble. Then the black-enveloped book will be distributed along with the only bequest of the dead. That bequest is the idealism which the fallen have entrusted to the living. As we assemble, we shall commemorate the names of those young men who abandoned the crowded cities and narrow towns for the glorious hills and broad deserts of Eretz Israel. And over our heads will hover the silent wings of the immortal spirit of the departed—the spirit of peaceful labor, of an emancipated land.

Note

In 1916 the American Poale Zion published a *Yizkor* (memorial) book in honor of the Shomrim (guards) who fell while serving in Hashomer (the guard), the Jewish self-defense group in Palestine. At the same time, Borochov published this in *Di Varhayt* (ed.).

16
Reminiscences: On the Occasion of the Tenth Anniversary of the Poale Zion in Russia, 1906-16

(1916)

This Purim will mark ten years since the founding convention of the Poale Zion Party in Russia. Ten years! It is impossible to transcribe the emotions that rise up in the mind of an "old" party worker like myself when he is reminded of that memorable event. However, let us narrate the rather dry historical facts of the small, hardly distinguishable beginnings from which the convention arose. Let us consider also those historical events which raised our weak and limited undertaking to its present high level.

Here are the facts. The convention, the jubilee of which we shall soon be celebrating, was not "the first." The party had actually existed five years previously and during that time had called several conferences. The Poale Zion idea, the concept of organic unity between socialism and Zionism, had already attained a respectable age. Our idea is not much younger than socialism proper. It was originally formulated by that celebrated German socialist and member of the First International, Moses Hess. A more concrete and modern form of Socialist Zionism was first propounded by our comrade Nachman Syrkin, who is justly considered in our movement as its spiritual father.

Nachman Syrkin first developed his new and militant concept in his speeches and articles on the Jewish question. His lectures were delivered to Russian-Jewish youths studying abroad, and his articles were published in *Das Deutsche Wort* in Vienna. Syrkin's propaganda continued from 1898 to 1901. Its first tangible result was the organization of a group of Socialist-Zionists. Under its auspices in Berlin, Syrkin issued in May 1901, his widely circulated Russian pamphlet: "An Appeal to the Jewish Youth." This was the first official manifesto of Poale Zionism, even though it did not bear that precise name. Syrkin's ideas were developed independently, having little connection with the forgotten philosophy of

Moses Hess. Similarly, in Russia proper there arose an independent Socialist-Zionist movement which had no relationship to Syrkin's propaganda abroad. The first group of socialist, class conscious Poale Zionists in Russia was formed in November 1900, in Ekaterinoslav. Its founders were the writer of these lines and Simon Dobin, who later went over to the Sejmist Party and earned a reputation for being a clever and wholesome Jewish writer.

Permit me to say a little more about this first organization. From September 1900 to May 1901, the writer, who belonged to the Russian Social Democratic Party in Ekaterinoslav, delivered a series of papers on Socialist Zionism to an educational club of intelligent young proletarians. It consisted of about 150 members. Dr. Shmarya Levin, who was then the government-recognized rabbi in Ekaterinoslav, delivered a series of lectures to the same club against the new idea. The lengthy and highly intelligent discussions, in which other prominent Zionist leaders participated (they were all against uniting Zionism and socialism), resulted in the club accepting the new viewpoint and calling itself the Zionist-Socialist Labor Alliance. Its first public appearance was in the organization of a self-defense group during the small pogrom of Passover 1901. Its second appearance was during the strike of men's tailors, during Sukkot of the same year. That was the first strike of Jewish workers in this big city. These things are being disclosed now for the first time. The facts show, above all, that the first Jewish self-defense group was organized by the Poale Zion two and a half years before the Jewish Socialist Bund (in Homel, in September 1903).

Let us now scan rapidly the history of the movement from 1901 to 1906. The name "Poale Zion" was first adopted by a club in Minsk in 1899, under the leadership of A. Litwin (the now well-known American-Jewish writer), Berger, and Rubentchik, after the same group had denied the value of class struggle in the *Galut*. They are the precursors of the so-called Minsker Poale Zion which united with the Socialist-Territorialists in 1907. In 1902 another socialist club called Poale Zion was formed in Odessa, under the influence of Ekaterinoslav and Poltava. Soon there were similar groups and organizations accepting the new ideology scattered all over western Russia. In 1902 they issued their own illegal organ in Russian. An interesting organization of socialist Poale Zionists arose in Vitebsk around 1903. Its theorist was Z. Hirsch, a man of outstanding intellect who had a most tragic fate. (His pupil Chashin is now a well-known party worker.) From Vitebsk, Poale Zionism penetrated into Bund territory in 1903-1905 and spread over Lithuania and Poland. In 1903 the movement was united with its spiritual father, Dr. Nachman Syrkin, through his paper *Haamon* (the masses). A year later the Vozrozhdeniye group was formed, which issued an interesting paper. This group later led to an unfortunate split within the party.

Many splits tore our youthful movement to pieces between 1904 and 1906. The Uganda issue awakened territorial tendencies in many of the young organizations. Even that early fighter for Socialist Zionism, Nachman Syrkin, was for a long time carried away by the current. The Territorialist sections seceded in January 1905 at their first convention in Odessa, wherein they named themselves the Zionist-Socialist Labor Party (the Z.S.). A second split followed in August of the same year, forced by the Vozrozhdeniye group which formed the party. They rejected Palestine together with all Zionist work. At the Kiev conference of the pro-Palestine Poale Zion in July 1905, the Jewish Social Democratic Party Poale Zion was constituted. Shortly after, it sent forty-seven delegates to the Sixth Zionist Congress in Basle. Following the congress, most of the delegates assembled in Zurich and chose a Central Committee. But the Sejmist influence was already being felt, and the Central Committee did not have a chance to see the light of day. In December 1905, the split was completed at a highly dramatic conference in Berdichev. Two organizational conferences were held almost simultaneously; ours in Poltava and the Sejmists' in Kiev.

Thus came that great historical event of our movement, the All-Russian Organizational Convention of the Jewish Social Democratic Labor Party Poale Zion, which finally put an end to all splits. It is the tenth anniversary of this convention that we are now preparing to celebrate. The conference began on Purim eve (February 1906) in Poltava, in the presence of thirty delegates. Meetings were held under cover in the small room of a Jewish bakery on the outskirts of the city. For seven days and nights we sat and slept there, not taking a step outside for fear the Czarist police would notice us. The profoundest theoretical questions and the most difficult organizational problems were courageously and enthusiastically dealt with in that uncomfortable environment. Finally the police did notice us, and we had to transfer ourselves hurriedly to a hotel in the center of the city.

Our "retreat" took place in perfect order, so that the enemy was unable to capture any prisoners of war. Our small army continued its deliberations quite peacefully in the hotel which we had forcibly captured by sternly warning the proprietor not to accept any other guests. The police discovered us even in our new abode, and two prisoners fell into their none-too-gentle hands; but the minutes and other documents were carried to safety in time. We hastily finished the most important organizational work, elected the first Central Committee, and appointed a commission to draw up the party platform. The commission hid itself in a small town in the province of Poltava immediately after the police had surprised us in the hotel. There again ferreted out by the Czarist minions, we transferred ourselves to Simferopol, once more leaving two prisoners in the clutches of the government. The result of the commission's deliberations was the ideological strengthening of our party. One of the resolutions of the conference was to establish the World Poale Zion Confederation.

In the course of these ten years, the Russian Poale Zion has played an important role in the world movement. Our party in Palestine is to some extent the product of the Russian party. The same comrades who organized the movement in Russia participated in establishing and leading the party in Palestine. Russia systematically contributed editors to the party periodicals in Austria, America, England, Palestine, and Argentina. Russia was for a long period the foundry in which Poale Zionist thought was molten and cast for the whole world. The secessionists, the Z.S., and the Sejmists, who in the beginning far surpassed the Poale Zion both numerically and intellectually, quickly disappeared. Their influence over the Jewish community soon evaporated, because everything that was vital in their platforms was already in the program of Poale Zion. We continued to grow in numbers and still more in influence. The day is not far off when the Poale Zion will assume the leadership of the whole Jewish working class. That will be history's judgment of the small, secret conference in the hot and dusty bakery where we were in constant fear of the police.

17
At the Cradle of Zionist Socialism
(1916)

We live in interesting times. Terrible, tragic, ugly, if you will, but interesting just the same. And it would be foolish to long for death before passing through them. But another time—I speak of ten years ago—was even more interesting; in any event it was more beautiful. That was the time that witnessed the founding of the Russian Poale Zion. This Purim will mark ten years since that event and Poale Zionists the world over will celebrate the anniversary. It will be a modest celebration, for our hearts are too heavy to indulge in merrymaking. However, those who were privileged to do battle in those revolutionary years will be filled with emotion. I related the historical facts of that dramatic gathering in the *Kemfer-shtime*, the central organ of America's Poale Zions,[1] but having the opportunity to address myself in these pages[2] to a larger constituency, I shall summon up even more dramatic scenes.

The Jewish Labor movement has been splintered into four distinct Jewish socialist parties. Foremost, claiming to be the "sole champion,"[3] is the Bund. The Bund has long made its reputation on spiritual platitudes, boorishness, irresponsibility, and a total inability for rational thought. But it acted like a Mr. Moneybags, a *nouveau riche*, dispensing favors through its kulak, intimidating all the Jewish artisans and petty bourgeoisie. The Bund always tried to ingratiate itself with the Russian Social Democrats, who were not impressed and refused to acquiesce to the former's ambitions. That's how the Russian socialists are by nature— they fawn over brilliant sophistry and go mad for piquant paradoxes. Some theoreticians! And this is just what the Bund lacked. Plekhanov used to break out laughing: "The Bundist theoreticians, ha, ha!"

But a Jewish socialist not wishing to court favor with his foes, a person who can think straight and wants to fight hard, will run from the Bund as if from a wilderness. And he will be welcomed by the Poale Zion with open arms. But then the Poale Zionists were tearing each other up over conflicting theories. The spiritual father of Socialist Zionism, Dr. Nachman Syrkin only made his amazing discovery a year after the sanctimonious Bund was ushered into life. Yet no one in Russia had an inkling of his new theorems. It was my lot to stumble upon the discovery of Socialist Zionism on my own. It happened in Ekaterinoslav in September 1900, and by November I had already founded the first Socialist Poale Zion group to appear on the globe. The group consisted of 150 souls— high school students who studied at home, and workers.

I belonged at that time to the Russian Social Democratic Party and worked under the supervision of the Ekaterinoslav Social Democratic Committee, which was responsible for the illegal paper *Iuzhnyi Rabochii* (southern worker). The members of that committee who still stand out in my memory are the Christian Pozdniakov (a fellow who was booted out of seminary for atheism), Tzvakoi the Georgian, and the Jew Taratatu. Pozdniakov—who had consumed prodigious amounts of knowledge— and I would drown ourselves in drink and heated discussions on Karl Marx and Richard Avenarius. Both of us—we were all of nineteen— knew Marx's *Capital* by heart, and we would go agitating among the workers, Jews and Gentiles alike, pressing illegal brochures into their hands. I was assigned to read whole chapters of Bogdanov's *Short Course of Economic Science* with the workers, explaining it with illustrations from everyday life. I do not remember what turned me into a nonbeliever. After meeting with both Jewish and Gentile workers, I came to see the truth of Socialist Zionism. The committee noticed my increasingly deleterious effect on the workers and charged that I was teaching them to think independently. I was quite unceremoniously given the boot by the Russian Social Democratic Party. Years later, Pozdniakov reverted into a devout Christian mystic, abandoning socialism altogether, and the Jew Taratatu adopted terrorist anarchism, falling in an armed clash with an entire pack of Cossacks. I have no idea what became of the Georgian Tzvokoi.

What does a banished Russian Social Democrat turned Zionist "infidel" do? He immediately marches off to a large Jewish home-study student union and converts them into the first Poale Zionists in Russia. Menachem-Mendel Ussishkin, the head of the Zionists in the Ekaterinoslav region, was a man of iron and steel. He actually boasted about living on the corner of "Iron" and 'Stubborn" Streets, since these were really their Russian names. Sternly and categorically he declared, "I won't let such heretical ideas past me." Dr. Shmarya Levin, then the official rabbi for Ekaterinoslav, was also not impressed by my socialist accomplishment and—in his inimitably refined and cultured manner—tried to drive home his polite but steadfast convictions. He even ventured to the seat of the heresy, the home-study union, to lecture against Socialist Zionism. The youngsters, however, paid their elders no mind and established themselves as the Zionist Socialist Workers' Alliance. Its first order of the day was organizing an armed self-defense operation during the flash pogrom which hit Ekaterinoslav on Passover 1901. This was the first such self-defense group in Russia—i.e. three years before the Bund organized one. The alliance's second action was leading the male garment workers' general strike on Sukkot 1901—the first major strike by Jewish workers in southern Russia. It included over 300 laborers.

We shall skip how our young movement grew and spread throughout all of Russia and, in the next three years, through Austria too. It finally split into three parties: the Territorialist Socialist Party (the Z.S.), the Diasporist Sejmists, and the Palestinian Poale Zionists. Fate determined that your humble servant was positioned at the heart of these raging, schismatic confrontations. That is why I remember them as if they happened yesterday. The Poltava regional committee convened the founding assembly of the Poale Zion, thus putting an end to the splintering process and making possible this tenth jubilee we are celebrating today.

The gathering occured on Purim 1906 in a cramped, smoke-filled storeroom of a Jewish bakery on Poltava's outskirts. I remember thirty delegates by name, and no less than thirty of them now work for the party. Such prominent comrades as Ben-Zvi, Zrubovel, Aleksander Hashon, Itzhak Zar, and Rachel Yanait were among these delegates. The thirty of us sat around for seven days and nights squeezed between four closed walls, not even once sticking our noses out the door, so that the Czarist police wouldn't catch on. Thirty delegates from across the width and breadth of Russia—from Warsaw, Lodz, Bialystok, Vitebsk, Odessa, Kishiniev, Simferopol, Kiev, Berditchev—all told fifty cities (several cities grouped into a region would send a delegate apiece to cut down on the participants—more people, more danger) eventually representing 16,000 party members in good standing.

Cramped between these four walls we ate together, slept on the hard floor and dispensed with mountains of theoretical and practical problems like the national question, the Jewish question, socialism, and the Russian Revolution, colonization in Eretz Israel, armed insurrection against Czarism, the notion of a World Confederation of Poale Zion, trade unions, and so on. In the end the police got wind of us and we had to rush willy-nilly into an inn in the center of town. This "express shuttle" took off without a hitch and the enemy could not claim a single "prisoner-of-war." We stormed the inn and took it by force—it was one of the town's showplaces—and warned the proprietor and waiters not to take on a single additional boarder. Here we spent the days like lords, going on with our deliberations. As God is my witness, we would have paid the proprietor cash for room and board had not the police finally broken in on us.

The enemy managed to grab two "prisoners-of-war," but no documents or protocols which we had safely secured. The authorities came out of all this shamefaced, since there was not a whit of evidence against the suspects. To this very day there are still seven pounds of dynamite buried in the bakery courtyard; another twenty pounds and seven set incendiary-bombs were discovered later when they arrested comrades B.Z.R. and me. But in any event, the Poltava regional committee held on to an arsenal in the event of a pogrom or any emergency which might arise. Following this debacle, most of the delegates rushed back to where they had come from, but not before selecting an ad hoc theoretical commission. The latter holed itself up for awhile in a hamlet in the Poltava district. In rapid flight before the scent of the Czarist spies, it reassembled in Simferopol. There it completed its mission of hammering out the party platform and, by the by, the Crimean region was usurped from the Sejmists; their illegal press was commandeered and the Poale Zion's hold over Crimea was consolidated.

This is how things were done in those days. . . . Our party was born in such trying circumstances. Its cradle was the Russian Revolution, and bursts of gunfire were the infant party's first lullabies. It's no wonder, then, that the child grew up molded not from cotton but from steel.

Notes

1. See preceding chapter (ed.).
2. I.e. in the newspaper *Di Varhayt* (ed.)
3. I.e. of the Jewish workers (ed.)

18
A. Lieberman:
Father of Jewish Socialism
(1917)

Forty years have elapsed since the Jewish socialist press made its first appearance. The Hebrew journal *Haemet* (the truth), the first Jewish socialist publication, made its debut in Vienna in May 1877. The journal and its publisher and editor Aaron Lieberman, are among the most interesting and extraordinary phenomena of modern Jewish history. To understand this first Jewish socialist publication and the period in which it originated, we must first study the man Lieberman, who truly deserves the title: "Father of Jewish Socialism."

Aaron Shmuel Lieberman (later known as Arthur Freeman, his pen names being *Bar Drora* and *Daniel Ish-Hamudot*) was born about 1848 in the town of Luna, in the province of Grodno, Russia. He received his education in the larger cities of Sowolke and Vilna. Independently, both he and his father (a Hebrew teacher tutoring in the homes of the well-to-do) fell under the influence of the Haskalah. Thus the young Lieberman was spared the conflict the free-thinking youths of that period had with their pious parents. In his father's home, Lieberman obtained the knowledge of Hebrew language and literature. Throughout his life he was a fanatical devotee of Hebrew, the language of his socialist propaganda. In accordance with the Jewish custom of those days, the future nihilist married at an early age and was already a father when he entered the Rabbinical school in Vilna. In the 1870s the Rabbinical school in Vilna was a center of enlightened, liberal, and even revolutionary thought. Several pupils were aware of the socialist movement among the Russian intelligentsia; and two. Aaron Liberman and his younger friend, Zundelevitch (born in 1854), were active socialist propagandists.

The years 1873-78 were important in the Russian revolutionary movement. That period marked the commencement of the interesting movement of "mingling with the people." The social-revolutionary intelligentsia learned manual trades, dressed as peasants and workers, and mingled with the masses, thereby spreading revolutionary ideas. The spiritual leader of this movement was P. Lavrov, who published a biweekly journal, *Vperod*, which was printed in London and illegally circulated in Russia. Jewish youth was not unaffected by this propaganda that gave birth to the *Chorni Peredial* and the terrorist activities of the Narodnaya Volya. Among the more prominent Jewish names actively identified with the underground movement of the 1870s were the Levinthal brothers, Axelrod, Aronson, Lazare Goldenberg, Goldstein, L. Zuckerman, Jessie Helfman, and Gotz. Jewish socialist writers such as M. Vintchevsky, L. Cantor, Yahalal, and M. Lilienblum appeared on the scene. The pogroms disillusioned the last three in the revolutionary ideals, and they joined the Hibat Zion movement.

Zundelevitch and Lieberman were original. Whereas other Jewish socialists agitated among the Gentile workers or were contented with merely writing Hebrew poetry on social problems, the two young students of the Rabbinical school attempted to win the Jewish masses over to socialism. This was a unique approach, for at that time not only Gentile but also Jewish intellectuals negated the economic role of the Jewish masses. Jews are not fit for productive work, they claimed; they are by nature brokers, merchants, money lenders and parasites—in short, an element that is not susceptible to socialist propaganda. Zundelevitch and Lieberman were more intimately acquainted with the Jewish masses. Being themselves proletarians and raised among the Jewish proletariat, they knew that the Jewish masses lived by their own toil—that the Jewish people was not a people of exploiters and parasites but of exploited and oppressed workers.

They therefore devoted themselves to the dissemination of socialist propaganda among the Jewish masses. With this aim in mind, Zundelevitch organized a group of young Jewish intellectuals in Vilna. But he was soon drawn into the Russian political movement and left for St. Petersburg, where he established an illegal press, fell into the clutches of the Czarist police, and was sentenced to Siberia. He was not freed until thirty years later, during the 1905 Revolution. Lieberman made a timely escape from the Czarist police by fleeing abroad, where he devoted the rest of his short life to spreading socialist propaganda among Jews. Immediately after his escape he organized in Berlin the Jewish Group of the Internationale, consisting of Jewish socialist émigrés from Russia. He then left for London, where he worked on Lavrov's *Vperod*. He also organized a Jewish socialist society—the first in Jewish history. The membership was a comparatively large one for that period, totaling thirty-seven, mostly workers. Lieberman was himself a worker, earning his living as a lithographer.

The records of this society are to be found in the archives of the Foreign Committee of the Bund at Geneva. Lieberman was the secretary of the branch. The title page reads:

RECORD OF THE SOCIETY OF
THE HEBREW SOCIALISTS OF LONDON

Founded Iyar 26, in the Year 5636, May 20, 1876

The record contains the program of the society, written in Hebrew as well as in Yiddish (although the minutes of sessions were in Yiddish). The first Jewish socialist program states in part:

> We are convinced that the present order, which holds sway everywhere, is ruthless and unjust. The capitalists, rulers, and clergy have taken unto themselves all human rights and property and have enslaved the working masses through the power of their money.

> As long as private ownership continues, economic misery shall not cease; as long as humanity is divided into nations and classes, hatred will not cease; as long as the clergy continues to sway the emotions of the people, religious hatred will continue.

> The liberation of humanity can be achieved only through a basic change in the political, economic, and social relations—by uprooting the existing order and constructing in its place a new society based on socialism, which will abolish the injustice and domination of capital and will eradicate the parasites and the system of "mine" and "thine."

> We Jews are an integral part of humanity, and cannot be liberated except through the liberation of all humanity.

> The liberation of humanity from misery and slavery can be achieved by the workers only if they unite in a struggle against their despoilers, destroy the existing order, and replace it by the reign of labor, justice, freedom, and the fraternity of mankind.

> The workers of Europe and America have united in various societies to achieve their aim and are preparing for a revolution, for the establishment of the reign of labor socialism [*Sotsialismus laavoda* in the Hebrew text]. Therefore, we, the children of Israel, have decided to affiliate ourselves with this noble Alliance of Labor.

This program was written by Lieberman and was unanimously accepted by the society. The society existed seven months, disbanding with Lieberman's departure from London.

During his stay in London, he published the first socialist proclamation in Hebrew. Commencing with *El Shlomei Bahurei Israel* (to the intelligent youths of Israel), he appealed to the youths to devote their energy to the public welfare and participate in the struggle for the emancipation of the working masses of all people. In a biblical style he portrays the awakening of the Jewish masses and their struggle against their Jewish exploiters. The Jewish people will soon recognize their enemies and will exclaim:

> Thus have your sins been visited upon us; your crimes have caused us sorrow. You have brought upon us the anger of the sword and the crash of thunder and lightning. Your sin has inflamed against us the hatred of the people; your treacherous hand has carried a blaze of religious hatred against us. Sharpened swords have been cast at us and have pierced through the bodies of thousands of our brethren. You have humiliated our people. Your deceit in trade has branded the Jewish people, the very same people whom your plundering has suppressed and tortured, to a much greater extent than all other evildoers on earth.

This proclamation was signed by the Loyal Volunteers of the People of the House of Israel. The proclamation showed deep love for the Jewish people and humanity. The opening of the proclamation was: "We, the friends of the Jewish people and of all the suffering masses. . . ."

After his departure from London, Lieberman settled in Vienna where he became acquainted with the conservative and nationalist publicist Peretz Smolenskin, and for a short time was a contributor to the latter's periodical, *Hashahar* (dawn). But he soon went his own way; and in May of 1876 he founded *Haemet*, the first Jewish socialist organ (mentioned above). Although Lieberman cloaked his writings in metaphors to escape Czarist censors, *Haemet* did not have a long life; the Viennese authorities shut it down after the third issue and arrested its editor. He was extradited by the Prussian police and was tried in Berlin with two other Russian-Jewish socialists (Hurwich and Aaronson, a brother-in-law of Eduard Bernstein). Lieberman was sentenced to prison (according to some, for fifteen months; according to others, for nine months) and was not freed until January 1880. All in all he spent two years in the prison of Vienna, in continuous danger of being handed over to the Russian authorities.

Prison life affected Lieberman's mental balance. A tragic love affair in London and America, where he went after his liberation, did not help restore it. On November 18, 1880, the father of Jewish socialism committed suicide in Syracuse, New York. His last written words were: "Long live the world! He who finds only misery and pain is doomed to die. Do not accuse me ere you have put yourself in my position."

Only three issues of *Haemet* appeared. It contained insufficient material from which to glean the *Weltanschauung* of that period in general and of Aaron Lieberman in particular. We do not even have a clear idea as to which articles and notices were Lieberman's own products. It seems that he was far from scientific socialism and Marx and Engels. Marxian literature forty years ago was little known and even less recognized. The socialism of *Haemet* has an idealistic and scholarly character. Lieberman's prospectus in *Haemet* stated:

> The darkness which to this day governs the minds of the majority is the father of all evil. It has penetrated to the base of society and has shattered its foundation. Darkness has paved the road for deceit. With its aid brutal rulers have enslaved the people. . . . The people knows endless pain . . . and is degenerating through ignorance. The people cannot choose between evil and good. Only truth can bring enlightenment to the human mind and distinguish good from evil.

> Champions of justice are to be found among all peoples. Only our Jewish literature has lacked *emet* (truth); for since prophecy ceased among the Jewish people, our writers have ceased to take an interest in the miserable life and needs of the people.

Characteristic of Lieberman was his uncritical assumption that the Jews understood Hebrew. The outstanding theoretical work in *Haemet* was Liberman's "The Struggle for Existence and Its Relation to the Life of Society" (the leading article of the second issue). He concluded that the struggle for existence was forcing humanity to unite into one society and that "solidarity is the best weapon in the struggle of life." The sketches and poetry of *Haemet* are replete with socialist thoughts and sentiments. A few articles, such as the leading one in the first issue, dealt with the Jews, including those of Hungary and London.

Immediately after Lieberman's death, J.A. Trivaush in his novel *Dor Tahapuhot* (the confused generation), pictured his hero Aaron Lieberman in the role of "Frank." He knew him intimately and portrayed him as a man of inner contradictions. On one hand he was a nihilist, discrediting the past and denying the right of existence of all nations, including the Jewish people; on the other hand, he was a fanatical Hebraist and lover of the Jewish people. Morris Vintchevsky, his personal friend, in his excellent "Memoirs" pictured Lieberman as stormy, paradoxical, and artistic.

The documents of the founder of Jewish socialism reveal his deep conflict: denying the existence of a Jewish people, while elsewhere expressing almost Zionist thoughts. S.L. Zitron (in *Hed Hazman*) and M.K. (in *Hashiloah*) relate that in his long discussions with Peretz Smolenskin, Lieberman "negated the historical past and dismissed the national problem." Lieberman's leading article in the first issue of *Haemet*, devoted to the Jewish problem, categorically denied the existence of a

Jewish people, as may be seen from this quotation: "We Jews do not possess a culture of our own which differentiates and isolates us from the nations among whom we live. . . . Any bond which may ever have existed between us has long been torn asunder." Thus wrote an author *who spoke to Jews in the name of Jews in the ancient Hebrew tongue* which for centuries served as the cultural tie of our scattered people!

The previously mentioned records of the London society illuminate a different characteristic of Lieberman. The minutes of the tenth meeting, held on the second of *Av*, 1876, contain Lieberman's motion that the next meeting, which should have been held on the ninth of *Av*, be postponed. This move was opposed by George Saper, who said: "We socialists are not interested in *Tisha b'Av*. We have renounced ancient tradition. . . . We are interested in the equality of humanity." To which Lieberman replied: "At the present time *Tisha b'Av* has the same significance for us Jewish socialists as it has for all Jews; for as long as the social revolution has not taken place, political freedom is of prime importance to every people. To the Jewish people it is of the utmost importance. On this day we lost our independence, for which our people has mourned for the past 1800 years." The society agreed to Lieberman's proposal and postponed the meeting.

Lieberman's cosmopolitanism came from the prevailing belief of the socialists of all nations that they were on the eve of the social revolution. Lieberman refused to publish advertisements in his *Haemet*. Expecting the social revolution at any moment, he avoided anything that might have identified socialism with the present order. He considered both nationalism and advertising to be capitalist phenomena, which might carry a bourgeois spirit into the Labor movement. The father of Jewish socialism did not succeed in creating harmony between his deep Jewish national instinct and his carefully construed socialist philosophy.

His picture of the Russian martyrs, published by M. Vintchevsky in the *Zukunft* (1909, p. 88), was an artistic achievement. Artistic tendencies were also noticeable in his handwriting, preserved in the archive of the Bund in Geneva and in the New York Public Library. These writings reveal a soul full of beauty and artistry. Lieberman's friend, Hurwich, relates a most unique incident in *Biloia*. He tells us that Lieberman presented a most extraordinary gift to his deified teacher, Lavrov. The gift was his own hat, with the following note: "As it is impossible for me to send you my head, I send you my hat."

Lieberman's tragic inner struggles drove him to suicide. The father of Jewish socialism died before the advent of the Russian pogroms—they might have clarified his attitude to the Jewish problem.

19
Facing Reality
(1917)

Zionism is facing reality, while the enemies of Zion are turning their backs on it. What we predicted about fifteen years ago, and again at the beginning of the World War, has now become a fact. The question of a Jewish national autonomous homeland has been placed on the agenda of world politics. For the present, this is all—no more but also no less. This is unquestionably a victory for all Zionists. Were it not for the twenty years of intense Zionist propaganda and for the ten years of practical revolutionary work in Palestine, this question would have never been seriously considered and world diplomacy would have never been seriously interested in it. Only people with a naive conception of politics could imagine that this question would have been given any consideration if there were no great Zionist movement. As a matter of fact, the Zionist movement has played second fiddle to none in bringing about this result—not even to the British march on Palestine. It will be well for our friends to remember this, and surely it will not be harmful for others to take note of it.

No question of rights is ever raised until those directly interested demand them. History proves that the Jews secured their rights only after they demanded them and only in that measure to which they fought for them. The English and Dutch revolutions of the seventeenth century did not bring full equality because the Jews made their demands too late. Before the revolution of 1848, the Jewish emancipation movement was very weak; and, therefore, that revolution brought them but little relief. For fifty years Jewish emancipation movements were active in Russia. Hence, the Russian Revolution immediately broke the chains of the Jewish people. The Russian Jews, however, were almost as instrumental in bringing about their freedom as was the Revolution. If our hearts are filled with gratitude to the Russian nation and the Russian working class for our emancipation, we must give the same wholehearted thanks and recognition to the Jewish *maskilim* of the 1860s and 1870s, to the Jewish Socialist Bund, and to the Socialist-Zionists, through whose struggles the result was made possible.

I go further. Outside agents often have less influence in bringing about the emancipation of an oppressed people than does the conscious effort of the people itself. Emancipation is after all the concern of the enslaved, of the working class, and of all oppressed peoples. Civil rights for the Jews of Central Europe in 1867-1870 were not effected by a revolution, but came as the result of an active struggle for these rights and as a result of the strengthening of constitutional principles in Austria, Hungary, and Germany.

The factors responsible for the recognition of our civil rights will also bring about the recognition of our national-political rights in Palestine and our autonomous national rights in the *Galut*. To be sure, external political situations must be favorable; but what we need primarily is a strong movement within Jewry to focus worldwide attention upon our interests—a movement which shall make use of every favorable political situation, and, whenever necessary, take advantage of every suitable alignment with other political forces.

From a political point of view, propaganda is less productive than action. *Establish facts and more facts—that is the cornerstone of political strategy.* Facts are more convincing than phrases. Accomplishments are of greater influence than proclamations. Sacrifices are better propaganda than resolutions. The Bund, for example, played a more important role in the emancipation of Russian Jewry than all the apologetic literature on the question of Jewish rights produced during a period of fifty years. The Bund did not content itself with talk but fought and made sacrifices. It established political facts, small and insignificant in their isolation, but in combination building up one great fact which has now borne fruit. (I refer, of course, only to the former *positive* achievements of the Bund.)

The same is true of Zionism. The practical colonization work in Palestine, with its experiences, sacrifices, and inevitable mistakes, has created those political *facts* which have paved the way for our present status. No matter how small and weak the Jewish colonies might be, no matter how great the shortcomings in their system of colonization—they did more toward enlightening the Jewish nation than a thousand beautifully worded programs and diplomatic negotiations. A fallen Shomer plays a greater role in the realization of Zionism than all declarations.

The best guarantee of Zionism lies not in a charter but in the Zionist movement. The guarantee lies in the organization of the Zionists and Socialist-Zionists. I said this fifteen years ago, and I will not cease reiterating it even now when the world is so carried away by current political and diplomatic events. I am not fearful of the disillusionment which may follow. The sole danger lies in confusion. One must not fail to see the trees because of the forest. The beautiful forest of political perspectives for Zionism can exist only because of its trees—the practical accomplishments of the Zionist movement.

Meanwhile, our goal has not been fully achieved. It is still in the process of realization. We must remember that Palestine is not yet ours. We still have no official promise that we are going to get Palestine. It is true, nevertheless, that Zionism has finally become a serious matter in world politics. This great victory for the Zionist movement must ultimately result in substantial dividends—even though we may suffer temporary setbacks. Ostensibly, the first Russian Revolution (1905) was a fearful fiasco, but today it has borne fruit with a vengeance. That tragic revolution with its tragic disappointment dealt the true deathblow to Czarism. Likewise, our latest victory has dealt a deathblow to the *Galut* ideology and to reactionary anti-Zionism.

Anti-Zionism has been mortally wounded. The world may now see that anti-Zionism has no sound psychological or social foundation, that it is thoroughly decadent, that it represents reactionary and obscurantist issues in Jewish life. The enemies of Zion, who brazenly turn their backs on life and freedom, do not realize that life has answered them in kind by turning her back on them. I repeat, the gain will be permanent even if the existing diplomatic negotiations bring no positive results. Let us hope that world events will so shape themselves that they will contribute to the highest interests of mankind and the Jewish people. The World War is progressing from its imperialistic phase to its revolutionary phase. Let us hope that it will end with a thorough emancipation of all peoples.

It is almost certain that England will conquer Palestine, Mesopotamia, and Syria. It is almost certain, too, that revolutions will make an end of the Hohenzollerns, the Hapsburgs, and the chauvinism of the Young Turks. If so, a Jewish republic in Palestine is destined to come. But, who knows? Is it not possible that the wheels of history will take a queer turn and Zionism, like other revolutionary hopes, will be disappointed; that the knights of Jewish assimilation and *Galut* opportunists, together with other reactionaries, will once again come out the "victors"? Yet, one positive fact will remain. Once placed on the table of world politics, the Palestine question will not be removed from there. The Zionist movement will, through its practical accomplishments, bring the problem to its ultimate solution—an assured and autonomous homeland for the Jewish people in Palestine. Zionism is the only answer to the economic and historic needs of the Jewish people. It will be realized through the Zionist movement, through the Poale Zion, and through our labors and struggles.

20
Eretz Israel in Our Program and Tactics

(1917)

Time in its flight has not passed us by; it has brought to the fore new slogans and deeds. Twelve years ago, our party, the Poale Zion, made its first appearance as an organized body. Since then, the proletariat in general and the Jewish proletariat in particular have made progress. Hitherto the proletariat sought to remove only its immediate obstacles; now it strives to create a new society. Our program, too, must keep pace with our growing aspirations. Our terminology must become richer and more elastic. Formerly we approached life from a naive, abstract point of view, and only our immediate demands were prompted by purely realistic conditions. Now, however, there have arisen in Jewish life cultural and aesthetic needs which demand immediate self-expression.

Socialism has several aspects. Economically, it means the socialization of the means of production; politically—the establishment of the dictatorship of the toiling masses; emotionally—the abolition of the reign of egotism and anarchy that characterizes the capitalist system. And so it is with Zionism. Economically, it means the concentration of the Jewish masses in Palestine; politically—the gaining of territorial autonomy; emotionally—the striving for a home. Recent times have witnessed a desire on our part to give expression to these emotions. And we need not fear what our neighbors will say. . . .

Twelve years ago, we clung to the epigram "Better a Jew without a beard than a beard without a Jew." Then we did not attach any significance to form and to the aesthetic aspects of life. It had to be that way, for then our battle was fought on two fronts: the Bundist and the General Zionist. Lest we be confused with the latter we had to be cautious in our terminology. But even then, we did not fear non-*kosher* terms. Our program of that time always employed the term *Jewish Nation.* But times have changed. The difference between our party and the others is sufficiently clear. No one will mistake our identity. It is therefore an opportune time to introduce a newer and richer terminology. Now we can and must employ an emotional terminology. Now we can and must proclaim: "Eretz Israel—a Jewish home!"

Our chief concern, however, is our program. The class interests of the Jewish proletariat remain unchanged. Our ultimate aim is socialism; our immediate need is Zionism. The class struggle is the means to achieve both. Our class struggle, however, is an abnormal one. It is largely thwarted by the prevailing conditions under which our people live and by the national struggle—the conflict between the forces of production and the conditions of production, as I have outlined elsewhere.[1]

In the past, the international socialist proletariat was weak. It was not interested in foreign policy nor in the national problem. But times have changed. The Socialist conferences in Zimmerwald and Stockholm indicate a new epoch in the struggle of the world proletariat. But does the Jewish worker keep pace with these new trends? In spite of his enthusiasm and tremendous revolutionary energy, the Jewish worker exerts but little influence. He is as impotent as the rock-bound Prometheus. This tragic plight compels him to demand a home for the Jewish people. This home will serve as a strategic base for the creative efforts of the Jewish worker in all fields of human endeavor.

Years ago we said: Zionism is a "stychic" process. Our only task is to remove all the obstacles which interfere with this process. And we left the creative work to the bourgeois Zionists. There are two types of stychic processes: the mechanical and the organic. We erred formerly when we contended that natural emigration waves were already under way. General Zionists were closer to the truth when they said that for the present only the organic process had begun. It is clear now that what motivated our previous mechanical conception was our reaction to the Zionists' assertion that the will of our nation is the *sole* determining factor in Zionism.

Our experiments in Palestine have taught us a new lesson. Colonization there is an especially difficult task. But in spite of the difficulties and temporary failures, colonization in Palestine is developing and is gradually approaching the socialist ideal. I refer, of course, to the cooperatives, particularly to those pursuing the Oppenheimer plan. Cooperative colonization in which the Jewish worker plays a very great role is also the way to a socialist society in Palestine. While this colonization is not in itself socialism, it does teach the Jewish proletariat the elementary lessons of self-help. Small as the *yishuv* is, the Jews enjoy an autonomous life and have their own courts, post offices, and banking system. Jewish labor has gradually become enrooted even in such a small *yishuv*. The Jewish working class is not as yet large; it nevertheless plays a prominent role.

Its organizations and institutions, such as Hashomer and the Palestine Workers' Fund, are publicly recognized.

It is important to note that Palestine is a semiagrarian country, and hence it is adapted to the Jewish city-bred immigrant. It is also the center of Jewish public interest. It may also be said that Palestine is the cynosure of all Jewish eyes—its every activity commands the attention of friend and foe. In the last analysis this is the best guarantee for its proper development. Many point out the obstacles we encounter in our colonization work. Some say that the Turkish law hinders our work; others contend that Palestine is insignificantly small; and still others charge us with the odious crime of wishing to oppress and expel the Arabs.

According to the latest investigations (e.g. Ben-Zvi's), Palestine's boundaries include eighty or ninety thousand square kilometers, a land capacity sufficient to hold tens of millions of inhabitants. But even in its present limited boundaries, Palestine's twenty-seven thousand square kilometers can accommodate up to nine million people, whereas now it is even short of a half-million. It is understood, of course, that the Turkish rule and prevailing system will cease. The war will create a change. When the waste lands are prepared for colonization, when modern technique is introduced, and when the other obstacles are removed, there will be sufficient land to accommodate both the Jews and the Arabs. Normal relations between the Jews and Arabs will and must prevail.

I repeat that we must originate independent activities in Palestine. We cannot merely content ourselves, as we have done until now, with the work of bourgeois Zionists and with our critical attitude toward it. We must define anew our stand toward the various Zionist institutions. We cannot participate in the Zionist Congress as long as it is a party tribune. We will, however, participate in a world Jewish congress because it will be a national tribune, having a semiparliamentary status. We are sympathetic to the Jewish National Fund, and as individuals we may even give it our support. But our official fund is the Palestine Workers' Fund, which deserves our full support. Similarly we must support the cooperative colonization movement. In short, we must initiate a socialist program of activities in Palestine. Then the Jewish worker, like the rock-bound Prometheus, will free himself from the vultures that torture him and will snatch the heavenly fires for himself and for the Jewish people.

Note

1. See chapters 2 and 3 of this volume (ed.).

Appendix:
Declaration to the
Hollando-Scandinavian Socialist
Committee Submitted by the Jewish
Socialist Labor Confederation
Poale Zion

(Stockholm, August 6, 1917)

In the name of all the organizations affiliated with the Jewish Socialist Labor Confederation Poale Zion, we heartily greet the activities favoring peace conducted by the Russian Council of Workmen and Soldiers' Deputies and the Hollando-Scandinavian Socialist Committee. We acclaim every step that can bring the world nearer to the ardently desired peace. We acclaim it the more heartily since the Jewish proletariat of all countries, in spite of all disappointments, has not for a moment during the war been shaken in its international sentiments and in its faith in mankind. The brotherhood of nations is a very ancient ideal of our people. The Jewish nation which has, as it were, hostages alike in all countries does not purpose to realize its national aspirations by armed force. The Jewish people is well aware that it can only prosper and strive for its national aims in an atmosphere of mutual benevolence and peaceful cooperation among peoples.

We see the main purpose of the impending deliberations to be: to oppose the war aims of the various states by the will to peace and the conditions of peace of a reunited world proletariat, and to organize the struggle for peace. The imperialist governments, which have on their consciences the horrible, universal slaughter, are unable to control the unchained elements of destruction: they have neither the power to consummate their war purposes nor the courage to relinquish them. The bleeding human race awaits its deliverer. The international proletariat must become conscious of its historical mission to take into its hands the destiny of nations, to establish a peace that will preclude the danger of future wars by the strength of its union and to pave the way for the social emancipation of mankind. The Jewish proletariat hopes that when the national questions are considered, the Jewish question will receive the position on the order of the day due it.

We beg leave to point to two factors which, in our opinion, combined very potently at the outbreak of the war to cause the crisis in the International. In the first place, it is common knowledge that authoritative groups in the International met the question of nationalities with rather little understanding and systematically ignored it. It thus occurred that sections of the working class, intimidated and excited at the critical moment by war inciters, could not clearly differentiate between *nationalistic* chauvinism and the wholesome leaven of *nationalist* thought, and succumbed to nationalistic ideology. To accomplish its lofty mission of the brotherhood of nations, the International must recognize the vital interest of nations and must become the guardian of all oppressed peoples. We agree with the opinion of the Social Democratic Party of Bosnia and Herzegovina that the *peoples* and not the states are to be considered as a basis for international negotiations. As to the composition of the International itself, the hitherto dominating practice of state representation shall be supplemented by representation of nations as well, so that the equality of nations without regard to political frontiers shall also be realized in its organization.

On the other hand, the International has never yet been anything but a loose alliance of the socialist parties of the various states. It could in no way avail itself of the united forces of the international workmens' movement. The International, only when it becomes the highest legislative and executive body of the organized proletariat of the world, will be able to oppose successfully the policy of force of the states and to implement the socialist policy of reconciliation of peoples. We agree with the proposal that all the participants of the next Stockholm Conference consider themselves bound strictly to abide by its decisions.

General Principles of Peace. We concur in the demand for *general disarmament, democratization of foreign policies, neutralization* of the *international highways* on land and sea, *free commerce* and traffic, *free immigration,* colonization and settlement, and the unlimited *right of every nation to determine its own destiny.* To realize these aims which will create a new international law, there must be established *extragovernmental bodies* invested with necessary authority to guard the conscientious observance of international treaties. The League of Nations, which has become a historical necessity, can have no prospect of duration if it should contain all the contradictions and antagonisms which ignited the world conflagration. It is an incontestable fact that national conflicts play a preeminent role in the present catastrophe. The war has clearly shown how every oppression of a nationality can disturb international amity and constitute a peril to mankind. The League of Nations can only be a union of free nations. The watchword "peace without annexation" appears in its full meaning only in connection with the simultaneously announced principle of the right of every nation to self-determination. But should this principle be realized, the settlement of the rights of national autonomy in states composed of different nationalities ought not to be left to the states, but should be internationally guaranteed in a treaty of peace; the various forms of national autonomy should similarly be decided in a treaty of peace.

The national question will certainly be resolved in nationally unified territories through the creation of new independent states and through the introduction of national territorial autonomy. In territories of mixed nationalities this question will arise again in another form and will become even more acute, unless provision is made for the *protection of minority nationalities.* As the rights of nations generally, so the rights of minority nationalities must be internationally settled and guaranteed. For the minority nationality, the principle of personal autonomy, i.e. of extraterritoriality, is essential. We concur in the demands of the Ukrainian and Czech delegations to the effect that: "on establishing an international Court of Arbitration, a special committee is to be created for the maintenance and protection of the rights of peoples. Each nationality considering its rights infringed by another nationality or by its own state is entitled to submit its grievance to the above committee and to demand international intervention."

The Jewish Question. We demand that an international guarantee of the rights of the Jewish people be included in the treaty of peace. In spite of the loss of their independence, of having been torn from their native soil, of being dispersed, and of continually wandering, the Jewish masses remain a *nation,* united by a common history, language, culture, custom, and peculiar economic position; and to preserve their national homogeneity and individuality, they have made the greatest sacrifices. The depriving of great masses of Jews of human rights in Russia and Rumania for decades, has beclouded the fact that the Jewish question is essentially a *national question.* The Russian Revolution civilly emancipated the Jews of that country, and it is to be expected that other countries where Jews are deprived of civil rights, will be forced to follow this example. But contrary to the French Revolution, the Russian Revolution will also be a pioneer. Thus in all countries where masses of

Jews are settled, the question of national emancipation is coming to the foreground.

The demand for the international guarantees of Jewish equality is much more justified since the Jewish question assumes an *international character*. The gathering of large Jewish masses in Eastern Europe, America, and the Near East, the influence of their situation in one country upon the other, their lack of national rights in most states, the fact that Jewish minorities are employed against their will as instruments of oppression of other nationalities, the continual flow of hundreds of thousands of déclassé Jewish emigrants from one country to another, the catastrophic character of Jewish emigration at moments of increased economic and political pressure—all raise the Jewish question to a position of international significance.

The settlement of the Jewish question by the treaty of peace is inevitable. Constituting a minority in all countries, our nation is threatened by the dangers of compulsory assimilation and national dissolution, which are calculated to make illusory even civil equality, unless the suggested guarantees are realized. At the same time, the Jewish nation is in need of organization for national self-administration to solve the unique problems of its existence. In accord with the entire Jewish proletariat, we demand a *personal autonomy* for our people in all countries where they are settled in masses, and particularly in states of mixed nationalities such as Russia, Austria, and the new territories of self-government and states which are to be created, such as Ukraine, Lithuania, Poland, etc.

We intercede for the establishment of an independent *Poland,* but demand at the same time securities and international guarantees for the rights of the Jewish people as citizens, and as a nationality. The attitude taken by Polish circles that the Jews renounce their nationality leaves no doubt that without such guarantees the new Poland will become a national burial ground for a great part of our nation. We deeply grieve that a majority of the Polish socialists agree with the overbearing point of view of the Polish bourgeoisie and nobility with regard to the Jews, and we invoke the judgment of the International on this vital question concerning three million Jews.

Rumania is an obvious example of the worthlessness of international agreements for the protection of feeble minorities when no extragovernmental organization exists to interfere when necessary. The Jews in Rumania have fewer rights than they had in Russia during the old regime. The alternating governments and the parliaments of the Boyars have within the purview of the nations of Europe shamelessly trampled the rights of the Jews solemnly guaranteed by the Treaty of Berlin. We do not hold the Rumanian people responsible for this state of affairs, but rather the ruling classes who oppress even their own people. We infer from this example that upon the establishment of a country's self-government, the democratic foundation and the protection of the minority nationalities must be settled. The peace Congress should apply effective measures to secure civil and national equality for Jews in the reestablished Rumania.

Palestine. The main source of all sufferings of the Jewish people is the loss of their historic homeland and their dispersion over many countries. The lack of a homeland has deprived the Jewish people of the possibility of independently controlling its own existence, and has brought its destiny into an unbearable dependence upon the rise and fall of nations under whose rule it lives. The lack of a homeland is the explanation of its abnormal existence and its exceptional position among the nations of the world; it is above the cause of the unwholesome economic structure and social grouping of the Jews; for their insignificant capacity for political and social resistance; for their unceasing migrations; and for their restlessness. It is not particularly necessary to indicate how far these abnormalities impede the development of the Jewish working classes.

The understanding of this situation and the uninterrupted spiritual association of the Jewish people with its ancient native soil called into being the Jewish national movement aiming at a *territorial solution to the Jewish question* by creating a Jewish settlement in Palestine. We see as inevitable for the recovery of the Jewish commonwealth of its normal existence a radical restratification of economic life, which presupposes an assignment of a possible large portion of the Jewish people to the soil and to the production of raw materials. The settlement of migrating Jewish masses in Palestine reveals already, in spite of all hindrances, very promising results. It is the beginning of a Jewish community of labor and culture, which in its growth is destined to become attractive for emigration and a hearthstone of free national development of a people secured in its existence.

The intense vital power of this national ideal manifested itself both in the self-sacrificial attitude of the Jewish masses in the cause of Palestine and in the fact that this ideal gave the Jewish people renewed faith in itself and has become a powerful lever in a tremendous national reju-venation in which all classes of our people are participating. Our demands in regard to Palestine today are not only the immediate aspirations of the popular movement initiated by Zionism, but also the demands of a large majority of the Jewish democracy.

The revolutionary transformation of the basis of the Jewish national existence by establishing a national homestead in Palestine can only be accomplished by the labor of the Jew himself. But we are justified in demanding from other peoples and especially from the organized international proletariat the elimination of those artificial hindrances which render more difficult or even threaten to undermine the progress of the Jewish national development in Palestine. The impeding of Jewish colonization contradicts the democratic principles of free movement of masses seeking employment and the right of national self-government. The striving of the Jewish people for national concentration in Palestine agrees fully with the colonization tasks of the human race. The making accessible to the land-hungry Jewish people the thinly populated and for the most part fallow land, which with the application of modern methods of production could employ millions of new settlers, would not only work a revolution for this people but would also be of great benefit to the population of the country and a step forward in the progress of the world.

It is clear that this colonization has nothing in common with the politics of colonial conquest, expansion, and exploitation. The Jewish people possessing no power of statecraft and seeking neither markets nor monopolies of raw materials for production in favor of a "mother country," cannot think of launching a policy of colonial politics in Palestine or of molesting the population of the country. The Jewish people aims at creating a secured place of employment for its déclassé, wandering masses: it seeks to increase the productive forces of the country in peaceful cooperation with the Arab population. The Jewish colonization is already a considerable factor in Palestine's economic development. The Jewish immigration brings progressive methods of labor, a higher standard of living, and a higher scale of wages. It can therefore only assist the Arab population to overcome their primitive standards of civilization and economics.

The new Jewish colonization in Palestine is therefore associated with the important colonization interests of the human race, which should be concerned with returning the only homeless people on earth to its own country, because the world cannot become peaceful as long as even one people is in vain awaiting its deliverance, and as long as the Jewish people, whose destiny is bound up in that of all peoples, is deprived of normal conditions for the development of its national individuality. The Jewish people, whose sons are shedding their blood in the tragic struggle against each other on all fronts, and which suffers the inevitable and avoidable horrors of the war behind the fronts, is justified in demanding that the approaching peace bring to it too an assurance of its existence and of its free development.

Summary of the Proposals

The harmonious dwelling of peoples among each other and the securing of a stable peace requires the regulation of international relations according to the following principles:

I. League of Nations

The establishment of an extragovernmental organization, of a League of Nations with the following purposes:

1. The codifying of *international law* including freedom of the seas.
2. Obligatory settlement of state and national conflicts by *courts of arbitration.*
3. Adoption of a uniform method of *democratic control of foreign policies* and international treaties in all countries.
4. *Disarmament* of all countries, and control over the industry of arms, which is to be the property of the state. Maintenance of an international militia strong enough to avert any infringement of international law and of international treaties.
5. *Administration of the commercial highways* which are to be made international.
6. Control over the maintenance and completion of *international socio-political* agreements which are to be included in the treaties of peace with regard to free migration, social insurance, working time, right of coalition, home industry, protection of workmen, women, and children.
7. *Regulation of the production of the world,* under which title should be considered:

    a) *Prevention of economic wars:* the politico-economic rapproachment of states by the removal of custom and traffic limits; simultaneous protection of the progress of production in territories where it may be required without limiting the economic freedom of any countries;
    b) maintenance of free immigration in all countries and *regulation of colonization* in virginal or thinly settled districts by agreement with the countries of immigration and emigration;
    c) *control over colonial administration* in the interest of the progress of the native population toward self-government and the promotion of production;

d) the effective accomplishment of the *open door* and *free trade* in the colonies that are to be guaranteed in the treaty of peace and, in an emergency, the *apportioning of importation of* indispensable *raw materials* in accordance with the needs of free industrial development in consuming countries.

II. Rights of Nations to Self-Government.

1. Realization of the right of each nation, i.e. each people, to national *unity and democratic self-government,* which would include:

   a) Restoration of Belgium, Serbia and Montenegro, Rumania;
   b) the unification and independence of Poland. According to the declarations of the delegates of Ukraine and Bohemia, the new Poland shall comprise territories where the Poles constitute the majority of the population;
   c) we agree with the demands of the Armenian, Ukrainian and Czecho-slavic delegations in regard to their nationalities;
   d) the transformation of Russia, Austro-Hungary, and Turkey into polynational federal states, i.e. into federations of ethnographically defined units of self-government.

2. The guaranteeing to each minority-nationality the right to maintain and develop its national peculiarity and to self-administration in national affairs.
3. The decision as to the disposition of contested districts shall be made on the basis of a plebiscite of the population itself, as for example in Alsace-Lorraine.
4. The federative uniting of states for the purpose of realizing national unity on the part of peoples living in such states, as well as federation and agreement for the purpose of satisfying economic interests of the participating peoples, such as free access to the sea, commercial highways, and to markets, e.g. Balkan Federation.

III. The Jewish Demands

Applying the above principles to the Jewish people, we demand:

1. Full civil equality for the Jews of all countries. Equal treatment of the Jewish population in the restoration of the districts affected by the war.
2. Free immigration and settlement of Jews in all countries.
3. National self-administration on the basis of personal autonomy and national equality within the state, province, and community, in countries where the Jews are settled in masses.
4. Security to unrestrained activity in Jewish colonization, aiming at the creation of a Jewish homeland in Palestine. For this is necessary:

a) Removal of all measures restraining the free immigration and colonization of Jews, extensive facilitation of naturalization, and free activity of the institutions created to promote Jewish colonization in Palestine;

b) establishment of modern legal relations and the settling upon sociopolitical measures for the purpose of developing the productive forces of the land. Further, the guaranteeing of economic facilities and the promotion of colonization by, first of all, the employment of ownerless and state domains and of the huge land properties for the settlement of immigrants and for the landless and landpoor agricultural population of the country;

c) transformation of Palestine into an autonomous and unified administrative district;

d) national autonomy of the Jewish people in Palestine.

The fulfillment of these demands is to be internationally guaranteed.

Glossary

Ben-Zvi, Itzhak (1884-1963). Early Poale Zion leader in Russia and Palestine; later, second president of Israel. Close boyhood friend of Borochov.

Bund. Founded in Vilna in 1897, the Jewish Labor Bund was an ardently anti-Zionist socialist organization, advocated national cultural autonomy for Diaspora Jewry, and claimed to be the "sole representative" of Jewish workers.

El Maleh Rahamin. Hebrew prayer for the dead.

Eretz Israel. The Land of Israel (Hebrew).

Forward. Popular daily Yiddish newspaper in New York City, edited by the socialist Abraham Cahan.

Galut. The Exile of the Jews from Israel (Hebrew). *Golus* in Yiddish.

General Zionists. Politically centrist Zionists who largely represented bourgeois interests.

Groupists. Semiassimilated middle class Jewish grouping in Russia.

Hashomer. The watchman (Hebrew). A pre–World War I Jewish self-defense organization in Palestine. A member was called Shomer (pl. Shomrim).

Haskalah. Enlightenment (Hebrew). A movement in modern Jewish life stressing the need to reconcile modernism with Jewish tradition. Adherents were called *maskilim* (enlightened ones). It originated in the eighteenth century.

Hasidim. The "pious ones," members of a popular Jewish religious movement originating in the Ukraine and Poland in the eighteenth century. The Hasidic movement emphasized prayer and religious ecstasy over traditional study as the focus of Judaism.

Heder. Literally meaning room, it was used to denote the traditionalist Jewish elementary school.

Helsingfors Program. Program of an important Russian Zionist conference in fall 1906 calling for national autonomy for Russian Jews and democratization of Russia.

Hibat Zion. Lovers of Zion (Hebrew). A pre-Herzlian Zionist organization founded in the early 1880s in Russia.

I.C.A. See Jewish Colonization Assocation.

Information Bureau. Was established by the Poale-Zion-founded Palestine Workers' Fund to aid immigrants to Palestine.

Jewish Colonization Assocation. Founded in 1891 by Baron de Hirsch, the J.C.A. (or I.C.A.) aimed to resettle Jews in the New World.

Jewish National Fund (J.N.F.). Zionist fund founded in 1901 to buy land in Palestine for the Jewish people.

Jewish National Party in Austria. A group of Galician Zionists who ran in local elections as advocates of Jewish national rights, rather than as Zionists.

Jewish Socialist Workers (Labor) Party. Also called the Sejmists or SERP (after its Russian acronym). Founded in 1906, close to the Russian Social Revolutionaries, this party believed a Jewish home to be a possibility only in the distant future, and thus concentrated their efforts on national political autonomy for Jews in Russia. They imagined each national group in the Russian empire having its own national *Sejm* (diet, Russian).

Kehilah. Community or Jewish community organization (pl. *kehilot,* Hebrew).

Loshn kodesh. Holy tongue, a Yiddish expression for premodern Hebrew.

Luftmensch. Slang for a person without an occupation (Yiddish).

Mame loshn. Mother tongue, a Yiddish expression for the Yiddish language.

Maskilim. See Haskalah.

Narodnaya Volya. The "people's will," a populist Russian terrorist organization.

Nordau, Max (1849-1923). Writer and critic, associate of Theodor Herzl as an early Zionist leader.

Oppenheimer Plan. Plan advocated to the World Zionist Organization by German Jewish sociologist Franz Oppenheimer. Aimed to turn Diaspora Jewish city dwellers into cooperative agricultural pioneers in Palestine.

Ostjuden. Derogatory term for East European Jews (German).

Pale of Settlement. Restricted areas of the Russian Empire in which Jews were permitted to live.

Palestine Workers' Fund. Established before World War I by Poale Zion as a fund to help workers in Palestine.

Pilpul. A term denoting Talmudic exposition which came to be used to designate overly fine, almost absurd knitpicking.

Poale Zion. Workers of Zion Party. Socialist Zionist movement unified in Russia in 1906 under Borochov's leadership. It had major sections in Palestine, Austria, and the United States. The World Confederation (Union) of Poale Zion was founded in 1907. During Borochov's "American period" the U.S. Poale Zion had competing Socialist and Social Democratic factions. Borochov belonged to the latter.

Sejmists. See Jewish Socialist Workers Party.

SERP. See Jewish Socialist Workers Party.

Shomer. See Hashomer.

Shtadlan. A prominent Jew who mediates between non-Jews and the Jewish community.

S.S. See Zionist Socialists.

Stychic Process. Spontaneous, elementary process.

Syrkin, Nachman (1867-1924). Born in Mohilev, a leading Socialist-Zionist theoretician and frequent foe of Borochov within the Poale Zion.

Talis. The Jewish prayer shawl.

Territorialism. Political movement based on the belief that the Jewish problem needed a solution entailing territorial concentration but not necessarily in Palestine.

Tisha B'Av. Ninth day of the Hebrew month *Av,* a traditional day of Jewish mourning as the anniversary of the fall of the Temples in Jerusalem.

Uganda Plan. British offer in 1903 to create a Jewish home in East Africa. The proposal caused a fevered debate in the World Zionist Organization but was eventually rejected.

Vozrozhdeniye. Renaissance (Russian). Founded in 1903 this "renaissance" group was a non-Marxist Jewish political organization close to the Russian Social Revolutionaries. While believing that ultimately the Jews needed territorial autonomy, they felt this to be a distant prospect and thus emphasized the need for the struggle for national rights in the Diaspora. They later merged with the Sejmists.

Weber-Fechner Law. Named after E.H. Weber and G.T. Fechner, this law claimed that the intensity of a sensation increases as the logarithm of the stimulus.

World Confederation (Union) of Poale Zion. See Poale Zion.

World Zionist Organization. Founded in 1897 by Theodor Herzl to promote the Zionist cause. Its supreme decision-making body is the World Zionist Congress.

Yarmulka. The Jewish skull cap.

Yishuv. Settlement (Hebrew). The Jewish community of Palestine.

Zhidi. Derogatory Russian term for Jews.

Zionist Congress. See World Zionist Organization.

Zionist Socialists (Z.S. or S.S.). Socialist Territorialists.

Printed in Great Britain
by Amazon

10624400R00129